NATIONAL GEOGRAPHIC

TRAVELER
Taiwan

![National Geographic logo]

NATIONAL GEOGRAPHIC
TRAVELER
Taiwan

Phil Macdonald

National Geographic
Washington, D.C.

Contents

Page 1: Men dressed as Taoist
gods dance during the annual
Dragon Boat Festival.
Pages 2–3: Alishan's mystical
"sea of clouds"
Left: Partaking in a ritual
celebration on Confucius'
birthday

How to use this guide

See back flap for keys to text and map symbols.

The *National Geographic Traveler* brings you the best of Taiwan in text, pictures, and maps. Divided into three main sections, the guide begins with an overview of history and culture.

Following are six regional chapters with featured sites selected by the author for their particular interest. Each chapter opens with its own contents list for easy reference. A map introduces the parameters covered in the chapter, highlighting the featured sites and locating other places of interest. Walks and drives, plotted on their own maps, suggest routes for discovering the most about an area. Features and sidebars offer intriguing detail on history, culture, or contemporary life.

The final section, Travelwise, lists essential information for the traveler—pretrip planning, special events, getting around, practical advice, and emergency contacts—plus provides a selection of hotels and restaurants arranged by area, shops, activities, and entertainment possibilities.

To the best of our knowledge, all information is accurate as of press time. However, it's always advisable to call ahead when possible.

282

Color coding
Each region of the country is color coded for easy reference. Find the region you want on the map on the front flap, and look for the color flash at the top of the pages of the relevant chapter. Information in **Travelwise** is also color coded to each region.

Visitor information

National Palace Museum
www.npm.gov.tw
 Map p. 57
✉ 221 Jhihshan (Zhishan) Rd., Sec. 2
☎ 2881-2021
$ $$
🚇 MRT: Shihlin (Shilin) station, then bus 225, 304, minibus 18 and 19 and Red 30

Practical information for most sites is given in the side column (see key to symbols on back flap). The map reference gives the page number of the map and grid reference, if relevant. Other details are address, telephone number, days closed, entrance charge in a range from $ (under $5) to $$$$$ (over $25), and nearest MRT station and most important bus routes for sites in Taipei and other relevant cities. Other sites have information in italics and parentheses in the text.

Chinese place-names
An ongoing frustration for visitors are the different transliterations of Chinese place-names into English—various city and county administrations can't agree on a standard method, tussling over the Wade-Giles, tongyong, and hanyu systems. This guide uses the tongyong method, followed by hanyu in parentheses if the spelling is different.

TRAVELWISE

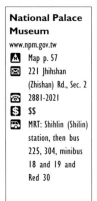

TAIPEI — Color-coded region name

🏨 **THE GRAND HOTEL** — Hotel name & price range
$$$$/$$$
1 JHONGSHAN (ZHONG-SHAN) NORTH RD., SEC. 4 — Address, telephone & fax numbers, e-mail address, website
TEL 2886-8888, FAX 2885-2885
www.grand-hotel.org
The red-columned facade, sweeping classical Chinese tile roof, and location atop a hill give this hotel a dominating presence. — Brief description of hotel
ℹ 490 🅿 ❚ 🚭 🚫 — Hotel facilities & credit card details
🏊 🛁 ♿ All major cards
🚇 Jiantan

🍴 **ANTOINE ROOM** — Restaurant name & price range
$$$$$
SHERATON TAIPEI HOTEL 12 JHONGSIAO (ZHONGXIAO) EAST RD., SEC. 1 — Address & telephone number
TEL 2321-5511
Top-notch ingredients and thoughtful presentation give this French restaurant much appeal. Try the luxurious seafood salad— fresh seafood mixed with Japanese seaweed, sticky rice, and vinegar and soy sauce dressing. — Brief description of restaurant
🍴 90 ♿ All major cards — Restaurant closures & credit card details

Hotel & restaurant prices
An explanation of the price bands used in entries is given in the Hotels & Restaurants section (beginning on p. 244).

REGIONAL MAPS

Adjacent chapter

Road number

Important featured site

Drive start point

Important featured town

• A locator map accompanies each regional map and shows the location of that area in Taiwan.

WALKING TOURS

Building outline

Direction of route

Walk route

Featured site on walk route

Start point

Red numbered bullets link sites on map to descriptions in the text.

District name

• An information box gives the starting and ending points, time and length of walk, and places not to be missed along the route.

DRIVING TOURS

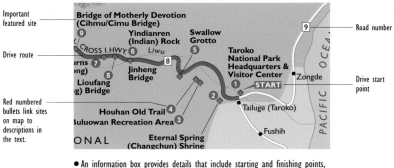

Important featured site

Drive route

Red numbered bullets link sites on map to descriptions in the text.

Road number

Drive start point

• An information box provides details that include starting and finishing points, places not to be missed along the route, the time and length of drive, and tips on terrain.

NATIONAL GEOGRAPHIC

TRAVELER
Taiwan

About the author

Phil Macdonald moved to Hong Kong from Sydney, Australia, in 1989 to continue a career in journalism that had begun eight years earlier in the west coast city of Perth. He worked for the *Hong Kong Standard* and the *South China Morning Post* for a number of years before settling— by way of Singapore and Laos—in Phuket, Thailand, in 1996. He now lives in Bangkok, working as a freelance journalist and writer, and contributing to a number of regional and international publications. His interests include Southeast Asian politics and recent history, and the beaches of southern Thailand. He is author of *The National Geographic Traveler: Hong Kong* and co-author of *The National Geographic Traveler: Thailand* guidebooks.

Brent Hannon contributed the features.

Rick Charette wrote the Mujha (Muzha) tea plantation, Jiufen, and Sun Moon Lake entries, and was the Editorial Consultant for this Second Edition.

History & culture

**Stylized stone lion statue:
a common Taoist temple
guardian**

Taiwan today

ON AN ISLAND AS DENSELY POPULATED AS TAIWAN, YOU MIGHT THINK THAT the last thing a local would want to see is another outsider coming in. Yet the Taiwanese are exceptionally welcoming to foreign visitors, sometimes disarmingly so. Speak to any traveler, businessperson, or expatriate who has spent time on the island, and the talk will likely drift to Taiwanese hospitality.

A stranger to Taiwan (officially, the Republic of China) is automatically taken in as a guest, and the locals—who pride themselves on being good hosts—treat their guests as guests should be treated, often going out of their way to make them feel at ease. So be prepared for largesse, take it all in stride, and accept it graciously. The notion of payback rarely enters the picture, although the conscientious guest should attempt to show generosity in return.

A common example of this hospitality comes when it's time to pay the bill at a restaurant. Forget about sharing. Dividing up the bill over the dining table is considered demeaning, and asking you, the guest, to pay your share is not even a consideration. In the West we settle for a coffee and polite conversation as an after-meal ritual; in Taiwan, the hosts argue over who will have the honor of paying the bill—with the host almost always winning the argument.

"BEAUTIFUL ISLAND"

This hospitality takes place in one of the most crowded places on earth. Twenty-three million souls jam into just 14,015 square miles (36,300 km) of land. That's an area slightly larger than Massachusetts and Connecticut combined. Add a chain of towering, mist-shrouded mountains that can't support human settlement and the squeeze is accentuated. The shortage of elbowroom means that about 1,600 people jostle for space on each square mile of land (640 people per sq km). In the capital, Taipei, the situation is more extreme, as 25,000 residents crowd into each square mile (10,000 people per sq km)—a tight fit by anyone's reckoning.

In the 16th century, Portuguese explorers were so impressed by the towering, green, mountainous island they saw from the decks of their ships that they called the place Ihla Formosa, meaning "beautiful island." Even allowing for the hyperbole of early explorers, these Portuguese seafarers were not far off the mark. The appellation stuck, particularly in the United States, and the names Taiwan and Formosa were interchangeable as late as the early 1970s.

Areas of the island's natural beauty that so awed early explorers are still intact. Those who imagine Taiwan as a crowded, clamorous, urban land are only partly correct. To be sure, the island's headlong rush into modernization has left its environmental scars, particularly on the heavily populated central west plains, but it has not totally eradicated the land's natural beauty, nor overwhelmed Taiwan's traditional culture.

The grandeur of the jagged peaks and alpine scenery of the Central Mountain Range matches that of mountains in better-known regions of the world. And in many cases, Taiwan's mountains are more accessible than those elsewhere. The Central Cross Island Highway cuts its way through the Central Mountain Range in such a miraculous fashion as to leave you wondering how the government managed to build it in the first place. You will be searching the rest of your life to find a more spectacular road.

While lacking the sheer drama of the Central Mountain Range, the island's east coast—the most isolated and unspoiled region of Taiwan proper—imparts a rare feeling of solitude in an otherwise crowded island. It's a place of spectacular gorges (its most famous, the stunning marble canyon of Taroko Gorge, is a world-class attraction), precipitous cliff faces rising from the Pacific Ocean, fertile hillsides, and bucolic valleys. Kending, at the southern tip of the island, is

A mere backwater just decades ago, Taipei has emerged as a modern, sophisticated, and vibrant city.

Taiwan's tropical playground, with sparkling beaches, abundant offshore corals, and pristine coastal scenery.

About 85 percent of the people living on the main island of Taiwan and its offshore islands consider themselves native Taiwanese, or *benshengren* ("this province people"), and they take pride in their unique culture and traditions. The Taiwanese dialect is heard in pop songs, on television and radio, and at the movies alongside the official Mandarin Chinese.

The two million people who followed Chiang Kai-shek's Nationalist government to Taiwan when it was evacuated from the mainland in 1949, as well as their descendants, are referred to as *daluren* (mainlanders). Until the lifting of martial law in 1987, the benshengren harbored a great deal of resentment toward the daluren, who occupied positions of power and privilege and suppressed Taiwanese language and culture after the Nationalists took power. The end to martial law was pivotal

socially, politically, and economically for the island. But the resentment still lingers, albeit to a lesser extent and at a level that is hardly noticeable to the visitor, except during the country's major elections.

Taiwan's indigenous minorities, referred to as aborigines and called *yuanjhumin (yuanzhumin)*, or original inhabitants, account for 1.5 percent of the population. Thirteen officially recognized tribes live in communities around the country.

Newlyweds in front of Chiang Kai-shek Memorial Hall, a marble-clad tribute to the late president of the Republic of China.

The Ami is the largest group, with 150,000 members. They live in the mountains and valleys of Hualien and Taitung counties, while smaller groups like the Dahwu on Orchid Island and the Thao—who live around Sun Moon Lake—number only a few thousand or fewer. Other groups include the Atayal,

Bunun, Paiwan, Puyuma, Rukai, Saisiat, Kavalan, Truku, Sakiraya, and Tsou.

The Hakka, a Chinese minority group whose ancestors came from the Chinese province of Guangdong, make up about 10 percent of the population. Along with the indigenous groups, they tend to refer to themselves as Taiwanese.

Most trips to Taiwan will begin and end in the modern capital of Taipei, a flat, urban sprawl contained within a ring of mountains that forms the Taipei Basin. Taipei is the social, business, cultural, and political hub of the island. Its three million smartly dressed and confident inhabitants go about their business along wide avenues and tree-lined boulevards, parting with cash across counters in gleaming shopping malls, trendy Japanese department stores, and brand-name fashion boutiques. They relax by surfing the World Wide Web on their wireless laptop computers and sipping on lattes in Starbucks, and by ordering drinks

and being seen in chic-this-week nightclubs, restaurants, and bars.

"Economic miracle" is the tag used to describe the transformation of some Asian cities and territories from underdeveloped outposts in the 1970s to modern and affluent urban centers that now demand to be taken seriously. Taipei is where Taiwan's economic miracle is on show, and Taipei's affluent citizens have no qualms about showboating.

The economic growth of Taiwan over the

Every October 10, crowds turn out uniformly across the island to celebrate Double Tenth National Day.

past four decades has been phenomenal. The island has emerged as one of the region's strongest economies, one of a group including Hong Kong, Singapore, and South Korea that has come to define Asia's economic success since the 1980s. It has proved itself resilient in the face of the disastrous Asian financial crisis

of 1997–98 and the economic havoc wrought by the SARS outbreak in 2003.

Like its Asian counterparts, Taiwan learned early that its future prosperity lay in changing its focus from producing and exporting inexpensive consumer goods, products that made the label "Made in Taiwan" synonymous with cheap and disposable.

After China opened up politically in the late 1970s and began to embrace a market economy, factories making low-cost consumer items have moved across the Taiwan Strait to the mainland, where labor was plentiful and inexpensive. Taiwan looked for a niche and found it in the manufacture of high-tech electronics.

Now the island rolls out computers, computer peripherals, and components like no other place on Earth. It makes more than a quarter of the world's desktop computers and half of its laptops. In the city of Hsinchu, to the southwest of Taipei, the Hsinchu Science Park rivals

California's Silicon Valley (see pp. 124–125).

The outstanding economic and political achievements of Taiwan stand out because many of them have taken place in difficult circumstances. For six decades, the country's powerful neighbor mainland China (officially, the People's Republic of China) has regarded Taiwan as a renegade province that one day must return to the fold. In recent times, China has reclaimed Hong Kong and the former Portuguese enclave of Macau and would like

Placid Carp Lake in Puli Township, central Taiwan, is a haven of natural beauty on an island beset with industrialization.

to add Taiwan to its holdings. Relations between the two lands are distinctly hostile.

While most Taiwanese were once resigned to—and in many cases in favor of—one day officially becoming part of China, that is less the case today. Democratic changes that began in the 1990s have brought a political

maturity to the island. This, coupled with increasing affluence and economic prosperity, has given the Taiwanese enough confidence to defy their huge neighbor, at least in word if not in deed. Today, more Taiwanese than ever before favor independence over reunification with mainland China. However, this is something that the People's Republic of China has strongly opposed.

One would think such a threatening political scenario would be oppressive, but this is far from the case. If the Taiwanese are afraid for their future, they certainly don't show it. Perhaps it's denial, but Taiwan and its people roll along with a palpable vibrancy and assuredness.

While some Asian countries rail against Western culture gnawing away at their traditions and values, Taiwan takes a more pragmatic view. It accepts elements of Western culture, but generally not at the expense of its own. As a decades-old ally of the United States, Taiwan

harbors very little anti-Western sentiment, making Western culture more acceptable.

But the modern gloss of Taiwan can be seen as a veneer covering a culture deeply rooted in Buddhist, Taoist, and Confucian beliefs, which are intertwined and often presented in riotously ornate temples. The Taiwanese honor dozens of deities, integrate folk and ancestral worship in their religions, and add in soothsaying to create a compelling spiritual mix.

The streets of Taipei's Simending (Ximending) quarter bustle with shoppers, theater-goers, and bar-hoppers at night.

People gather in thousands of temples around the country—from makeshift shrines to astonishing achievements in religious architecture—to pray, burn incense, and offer food to myriad deities. Taiwanese religion (and Chinese religion in general) incorporates around one hundred deities of varying

Taipei's modern, stylish, and convenient Mass Rapid Transit system, or MRT, is the most extensive of any in Asia.

popularity and spiritual influence. A student cramming for exams will find time to visit a temple honoring a scholarly god; sharp-suited businessmen will lay food offerings before the image of a god who will bestow riches; a person worn down by sickness will pay homage to a deity that can restore health; while a fisherman faced with weeks at sea will visit a temple that honors a deity who will ensure a good catch and a safe return. Fortunetellers have co-opted this religious hodgepodge and linger outside temples, lending counsel to those impatient to see if their prayers will be answered. The Taiwanese don't like to leave things to chance.

Temples erupt with color and noise around the time of a particular deity's birthday. The sounds of beating drums, pounding cymbals, and earsplitting firecrackers accompany the throngs of devotees who follow the deity's icon as it is carried on a sedan chair through city streets.

Superstition pervades daily life. Certain dates and numbers portend success or failure. There are good days to do things, and there are bad days to do things. To make sure a marriage is a long and happy one, young couples will choose a suitable time and date for the ceremony as ordained by tradition or confirmed by a soothsayer. A businessman well versed in the ways of international wheeling and dealing may attribute his latest success to the way his *fengshuei (fengshui)* master arranged his office. Families will not travel during Ghost Month (see p. 44) because they are more likely to run into trouble when angry ghosts are about, and if a family member is killed in an accident, then that person's passage to the afterlife will be fraught with peril.

Early Christian missionaries had some success converting the locals, especially the aborigines, who were more amenable to the religion's tenets than the Chinese. Just over a million Taiwanese are Christians, about three-quarters of them Protestant, and they worship in some 3,000 churches around the island.

Like other Asians, people in Taiwan take the concept of "face" seriously. The customs, hierarchies, and rules that apply can vary from

A researcher at one of Taiwan's many biotechnology firms "pipettes," or transfers, materials to a tray. The country reigns as one of Asia's leaders in high technology.

country to country in Asia, but they share the theme of showing respect and avoiding embarrassing others.

Being rich and powerful will earn you a lot of respect (and therefore allow you to gain face) in Taiwan. The reason is simple: To become rich you must be diligent and hardworking, qualities that will necessarily command respect.

Obviously no one is going to give you the respect you deserve as a rich or powerful person if they don't know you are rich and powerful. This explains the common and ostentatious displays of wealth you may see in the country (luxury cars, expensive jewelry and watches, designer clothing, etc.).

Face works at all levels of society and exists to maintain harmony. Raising your voice in anger or frustration causes much embarrassment—and hence loss of face—for the person at whom your ire is directed. The result is invariably negative and potentially dangerous.

Compliment freely and you will give people face, but even the slightest personal criticism, even one that would be considered

harmless or even helpful in the West, can cause loss of face, embarrassment for the target, and a period of uncomfortable silence. Even in the most frustrating moments, a smile and some patience will get you a lot further than a scowl and fist-thumping.

The peculiarly Chinese concept of *guansi* (*guanxi*) also pervades interpersonal relationships. In mainland China, a stifling bureaucracy can make it impossible to get anything done, so individuals need to form relationships with the people who can get wheels turning. However, the person who turns the wheels for you will, at some point, want to have the favor returned.

To accumulate guansi you need to do things for people: Give them gifts, take them to dinner, lend them your car, and so on. Once you have built up guansi, an unspoken understanding develops that favors will be returned repeatedly in an ongoing relationship. Visitors to Taiwan will rarely become involved in *guansi*, unless there often on business.

Most Taiwanese people, especially in the

cities, dress well and expect you to do the same. The way you dress often says a lot about your character and can determine how you are treated. Always dress neatly. For men, clean T-shirts, shorts, and sandals are the minimum dress standards for streetwear. Don't wear skimpy shirts or flip-flops. Women should dress modestly.

A Taiwanese peculiarity that can confuse visitors is the use of different English translations for Chinese. The problem stems from the number of transliteration systems that follow different criteria and the inability of governments and municipal authorities to agree on a single one. The same major road may be called Zhongxiao, Chunghsiao, and Chung Hsiao; another Zhongshan and Chungshan; and another Ta an, Da an, and Daan. Applying some logic will usually solve the problem, although it is sometimes a little tricky (e.g. Pateh Road at times is also called Bade Road and Pate Road). Among the main transliteration systems are Wade-Giles, tongyong, and hanyu; however, the situation can become frustrating when individual sign writers and mapmakers add their own interpretations. This guidebook uses the tongyong method, followed by hanyu in parentheses if the spelling is different.

The transformation of Taiwan over the past 30 years from a backwater into an Asian economic powerhouse has generally not been at the expense of its traditional culture and values. A trip to a Taoist temple to burn incense and make offerings of food is still as much a part of everyday life as a trip to a shopping mall to buy the latest brand-name fashion. Seeking counsel from a fortuneteller is no more unusual than meeting with a stockbroker to discuss investment opportunities. Burning paper "hell money" to appease wandering spirits is as run-of-the-mill as handing over a wad of notes in a trendy bar for overpriced cocktails. Indeed, much of Taiwan's appeal for the visitor lies in this unaffected blend of a modern, consumer-driven Western lifestyle with the vitality of a culture whose values are richly steeped in tradition. ■

Nets and trawling poles form sharp silhouettes at sunset in Kaohsiung Harbor.

Food & drink

THE FLOOD OF IMMIGRANT CIVILIANS AND NATIONALIST SOLDIERS TO Taiwan after China's civil war ended in 1949 brought with it a wide variety of culinary habits and traditions. Over the years these traditions have been maintained and refined. Today, Taiwan can boast the best Chinese food in the world and find little argument. The island's multitude of restaurants runs the gamut of major Chinese regional cuisines, taking you on an instant culinary tour of China.

Food is very much a part of Chinese culture. Confucius, who believed social ritual taught virtue, laid down the ground rules for customs and etiquette at the dining table. In classical Chinese teaching, a true scholar not only mastered the arts of poetry, calligraphy, music, and strategy, but also needed to be a dab hand in the kitchen, able to turn out

a superb meal for family, friends, and guests.

Although the lofty ideals of aligning food and fine art may have dissipated over the centuries, the Taiwanese—like all ethnic Chinese—still take their food quite seriously. Food and eating play a far more important role in ritual, language, symbolism, and social interaction than they do in even the

most gregarious of Western cultures.

To the Chinese, the most important elements of taste are color, aroma, flavor, and texture, all of which must be combined into one harmonious whole. Herein lies the art of Chinese cuisine. Dishes will have a main ingredient and a number of supplementary ones that bring it into a coordinated whole. Traditionally, dishes are brought to the table in a sequence that reflects a particular harmonic relationship among the foods.

TAIWANESE

Taiwanese food combines local ingredients with the culinary influences of the nearby Chinese province of Fujian and ex-colonial master Japan. Oyster omelets are popular, as are taro cakes doused with pork-based sauce.

Other offerings include squid balls, fried fish with peanuts, and simmered cuttlefish. Taiwanese food is often eaten as a snack and sold at night markets. Shilin Night Market (see p. 67) is one of the best places to sample some of the dishes.

CANTONESE

To Westerners, Cantonese cuisine—from the southern Chinese province of Guangdong—is the most familiar style of Chinese food. The vast majority of Chinese restaurants found in the West are Cantonese, but this probably has more to do with the Cantonese propensity for migration than anything else.

Cantonese cuisine emphasizes freshness and natural flavor; food is lightly seasoned. Many dishes are stir-fried or steamed to allow

Taiwan holds no end of restaurants to satiate the Taiwanese appetite for both food and company (left). With dishes from all regions of China, the country is a great place to try out foods such as *dan-zi mian*, a noodle dish (above).

Fresh produce is the hallmark of Chinese cuisine, and Taiwan's many food markets offer an abundance of locally grown fruits and vegetables.

the foods to retain their natural taste. Guangdong's tropical climate encourages abundant, varied produce. Cantonese dishes often include seafood along with tropical fruits, rice, and a wide array of vegetables. Beef, chicken, and pork are typical meats. Popular Cantonese offerings include steamed sea bass, stir-fried garoupa, steamed chicken, beef with oyster sauce, and fried rice. Vegetable dishes come in wide variety. Elaborately prepared shark's-fin soup and bird's-nest soup are two of the most exotic (and expensive) dishes on offer.

Cantonese cuisine is also famous for its roast meats, such as pork and duck, as well as the assortment of mid-morning treats known as dim sum (see p. 27).

BEIJING-STYLE
Beijing-style cuisine reflects its origins in the northern Chinese provinces. These cooler climes prohibit the growing of rice as a staple, so the emphasis shifts to wheat-based foods. The cuisine, therefore, consists of a variety of dumplings, baked and steamed breads, and buns and noodles.

A typical meal consists of vegetable dishes, soups, tofu (soybean curd), and fish, often with garlic or vinegar. Meats may be braised or stewed, and the food is not heavily spiced.

The variety of buns, dumplings, and noodles makes Beijing cuisine ideal for snacks. Round flat buns filled with meat are pan-fried or baked. Dumplings usually hold a mixture of meat or vegetable (or both) and are steamed, boiled, or fried. Noodle-making at some Beijing-style restaurants becomes part of the evening's entertainment, with chefs expertly twisting and twirling the dough while peeling off thin strands.

Peking duck, the most famous Beijing dish, is often served at banquets. Slices of oven-roasted duck with crispy brown skin are wrapped in thin pancakes and served with sauce and scallions.

SHANGHAINESE
Shanghai cuisine comes from the central coastal region of China. The area's coast and lakes provide saltwater and freshwater seafood, while both rice- and wheat-based dishes, such as buns and noodles, are available as accompaniments. Sauces are rich and slightly sweet. Shanghai cuisine tends to be heavier than Cantonese, lightly spiced and relatively oily. Popular Shanghainese dishes include

Fashioned into such unexpected shapes as fish and squid, the Taiwanese pastries called *gao* are popular during holidays and festivals and as snacks year-round.

fried prawns, drunken chicken, and steamed crab. Its West Lake vinegar fish (a whole carp is sliced opened and splayed, lightly poached, then smothered with minced ginger and sweet-and-sour sauce) can be superb.

SICHUANESE

The cuisine of southwestern China's Sichuan province features generous sprinklings of garlic, peppercorns, fennel, anise, coriander, and chilies, making it the spiciest of all Chinese foods. Traditionally prepared Sichuan food—often soaked and simmered in chili oil—can be too fiery for the unprepared Western palate, although milder dishes are available. Popular ingredients include chicken, pork, and river fish. Bean curd with spicy minced pork is a favorite dish, along with tasty stir-fried diced chicken with tiny, dry, and extremely hot chilies.

DIM SUM

Originally a Cantonese custom, these days dim sum is found throughout China, although the Cantonese still serve up the best.

Dim sum consists of a variety of steamed or fried dumplings stuffed with an assortment of either savory or sweet mixtures, along with bite-sized items ranging from spareribs and meatballs to egg custard tarts. Most people eat dim sum mid- to late-morning, similar to brunch in the West, although restaurants may open as early as 6:30 a.m. and not close until mid-afternoon.

Once you are seated, waiters with food-laden trolleys push their way around the restaurant. You choose the snacks you want from the trolley and share them with others at the table. It is best to go with a group, as that way you can try a greater variety of treats. You wash the food down with an endless supply of green tea.

Dim sum favorites worth sampling include spring rolls, shrimp and pork dumplings, steamed pork spareribs, sesame seed balls filled with a sweet potato paste, egg custard tarts, and mango pudding.

TEA

You will never believe that tea can taste so good until you visit Taiwan. Even the most uncompromising coffee drinker could be converted to the delights of Taiwanese teas during a visit to the island. Taiwan's mountains and mild climate, along with Chinese tradition and expertise in cultivation, have collaborated to

produce some of the world's finest brews. Teas in Taiwan are aromatic and renowned for their sweet and pure flavor. The most famous are Baojhong (Baozhong), known for its subtle taste and aroma; Tie Guanyin (Iron Goddess), with a pure flavor; the full-bodied and refreshing Dongding Oolong; and Pekoe Oolong, which has a distinctive fruity, sweet taste.

Taiwanese restaurants will automatically provide tea with meals, and coolers at convenience stores are stacked with a large variety of refreshing iced teas. But to get the best out of the tea-drinking experience, sit down for some *yum cha* (literally "drink tea") at one of Taipei's delightful teahouses.

ALCOHOL

Taiwan Beer is Taiwan's best-known locally made brew; it is an acceptable beer, not a great one, but cheaper than imported beers. The

selection of imported beers is reasonably varied, with ubiquitous global brands Heineken and Carlsberg widely available. U.S. beers Budweiser and Miller can be found in most bars, as can China's well-known Tsingtao.

Local liquor falls into the firewater category, with powerful Kaoliang coming in at 58.5 percent alcohol. The most popular liquor is Shaohsing, a rice wine with a much more moderate alcohol content. The island also produces a couple of quaffable grape wines, as well as more exotic plum wine.

Dining out and drinking are often combined into one convivial social event involving a great deal of toasting. To impress, hosts may splurge on an expensive bottle of brandy, and you will be required to have some even if you have not been drinking beforehand. Diluting even expensive brands with cola, however, is perfectly acceptable.

Taiwan's younger set has enthusiastically embraced nightclubs such as Taichung's Anole Versus Dance Pub (left), as well as Western-style pubs.

number of rules attached. As a foreigner you will be graciously given some leeway—but just because no one says anything (that would be impolite), don't think you are not breaking any rules. Try to become familiar with some basic etiquette for formal meals.

Waiters place dishes of food on the table throughout the meal. Many dishes come with their own serving spoons or chopsticks. Diners get their own rice bowl—which is refilled by waiters during the meal—and sometimes an empty plate to place food on before transferring to their rice bowl.

While waiting for the food to arrive, don't play with your chopsticks, and never leave them standing upright in your rice bowl, as it evokes the funerary tradition of burning incense. Don't use your own chopsticks to take food from communal plates; use the spoons provided. And don't root around for the tastiest morsel; it's seen as selfish and impolite.

There are a number of things that you can do that would be considered impolite in the West. It's okay to spit bones on the table, slurp the noodles and soup, and even let out a discrete burp now and again. Holding your rice bowl close to your lips and rapidly shoveling the food into your mouth with chopsticks is an accepted way of eating.

The host and others will interrupt dining with toasts, and your glass will regularly be topped up. You are expected to join in the toasts, but it's fine to just touch the glass with your lips. You may choose soft drinks over alcohol, although it is polite to accept a glass of alcohol if offered.

Lingering at the table after a meal for coffee, tea, or a chat is not a Taiwanese habit. When the host signals the end of a meal—sometimes by standing and offering a toast—it's over. As a guest, you are not expected to pay the bill, or even to offer to do so. Just sit back and enjoy the ritual argument over who pays. It will always end up being the one who made the invitation, or the boss, who pays. Never suggest splitting the bill, as this will demean the occasion. ■

BEER HOUSES

Taiwanese beer houses (*pijiu wu*) go beyond the usual notion of a pub or bar. The typical beer house is a cavernous place enlivened with over-the-top theme decoration. Some are able to comfortably seat more than a thousand patrons at a time.

Beer house food includes such perfect beer accompaniments as chili clams, crab stir-fried in garlic and onion, grilled oysters, spareribs, deep-fried bean curd, steamed mussels, fried squid, and dozens of other dishes. Beer houses are clamorous, frenetic, and friendly places where groups of friends relax after a hard day at the office with some food, beer, and chatter.

ETIQUETTE

Dining, whether at home or in a restaurant, fulfills an important cultural function in Chinese communities and, as such, there are a

History of Taiwan

IN THE MID-16TH CENTURY, JAN HUYGEN VAN LINSCHOTEN, A DUTCH navigator, was traveling on a Portuguese ship to Japan when the vessel came upon the island of Taiwan. Van Linschoten was enthralled by the lovely island, and in the centuries to come, the Dutch, Portuguese, Spanish, and Japanese would all attempt to settle this scenic but strife-torn land.

By the time the first European visitors arrived, indigenous peoples had been living on Taiwan for thousands of years. Finds at more than 500 prehistoric sites in Taiwan—some of which date back 10,000 years—offer clues to the origins of Taiwan's first settlers, but not enough evidence has been discovered to provide any definite conclusions.

Digs have unearthed dwelling areas, tombs, shell mounds, megaliths, flat axes, red unglazed pottery, and decorated bronze implements, indicating that the island's earliest peoples were likely from Malayan-Polynesian groups of Southeast Asia and the Pacific. Other archaeological sites have yielded implements that suggest that some of Taiwan's earliest settlers might also have come from the Chinese mainland. These various indigenous groups—13 are now officially recognized in Taiwan—operated independently and were often hostile, lending weight to the argument that they may have had different origins.

By the time Chinese immigrants—mainly from the province of Fujian—began arriving from the mainland in relatively large numbers in the 15th century, they found two distinct indigenous groups. One had settled on the fertile plains of the island, mostly in the southwest, hunting, fishing, and farming. The other, whose practices of tattooing, headhunting, and constant conflict pointed to Pacific-island origins, gathered in mountains, living a semi-nomadic existence.

PIRACY

From the 14th to 16th centuries, marauding Chinese and Japanese pirates used Taiwan as a stronghold, retreating to this ungoverned, unruly island after attacking Chinese and Japanese trading ships and pillaging coastal towns on the mainland. The ruling Ming dynasty (1368–1644) government could do little to stop this piracy, and warships would rarely chase the opportunistic pirates beyond the Ming outpost on the Penghu islands (known to Europeans as the Pescadores) in the Taiwan Strait.

The Portuguese established a trading settlement in the north of the island in 1590, only to pack up and leave soon after. The Dutch were the next European power to try its luck, and they proved to be much more resilient. They originally set up fortifications on the Penghu islands in 1622. However, after an overpowering Ming fleet threatened them in 1624 and forced a truce, they moved to Anping (now part of Tainan) on the southwest coast of Taiwan. It proved a convenient arrangement for both parties. The Ming had little interest in the island and held no sovereign claim to it.

THE DUTCH & SPANISH

The Dutch East India Company, which managed Holland's colonial business, gained exclusive rights to sugarcane and camphor, along with anything else it could trade. Local Chinese were herded into villages and farming cooperatives and burdened with heavy taxes, while missionaries—with a marked degree of success—set about converting aborigines to Christianity. (The fact that aborigines who refused to be converted often ended up on the wrong end of a musket may have proved a powerful incentive.)

The Spanish looked on the initial success of the Dutch in Taiwan with envy, seeing the island as a perfect midway trade point between the Philippines—which they had conquered in the 1560s—and Japan, with which they were trying to establish trade. In 1626, the Spanish launched a small fleet from Manila and landed in the northeast of Taiwan, establishing garrisoned trading posts at Keelung and Danshuei (Danshui). The fort at Keelung was christened Fort San Salvador,

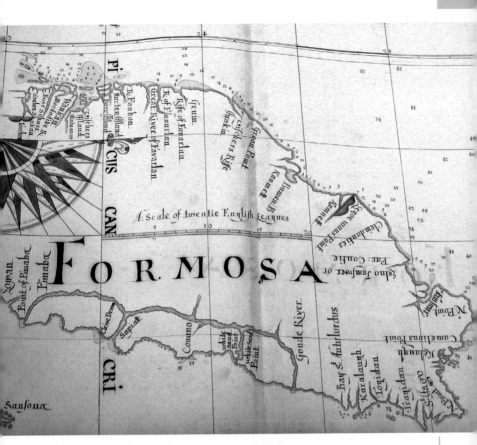

X marks the spot: Well-known British buccaneer William Hacke drew this map around 1690, complete with soundings, distances, and facts regarding anchorages and navigation of rivers that might come of use in his pirating activities.

and the smaller fort at Danshuei was named Fort San Domingo.

The Dutch made two attempts to drive out the Spanish in 1630 and 1641, but both times failed. Feisty local aborigines were also a thorn in the side of the Spanish, while many soldiers succumbed to illness and died. Finally, a threatened rebellion in the Philippines forced the recall of three-quarters of the Spanish garrison. The Dutch overran Fort San Salvador in the summer of 1642, ending 17 years of Spanish adventurism on the island.

By 1650, nearly 300 Chinese and aboriginal villages were under the direct jurisdiction of the Dutch East India Company. Chinese immigrant farmers were organized into collec-

tives, with leaders responsible for keeping local law and order. Areas of land under cultivation continued to increase and new crops such as cabbages, peas, tomatoes, mangos, and capsicum were introduced.

By this time, Taiwan had become one of the most profitable outposts of the Dutch East India Company in the Far East. Spices, amber, kapok, and opium arrived from Southeast Asia through Batavia (Java in Indonesia), silver from Japan, and silk, pottery, herbs, and gold from China. All this was exchanged for sugar, camphor, venison, and deer hides from Taiwan. The Dutch enlisted the help of local pirates to guarantee the safety of their vessels at sea. Sporadic uprisings by both aborigines and Chinese living on the island were swiftly and severely dealt with.

Meanwhile, turmoil had erupted in mainland China, with Manchu armies in the north threatening to overthrow the Ming dynasty. Mainland Chinese began pouring across the Taiwan Strait to escape the fighting.

At first the Dutch welcomed the new settlers and provided them with oxen, seeds, and agricultural tools. The Chinese cleared new land, agriculture continued to flourish, and the Dutch landowners profited handsomely from the rents and taxes paid by their industrious Chinese tenants.

But the Chinese farmers were becoming dissatisfied with the Dutch refusal to sell them the land they worked, forcing them to pay rent instead. The settlers asked to be allowed to buy land and pay taxes in lieu of rent, but the Dutch were not interested. The situation came to a head in 1652 after the Dutch introduced a poll tax. The Chinese revolted, but the uprising was easily and violently suppressed. Up to 6,000 poorly armed Chinese peasants were slaughtered.

KOXINGA

On mainland China, the Ming dynasty was crumbling under a relentless southward push by the Manchu, who had by now built up a huge army. After the Manchu took Beijing, Ming loyalists headed south and continued to resist. Among these resistance fighters was the pirate, Jheng Jhih-long (Zheng Zhi-long), who led a formidable mercenary army. One of his sons, Jheng (Zheng) Cheng-gong, known in the West by his title Koxinga, eventually took over his father's army and pledged to use it to reestablish Ming rule.

From 1646 to 1658, with an army of 100,000 men and a flotilla of 3,000 ships, Koxinga was a scourge to cities along the Chinese coast. The Manchu eventually forced the inhabitants of coastal towns to move inland, robbing Koxinga of both his safe havens and supplies. With the Manchu pressing in on his coastal base, Koxinga set off to Taiwan to regroup.

In 1661, Koxinga's army laid siege to Fort Zeelandia at Anping. The Dutch managed to hang on for eight months before surrendering and eventually leaving the island. Koxinga

Central panel of an 1859 triptych portraying warrior Koxinga, famous for expelling the Dutch from Taiwan in 1662

chose Anping as his capital and set about transforming the Ming enclave into a base from which one day to defeat the Manchu, who had by now established control over almost all of China. However, Koxinga's rule was short-lived. Just a few months after defeating the Dutch, at the age of 38, he succumbed to illness and died.

QING DYNASTY RULE

Koxinga's son Jheng Jing succeeded his father and ruled for the next 19 years until his death, when his son, only 12 years old, was placed on the throne. Two years later, in 1683, the Jheng navy was all but wiped out near the Penghu Islands. The Manchu, or Qing, took control of Taiwan, and it became a part of China's Fujian Province.

Initially, the Qing were intent on seeing that Taiwan did not become a haven for pirates and anti-government forces. One hundred thousand Chinese were repatriated to the mainland and immigration was banned.

Other Chinese were prohibited from living in aboriginal territories lest they foment revolt and form alliances; intermarriage was also forbidden. But concerted resistance continued. During the 212 years of Qing rule on Taiwan, there were over 100 uprisings and revolts, as the people railed against an undisciplined army and bald-faced corruption and mismanagement by officials.

Despite all this, Taiwan thrived. Farms, which were previously owned by the state and the army, fell into private hands. The immigration ban had little effect, and Chinese continued to pour across from the mainland. Camphor became a major cash crop, sugar plantations expanded, and rice fields and tea plantations sprang up.

Taiwan's newfound wealth and strategic position didn't escape the notice of foreign powers. In the 19th century the British, in almost constant conflict with China since the establishment of Hong Kong in 1841, sent their warships out to patrol the coast of Taiwan, searching for movements by Qing forces. Matthew Perry, commander of the U.S. East Indian Fleet, who had earlier forced Japan to open up to trade after two centuries of peaceful isolation, also realized the strategic importance of Taiwan, and pushed for it to become a protectorate of the United States.

The grisly fate awaiting shipwrecked sailors who frequently washed up onto Taiwan's shores did not help matters. These unfortunate souls were subject to beatings, imprisonment, and sometimes beheading by the Chinese or hostile aborigines. Calls for justice were met with shrugs in the Chinese capital of Beijing, whose official influence over Taiwan remained minimal. Europeans often resorted to gunboat diplomacy, bombarding coastal settlements in retribution for the attacks.

The Treaty of Nanjing, signed after the end of the Second Opium War in 1858, led to the opening of four Taiwanese ports, Anping, Danshuei, Dagou (Kaohsiung), and Keelung, to foreign trade. Trading companies quickly established themselves, trade boomed, and expatriate communities flourished.

But skirmishes continued. In 1866, American warships bombarded a tribal area in southern Taiwan in revenge for the murder of two shipwrecked American sailors. In 1869, British warships attacked Anping and demanded better terms for the camphor trade. In 1884, France attacked and temporarily shut down the ports of Keelung, Danshuei, and the Penghus to challenge Qing power.

Taiwan remained an unruly place, virtually ignored by the central government in Beijing and the provincial leaders in Fujian, which left it sorely lacking in law and order.

Much of Taiwan was still in the hands of the aborigines, who begrudgingly shared the island so long as others did not encroach on their territory. The Chinese who did—often in search of new land to clear and farm—were often killed by the land's original inhabitants.

THE JAPANESE

In 1871 the Japanese ship *Miyako* foundered off the southeast coast of Taiwan. Sixty-six men came ashore to be met by a particularly hostile group of Botan aborigines, who duly slaughtered 54 of them.

Japan was set for retaliation, but Foreign Minister Soyeshima Taneomi convinced the Meiji government that a diplomatic solution would be in its best interests. He set off for Beijing with Meiji adviser Charles Le Gendre, a retired American Consul from Amoy (Xiamen) and an American Civil War hero, who had previously negotiated settlements of similar incidents between aborigines and American sailors.

The Qing government sought to escape responsibility for the incident by claiming that China's sovereign rights did not extend to the eastern and southern part of the island inhabited by aborigines. So on May 17, 1874, 2,500 Japanese troops left Nagasaki and headed to Hengchun in the south of Taiwan to confront the Botan. After a few attacks on the tribe to teach them a lesson, the Japanese showed no signs of leaving. After protracted negotiations, Beijing agreed to pay compensation to the families of the victims and for the construction expenses of the Japanese during their six months of occupation.

The affair shook the Chinese into action as they realized that the Western powers and Japan were eyeing the island. Shen Bao-jhen (Bao-zhen), the administrator of shipping affairs, was put in charge of Taiwan's defense in 1874. He organized local militias and

Sun Yat-sen, who established the Republic of China in 1912, has the unusual distinction of being revered both in Taiwan and mainland China.

constructed cannon emplacements along the coast. A law prohibiting contact between immigrants and aborigines was lifted, and immigration from the mainland encouraged.

In 1885 the Qing government made Taiwan China's 22nd province. Its new governor, Liou (Liu) Ming-chuan, continued to modernize Taiwan's defenses and implemented tax reforms in an effort to make the island financially independent. Telegraph lines soon linked Taipei, Keelung, Danshuei, and Tainan, and a submarine cable between Danshuei and Fuzhou in Fujian was completed in 1888. The same year, China opened its first post office, and a railroad connected Keelung and Hsinchu in 1893. The government established a trade office to encourage foreign trade, and Western-style schools sprang up.

JAPANESE OCCUPATION

War between China and Japan broke out in 1894 when the Japanese invaded the Chinese vassal state of Korea. It ended in a humiliating defeat for the Chinese, and the ensuing Treaty of Shimonoseki forced China to cede Taiwan and the Penghu Islands to Japan.

The move, naturally enough, shocked the people of Taiwan. In a futile act of defiance, Qing officials on the island boldly declared a new country, the Taiwan Republic, on May 25, 1895, and pledged to resist the Japanese takeover. It was a disaster. Between June 6, 1895, when Japanese troops formally entered

Taipei, and October 21, when they took Tainan, 7,000 Chinese soldiers died, along with thousands of civilians. The Tapani Incident, another uprising in 1915, proved even more calamitous, resulting in the death of thousands of Chinese.

Japan set about modernizing and remodeling Taiwan in its own image. It built roads and railways linking major towns and cities; constructed dams for hydroelectric power; and created irrigation systems that greatly increased the productivity of land for rice and sugarcane cultivation. Schools, hospitals, and public buildings sprang up, industry developed, modern agricultural methods were introduced, and public health improved tremendously.

Taiwan's first census in 1905 found 3,040,000 people living on the island, 97.8 percent of whom were Chinese and 1.9 percent Japanese. But the census neglected to count aborigines and "bandits," both groups with sizable populations.

The Japanese also managed to do something all previous administrations had failed to accomplish: bring law and order. During their initial years of occupation, the Japanese established administrative mechanisms, monopolized important industries, and suppressed armed resistance. Strict police controls were brought to bear; the infamous Bandit Penalties and Punishments Decree resulted in the executions of more than 10,000 Chinese and aborigines between 1898 and 1920. Later the occupiers introduced compulsory Japanese education and forced cultural assimilation. Economic development began to focus on building the Japanese war machine and providing a launch pad for its forays to the south.

In the later years of Japanese rule, Taiwan's residents were forced to become Japanese subjects, adopt Japanese names, wear Japanese-style clothing, eat Japanese food, and observe Japanese religious rites. Japan drafted tens of thousands of young Taiwanese men into the Imperial Japanese Army, and many thousands were killed.

RETROCESSION

After the Japanese surrender in World War II, Taiwan was officially restored to Chinese rule on October 25, 1945, as agreed to by Nationalist leader Chiang Kai-shek and the other Allied powers.

At war's end, Taiwan's population consisted of 6.7 million Taiwanese, 285,000 Japanese civilians, and 158,000 Japanese military personnel; about 200,000 Japanese wanted to remain in Taiwan, but only 28,000 technical personnel were allowed to stay. Each departing Japanese was allowed to take two rucksacks worth of personal belongings and 1,000 yen. All property and real estate once owned by the Japanese was co-opted by the incoming Kuomintang (KMT) government.

In October 1945, 12,000 Chinese military personnel and 200 officials landed on the island. The joyous welcome that greeted them was soon replaced by despair, as undisciplined troops and officials were more intent on plundering than governing and maintaining order. The Republic of China installed a particularly brutal administrator, Chen Yi, who appointed only mainland officials. The Taiwanese soon

Nationalist headman Chiang Kai-shek joined Allied leaders Franklin Roosevelt and Winston Churchill in a World War II alliance to defeat the Japanese.

Chiang Kai-shek and his wife, Soong Mayling, wave to followers at a mass rally in Taipei in 1970. Chiang ruled Taiwan with an iron fist from 1949 until his death in 1975.

came to feel that they had just traded one colonial government for another.

Newly liberated Taiwan was suffering food shortages, skyrocketing unemployment, and rampant inflation. Its people became second-class citizens in their own land as corrupt KMT officials took what they could and did what they liked.

Festering anger and resentment came to a head on February 27, 1947, when a street vendor in Taipei was beaten by officials for selling contraband cigarettes. In the ensuing melee, a bystander was accidentally shot dead. The

following day a crowd gathered in front of government offices to protest. Sentries fired on the crowd and many were killed. Shops and factories closed in protest, and students went on strike. Governor Chen Yi declared martial law (which was to remain in place for 40 years), called for reinforcements from the mainland, and unleashed a wave of oppression that became known as the White Terror.

Within a few months the number of deaths ran into the thousands, with students, lawyers, and intellectuals the main targets. On March 29, 1948, *Newsweek* reported 10,000 murders.

"Police on trucks roamed Taipeh [sic] shooting into unarmed crowds. Troops knocked on doors of houses and shot the first person who appeared. They looted left and right. ... It was evidently a common practice to bind prisoners with thin wire. The dead bodies of bound men were found every morning on the streets, some beheaded or castrated."

Between 18,000 and 28,000 people were killed, and in the ensuing decades thousands more were imprisoned. The incident that sparked the killings, which occurred on February 28, became known as "er er ba" or 2-2-8, and remained a taboo subject until the lifting of martial law in 1987. On February 28, 1997, the day was named a national holiday.

THE REPUBLIC OF CHINA

Chiang Kai-shek, an ardent Nationalist, had earlier joined Sun Yat-sen in his revolutionary activities in China in a bid to overthrow the Qing dynasty. Sun became first president of the Republic of China in 1912. After Sun's death in Beijing in 1925, Chiang set about consolidating power, leading successful expeditions into northern China and shattering the control of the powerful warlords. He then turned to fighting the Communists before joining Communist leader Mao Zedong to fight the Japanese during World War II.

Following the war, the Communists and Nationalists took up where they left off and unleashed a bloody civil war that ended with Mao proclaiming the People's Republic of China in October 1949. Chiang, who only a year earlier had had himself elected president of the Republic of China by the National Assembly, was forced to flee to Taiwan with his army, where he set up a Nationalist base and vowed one day to retake the mainland—an ideal not officially abandoned until 1991.

At first the United States refused to support Chiang, seeing his KMT party as brutal and corrupt. On January 5, 1950, President Harry Truman told reporters that the United States would not use its armed forces to interfere in any situation involving the Republic of China and the People's Republic of China. But its position soon changed with the advent of the Korean War the same year, and Truman declared: "In these circumstances the occupation of Formosa by Communist forces would be a direct threat to the security of the Pacific area and to the United States forces performing their lawful and necessary functions in that area. Accordingly I have ordered the 7th Fleet to prevent any attack on Formosa." In January 1951, military aid was provided for the KMT, with the proviso that Chiang root out corruption within the KMT.

Millions of Chiang's supporters had followed him to the island, and Taiwan's new leader—who had an affection for the title "Generalissimo"—set about reforming the KMT and planting the seeds for Taiwan's phenomenal economic growth over the ensuing decades. Chiang instituted liberal economic reforms, dismantling state monopolies and encouraging free enterprise and freeing up the entrepreneurial spirit of the island's people in the process. However, political freedom did not come as quickly and challenging the authority of the KMT was not an option.

The Republic of China's insistence that it was the representative of all of China led to the loss of its seat in the United Nations in 1971. In 1972, President Richard Nixon made

Madame Chiang

Western educated, shrewd in politics, charming as could be, Soong Mayling reigned as one of the 20th century's pivotal figures in the struggle between the Nationalists and the Communists for control of post-imperial China. Married to Chinese Nationalist leader Chiang Kai-shek in 1927, Madame Chiang, as she became known, rose to prominence during World War II. In 1943 she became the first Chinese and the second woman to address a joint session of the U.S. Congress. Her influence in Washington during those years played a big part in the close relationship that exists today between the United States and Taiwan. After her husband's death in 1975, Madame Chiang moved to New York; she was left shattered by President Jimmy Carter's announcement in 1978 that the U.S. was breaking off diplomatic ties with Taiwan and establishing relations with China. She remained in seclusion in New York until her death at the age of 106 in October 2003. ■

Supporters of Democratic Progressive Party candidate Chen Shui-bian celebrate his election as president in 2000.

a historic visit to mainland China, giving de facto recognition to the Communist regime. In December 1978, President Jimmy Carter ordered a shift of the United States embassy from Taipei to Beijing.

From the time Chiang took control of Taiwan in 1949 until his death on April 5, 1975, the population of Taiwan more than doubled to 16 million. Chiang's model of capitalism propelled Taiwan from an agricultural economy to a leading exporter of manufactured goods. The island had reached new heights of prosperity and economic growth, and it enjoyed a standard of living well above that of most economies in the region, certainly far above that of the mainland.

But all this came at a price. Chiang was a ruthless dictator and the KMT monopolized power at national and provincial levels. Dissent was not countenanced. The government commonly imposed long jail terms and executed citizens without trial. Citizens were not allowed to leave the country without government permission (a law not repealed until the lifting of martial law in 1987), and the Taiwanese language and customs were suppressed, as were those of the Hakka and aboriginal populations.

THE ROAD TO DEMOCRACY

Chiang's son Chiang Ching-kuo took over as head of the KMT and was elected president in 1978. He was a more personable figure than his father, willing to talk and listen to the growing opposition forces within Taiwan. Eventually he gave tacit approval for opposition parties to operate openly.

In 1979, in the southern city of Kaohsiung—a stronghold of anti-government dissent—150,000 people rallied to protest against the government. Police swamped the demonstrators with tear gas, and the rally soon disintegrated into a riot. When the dust settled, organizers were arrested and charged with sedition, and a number received long jail sentences. The Kaohsiung Incident, as it became known, proved to be a watershed in Taiwan's movement toward democracy.

Chiang Ching-kuo died in 1988. His vice-president Lee Teng-hui succeeded him and immediately set about steering Taiwan toward democracy. He legalized opposition parties, giving more credence to the increasingly popular, pro-independence Democratic Progressive Party, formed in 1986, and out-maneuvered KMT hardliners to cement his position as KMT chairman.

Lee then turned his attention toward mainland China. He boldly announced his pro-independence feelings (a sentiment shared by much of the population), and further inflamed the situation by first lobbying for a seat at the United Nations before making a high-profile visit to the United States in 1995.

Taiwan's first democratic presidential

elections were held the following year. China, in an unsubtle attempt to dissuade people from voting for pro-independence Lee, began lobbing missiles near the island as part of "military exercises." The bullying backfired; the Taiwanese, fed up with the mainland's belligerence, elected Lee with an overwhelming majority.

Lee fired a final political salvo at the mainland when he declared that China and Taiwan were two separate states, going against his previous statements that the two were one country with two different governments.

THE FUTURE

After 55 years in power on the island, the KMT lost the presidency in 2000, when the pro-independence Democratic Progressive Party's leader Chen Shui-bian was elected. Chen, narrowly re-elected in 2004, has worked to institute social reforms, but many promises remain unfulfilled, and his popularity has waned. His popular pro-independence policies remain muted in the face of ongoing threats from mainland China.

Mainland China sees Hong Kong's "one country, two systems" handover in 1997—which guarantees 50 years of autonomy for the territory—as a precursor to a similar political solution for Taiwan. But the mainland's often overt political interference in Hong Kong since the handover has convinced many Taiwanese that a similar agreement is not the best option. A solution to the "one China" problem remains far off. ∎

The land

MUCH OF TAIWAN'S NATURAL BEAUTY IS FOUND IN THE TOWERING Central Mountain Range that runs for 167 miles (270 km) along much of the island's length from north to south, forming Taiwan's most dominant topographical feature. Visitors are often surprised at the pervasive presence and majesty of these heavily forested mountains. More than 200 peaks rise above 10,000 feet (3,000 m), and the range is rarely out of view from anywhere on the island.

Taiwan's modest size accentuates the dominance of its mountains. The island is only 245 miles (394 km) long and 89.5 miles (144 km) across at its widest point, making it just 14,015 square miles (36,300 km) in total area, including offshore islands. It straddles the Tropic of Cancer and is the only good-size island in a swath of Pacific Ocean between the Philippines 221 miles (356 km) to the south and Japan's Okinawa island 370 miles (595 km) to the northeast.

The island's mountains are the result of a collision of monumental proportions. Taiwan sits about 80 miles (130 km) from the Chinese mainland on the westernmost edge of the Rim of Fire, the term given to the perimeter of the vast Pacific Ocean, where ocean tectonic plates are in constant conflict with continental tectonic plates. Twelve million years ago, the Philippine plate collided with the Eurasian landmass, buckling the Earth's crust. Land heaved upward, then folded and twisted to form Taiwan's chains of mountains.

This geologic stress deep inside the Earth builds volcanoes around the Rim of Fire, and the continuous friction and grinding between the plates causes frequent and violent earthquakes. The Rim of Fire is in fact the most volcanically active and earthquake-prone region in the world.

Although Taiwan has no active volcanoes, it has its fair share of earthquakes. Many fault lines crisscross the island. As the Eurasian and Philippine plates continue to collide, enormous pressure builds. When released, this pressure rocks the Earth's surface with violent and sometimes devastating temblors.

Taiwan has had 19 earthquakes measuring more than 7 on the Richter scale since the beginning of the 20th century. Among these were a 7.1-magnitude earthquake that killed more than 3,250 people in 1935, and a 6.8-magnitude quake on November 14, 1986, that killed 15 and injured 44.

In the early hours of September 21, 1999, the island was shaken awake by one of its most devastating quakes. The earthquake (now called the 9-21 Earthquake) measured 7.3 on the Richter scale and was so violent it toppled buildings in Taipei, 93 miles (150 km) away from its epicenter at Jiji township in Nantou County, near the resort area of Sun Moon Lake. It killed 2,415 and injured 11,305. Around 30,000 buildings were destroyed and 25,000 damaged. The worst-hit area was the Central West, where just about every city, town, and village suffered damage. More than 1,300 aftershocks were reported within 24 hours of the major quake.

REGIONS

On the island's relatively isolated east coast, the eastern flank of the Coastal Mountain Range rises dramatically from the Pacific Ocean, climbing to over 5,000 feet (1,500 m), before dropping down to the rich alluvial plains and bucolic scenery of the East Rift Valley—a fault that cuts through the mountains for 100 miles (160 km) between the east coast cities of Hualien and Taitung.

On the western side of the valley, mountains again rise steeply to form the Central Mountain Range. On the range's southeastern flank, the jagged and exposed peaks of Yushan reach as high as 12,966 feet (3,952 m), forming Taiwan's tallest mountain.

Erosion has carved spectacular gorges and left expansive valleys throughout the Central Mountains, while at the highest altitudes, sheer pinnacles of rock jut out above heavily

The spectacular Cingshuei (Qingshui) Cliffs on Taiwan's east coast are typical of the island's spectacular coastal scenery.

forested mountainsides.

To the west and northwest the mountains yield to foothills cut through by narrow valleys laced with rocky gullies and tablelands. From the base of the hills and tablelands, broad, fertile plains fed by convoluted rivers and streams stretch to the west coast. These rich alluvial plains account for most of Taiwan's agricultural output.

Wide tidal flats, swamps, sandy spits and lagoons characterize the island's west coast. These coastal areas are heavily industrialized and densely populated. Cities, towns, and factories merge to form an almost unbroken string of urban sprawl.

Fringing coral reefs with an abundance of marine life line Taiwan's south coast, where coastal land areas are marked by uplifted coral outcroppings.

HOT SPRINGS

While Taiwan has no active volcanoes, it does have plenty of bubbling geothermal activity in the form of hot springs. Around 100 hot-spring resorts around the island give weary citizens the opportunity for revitalizing soaks.

As rain falls in the mountains, it seeps into porous sedimentary rock, picking up the rock's minerals—anything from radium to sulfur—along the way. Water seeping deeper beneath the Earth's surface is warmed by the Earth's heat. When it eventually encounters a large fault, the hot, pressurized water rises to the surface within the fault line until it bubbles into a hot-springs pool. The fault line needs to be wide enough so the water can be forced to the Earth's surface quickly. If it moves too slowly, the water will cool down before it emerges at the surface.

Over time, sediment on the walls of the fault lines dissolves under pressure from the rising water, enlarging them. The escaping water also wears the surface opening of the fault lines wider. This creates a type of pipe-line, allowing the heated groundwater to run to the Earth's surface quickly and efficiently.

Autumn leaves add a splash of color along the Cijiawan (Qijiawan) River in Alishan, in the heart of Taiwan's central mountains.

mammal on the island, distinguished by a white V-shaped mark on its chest and long curved nails that help it dig into the ground in search of food.

The slopes of Taiwan's highest mountain, Yushan—found in Yushan National Park— harbor 28 species of mammals, 125 species of birds, and 17 species of reptiles, including possibly the largest selection of rare and endangered wildlife on the island. Although there is a good chance of spotting Formosan macaques on the forested slopes of Yushan, sightings of other singular species such as Formosan sambar (a type of deer), Chinese pangolin, serow, and Formosan wild boar are much rarer.

Rare and beautiful, the Formosan clouded leopard may have its last refuge in the Central Mountain Range south of the Tropic of Cancer. The lack of recent sightings leaves conservationists unsure whether the mammal still exists in the wild.

Taiwan's extensive network of estuaries, coastal marshlands, and sheltered areas along the coast and in the mountains make it an appealing stopover for a number of migratory birds. About 480 local and migratory bird species have been identified on the island, and bird-watching is a popular pastime for locals and visitors alike.

The island was once almost totally carpeted with forest. These days, forested areas take up about 7,336 square miles (19,000 sq km). Hardwoods, conifers, and bamboo are common in the hills and lower reaches of the mountains, giving way to temperate and sub-alpine coniferous forests at altitudes of between about 8,200 feet and 11,450 feet (2,500 m and 3,500 m). At higher altitudes forests are primary and virgin. On gravelly slopes beyond the tree line—above 11,450 feet (3,500 m)—brushwood and herbaceous vegetation dominates.

In the south of the island, varieties of palm and other tropical-plant species are common. Kending National Park, at the southern tip of the island, contains small pockets of protected primal tropical forest. ∎

As the water percolates deep beneath the Earth's surface, pressure increases and anaerobic bacteria set to work converting dissolved sulfates in the water to hydrogen sulfide. This process is what causes the common "rotten-egg smell" given off by some hot springs.

To retain the created hydrogen sulfide, the water must travel quickly to the surface. If there is no oxygen along the route to the surface, then conversion continues. However, if the fault contains oxygen (generally the case in wide fault lines), the hydrogen sulfide is oxidized before it reaches the surface, and there is no rotten-egg smell.

FLORA & FAUNA

With much of Taiwan either cultivated, industrialized, or urbanized—particularly the north and west in areas below 1,640 feet (500 m)— the sparsely inhabited mountain regions have become a sanctuary for the island's wildlife.

Areas above 6,560 feet (2,000 m) are home to the Formosan black bear, the largest land

A year of festivals

Taiwanese festivals, which have their origins in Taoism, Buddhism, and folk religion, are colorful affairs rich in costume, action, and symbolism. They are celebrated according to the lunar calendar, so dates vary from year to year. It is worth planning your visit to Taiwan to coincide with a festival; some of the major ones are outlined below.

Chinese New Year (January/February)
First day of the first moon (lunar month). Celebrations officially run to the 5th day, but traditional holidays run to the 15th. This is Taiwan's most important holiday: the time to get rid of the old and welcome the new, so debts are cleared, houses cleaned, and feuds ended. Many people take time off during the holiday to travel, and most shops and offices close. It is best to avoid Taiwan at this time, as transport and hotels are fully booked in advance. *Dates: Feb. 18, 2007; Feb. 7, 2008; Jan. 26, 2009; Feb. 14, 2010.*

Lantern Festival (February)
Fifteenth day of the first lunar month. This is one of Taiwan's most colorful and popular festivals, celebrated to mark the end of Chinese New Year. Temples, homes, shops, and restaurants display traditional lanterns. Enormous lanterns displayed at Chiang Kai-shek Memorial Hall, a carnival in Kaohsiung, and other large-scale official celebrations also mark the festivities. *Dates: March 4, 2007; Feb. 21, 2008; Feb. 9, 2009; Feb. 28, 2010.*

Birthday of Mazu (April/May)
Twenty-third day of the third lunar month. The goddess of the sea is one of Taiwan's favorites. On her birthday, noisy celebrations erupt at the more than 400 temples devoted to Mazu. Expect fireworks, dragon dances, and images paraded on sedan chairs. *Dates: May 9, 2007; April 28, 2008; April 18, 2009; May 6, 2010.*

Dragon Boat Festival (June, occasionally late May)
Fifth day of the fifth lunar month. This festival celebrates the life of Cyuyuan (Quyuan), a hero from ancient times. Dragon boats manned by rowers plow though waterways in a series of competitive events. *Dates: June 19, 2007; June 8, 2008; May 28, 2009; June 16, 2010.*

Ghost Month (August)
First to 29th day of seventh lunar month. The time of year when the gates of the netherworld are open and restless spirits wander the Earth. Devotees appease the ghosts through rituals such as offering food and burning wads of "hell money." People tend to be cautious during this period, so traveling and celebrations are curtailed. Visit a Taoist temple if you would like to see the appeasement rituals. *Dates: Aug. 13, 2007; Aug. 1, 2008; Aug. 20, 2009; Aug. 10, 2010.*

Mid-Autumn Festival (September/October)
Fifteenth day of the eighth lunar month. Also known as the Moon Festival, it is a celebration of the harvest moon. Disc-shaped moon

cakes—symbolizing family unity—appear in bakeries. This is a time of family get-togethers, evening strolls, and moon-gazing. *Dates: Sept. 25, 2007; Sept. 14, 2008; Oct. 3, 2009; Sept. 22, 2010.*

ABORIGINAL FESTIVALS

Taiwan's indigenous minorities celebrate their cultures in a number of annual festivals. Most are open to the public, but ask permission to join activities or to take photographs; avoid certain no-go areas.

Bunun Festival (April/May)
Held between the end of April and the start of May, this festival honors farming and hunting.

Dahwu Flying Fish Festival (generally March/April)
The Dahwu (Yami) live on Orchid Island off Taiwan's southeast coast. For the long festival, they build traditional fishing boats, launching them amid blessings and ceremonies.

During the Divine Palanquin Crossing the Fire—a temple ritual that is part of the Lantern Festival—palanquin guards dash into fierce flames.

Ami Harvest Festival (July and August)
This is when Taiwan's largest indigenous group welcomes, feeds, and says farewell to the spirits in thanks for a bountiful harvest.

Saisiat Sacrifice to the Short Spirits (October/November)
Held biannually around the 15th day of the tenth lunar month. The Saisiat honor the spirits of a fabled neighboring tribe of short people who befriended the Saisiat tribe.

Puyuma Annual Festival (late December)
The festival, in which boys are set a number of trials, revolves around the passage from boyhood to manhood. ∎

The arts

WITH A FEW EXCEPTIONS, TO TALK OF TAIWANESE HERITAGE IS TO TALK OF
Chinese cultural traditions in art and theater. In fact, Taiwan, with its stunning wealth of
Chinese art and antiquities, is probably the best and most convenient place to enjoy
these expressions of the long history of China's religion, tradition, and art.

The National Palace Museum (see pp. 80–85)
in Taipei houses the largest and most
magnificent collection of Chinese art and
antiquities in the world. Taipei's National
Museum of History also holds a rich repository
of Chinese artifacts. To see the development of
contemporary Taiwanese artistic styles, a visit
to the Taipei Museum of Fine Arts, as well as
the Museum of Contemporary Arts, is a must.
Traditional performance art, such as Chinese
opera, is popular in Taiwan, especially the
Beijing and homegrown versions. Other arts,
such as cinema, have evolved into something
uniquely Taiwanese.

CHINESE OPERA

To the Western ear, traditional Chinese opera
can take a bit of getting used to. The voices of
the performers are shrill; banging gongs and
drums are loud and erratic; string instruments
twang uncomfortably; and wind instruments
screech. But amid this cacophony is a dazzling
visual feast of elaborate and colorful costumes,
symbolic makeup, absorbing pantomime, and
exciting acrobatics and martial arts.

Chinese opera has its origins in the third
century, when simple plays were performed
for court entertainment. The form went
through transformations over the centuries,
gradually gaining popularity. In 1790, an
Anhui opera troupe performed before the
Qing royal family at the Forbidden Palace. The
troupe used themes and techniques co-opted
from other opera styles, giving birth to Beijing
opera. Performances evolved between 1840
and 1860, and Beijing opera took on its own
identity, eventually becoming the most popular form of theater in China.

More than 350 forms of Chinese opera
exist in mainland China, most acted out using

local dialects and differing melodic forms.
Most are named after the area in which they
originated and remain obscure. One exception
is Cantonese opera, which is popular in the
southern province of Guangzhou and neigh-

**Elaborate costumes, heavy makeup, and
stylized expressions and movements
characterize Chinese opera.**

boring Hong Kong. Like the Cantonese themselves, this opera has a more rough and ready nature (performed in the Cantonese dialect and using down-to-earth themes) than the refined Beijing opera.

Taiwanese opera shares popularity with Beijing opera in Taiwan. Taiwan's version is generally performed outdoors on makeshift stages in marketplaces and during festivals. Performers use the Taiwanese dialect, stages are elaborately decorated, and facial makeup is restrained.

Chinese opera depicts action and emotions through universally understood symbols embodied in the actors' gestures, costumes, and makeup. Themes are mainly melodramatic and epic (such as good triumphing over evil), drawn from ancient folklore and legends familiar to the audience.

When the hands and body tremble, a character is angry. A curt flick of the sleeve indicates disgust. A hand thrown in the air and sleeves flicked back symbolize surprise. To portray embarrassment, the face hides behind a sleeve. A performer rubbing his or her hands together for a few moments is enacting worry. A chair

on the stage is a chair, but when placed on a table it's a mountain, and when used as a seat after being placed on a table is a throne. Opening doors, climbing steps, riding in carriages, rowing boats, eating, embarking on long journeys, and so on, are all symbolized by stylized movements.

Color and design in both costumes and makeup indicate social status and temperament. Red makeup shows loyalty and honesty, while white means cunning. A student usually wears a blue gown, while an emperor is decked out in a "dragon," or imperial yellow, robe.

Performances can last for hours, and the audience doesn't always remain rapt. People chat among themselves, eat and drink, come and go, snooze, and generally cause a good deal of clatter. Attention reverts to the stage during popular and exciting scenes.

BRONZEWORK

Some of the earliest examples of China's rich artistic heritage are found in its ancient works of bronze, mainly created between the Shang (ca 1766–1122 B.C.) and Han dynasties (206 B.C.–A.D. 200). Artists typically cast bronze into ritual and utilitarian vessels, musical instruments, and weapons with highly decorative elements. Many were inscribed with Chinese characters honoring the ancestors of royalty and highly placed officials.

The most famous piece of ancient Chinese bronzework is the "Mao Gong Ding" tripod vessel, now on display at the National Palace Museum in Taipei. The inscription on the inside of the bowl is made up of 497 characters, the longest ancient Chinese bronzework inscription unearthed so far.

Decorative elements changed with the times. Reliefs and three-dimensional designs gradually replaced engraved lines and embossed patterns. Later advances included inlays using gold, silver, copper, and turquoise. The fierce-looking tao tieh (tao tie), or beast of gluttony, said to be a symbolic composite of various wild animals, became the most prominent element during the Shang period.

During the Western Zhou period (ca 1122–771 B.C.), bird and other animal motifs came into vogue. Later, encircling chain-link patterns became popular. The Eastern Zhou period (ca 771–256 B.C.) introduced vertically

interlocking geometrical animal-band designs.

Besides relics found in Taiwan's museums, superb bronzework can be spotted in many temples. These include large incense burners with dragon-themed handles, doors, ritual vessels, and, sometimes, dragon columns.

CALLIGRAPHY

Calligraphy is regarded as one of China's highest art forms. It was once a pursuit of the literati and privileged classes—the only ones who could afford the time to master it. Those seeking admission into the mandarin class needed to be skilled in calligraphy. The art demands careful planning and confident execution, qualities admired in administrators and executives.

Calligraphy developed as the Chinese written language became more sophisticated. It was both a means of communication and a form of artistic expression; calligraphers chose a style that would best express a passage of text, often adding imagination and beauty to practical government laws and decrees.

The earliest examples of calligraphy come from rubbings taken from bronzes and other metalwork. The National Palace Museum in Taipei has a treasure trove of calligraphic art, the earliest being Shang-period inscriptions. Its earliest authored piece is *Pingfu Tieh (Tie) (On Recovering from Illness)* by Lu Ji (261–303).

Lu Chang, an 11th-century biography of calligraphers of the Five Dynasties (907–960) and Northern Song periods (960–1127), describes the methods used to achieve the best calligraphic results:

"To display brushstroke power with good brushwork control; To possess sturdy simplicity with refinement of true talent; To possess delicacy of skill with vigor of execution; To exhibit originality, even to the point of eccentricity, without violating the *li* [the principles or essence] of things; In rendering space by leaving the silk or paper untouched, to be able nevertheless to convey nuances of tone."

The Song dynasty (960–1279) produced a number of noted calligraphers, who made paper rubbings after first carving wood or stone. The Yuan period (1279–1368) also had its share of masters. But it was during the Ming (1368–1644) and especially the Qing periods (1644–1911) that calligraphy truly developed and flourished.

A craftsman puts the finishing touches on a lantern. Colorful, bold, and detailed, these lanterns are a uniquely Chinese art form.

CERAMICS

Pottery in China dates back to the Neolithic period, but it wasn't until the development of kiln firing during the Han dynasty that ceramics were widely produced.

Improved glazing techniques during the Jin period (265–420) and the Northern and Southern dynastic periods (386–589) allowed for the inclusion of more detail. Tang dynasty (616–906) potters took the craft a step further by developing *sancai*, or tri-color, glazes in green, yellow, and brown. These ceramics, most often horses, camels, and tomb guards, are among the most famous of Chinese porcelains. The Song dynasty saw the introduction of monochrome ceramics, which became renowned for their technical detail.

The familiar underglaze cobalt-on-white painting, usually landscapes or theatrical scenes, was the signature of Ming dynasty ceramics. Initially, the quality was poor, but as potting and glazing techniques improved the pieces achieved remarkable delicacy.

Wucai, or five-color, wares of the mid-to-late Ming period were enlivened with colorful motifs in reds, yellows, light and dark greens, browns, aubergines, and underglaze blues.

Quality and production of ceramics reached their peaks in the early decades of the Qing dynasty, aided by a string of technical breakthroughs that allowed for more creativity in shaping and vibrancy in color. Vases became reticulated, oversized, and painted with detailed landscape scenes. Breakthrough *fencai*, or powdery color, enamel for decorating porcelain appeared during this period. Subsequent improvements in the technique meant a wider range of colors and tones could be used, resulting in highly detailed compositions of plants, humans, and animals. The Qing era also introduced another famous color known as "tea dust," an opaque glaze finely speckled with green, yellow, and brown.

The height of technical perfection was reached during the Qianlong period (*R.*1736–1795) of the Qing dynasty. Subsequently, the craft fell into decline as the popularity of porcelain waned and political upheaval took hold. By the time the second Sino-Japanese War erupted in 1937, all kilns were closed and most of the artisans who were left headed to the south of China to make a living.

China reestablished its pottery industry after World War II, and it slowly gained

momentum. Leaps in technology over the past few decades mean that excellent porcelains can be had for affordable prices in Taiwan. The town of Yingge (see p. 121), just south of Taipei, is Taiwan's pottery capital. Here, hundreds of factories turn out an overwhelming selection of porcelains and other ceramics. If you are in the market for modern porcelain, this is the place to go.

CLOISONNÉ

Cloisonné is the technique of applying enamel decor in various colors to the surface of metal objects. It came to China from Persia in the eighth century, but was then all but forgotten until around the 1200s. The Chinese, already masters of firing techniques for ceramics, glass, and metals, improved and refined the technique, and by the mid-15th century cloisonné products reached new levels of delicacy and quality.

The cloisonné technique involves first soldering brass wire to the surface of a metal object to form a pattern or illustration. The craftsperson then fills in the patterns with colored enamel paste (made by crushing enamel pieces into powder and mixing them with water) and fires the piece in a kiln. After firing, the enamel surface is smoothed and the exposed brass wire and metal gilded.

Popular cloisonné pieces include screens, tables and chairs, boxes, chopsticks, earrings, and smoking accessories.

JADE

Even though found in relative abundance, jade is highly prized in China for its soft sheen and subtle hues, while jade sculpture from the Qing dynasty to the present day is perhaps the most sumptuous form of Chinese art.

Ancients believed that wearing jade would increase longevity, allowing them to live as long as the gods. Jade figures and jade robes sewn with gold thread have been found in Han dynasty tombs. Many people in Taiwan today wear jade jewelry for good luck.

Some simple jadestone artifacts in China date back 12,000 years. Discoveries of small disks, likely used for personal decoration, date back more than 7,000 years, while finely crafted jade objects 4,000 years old point to the stone being used in ritual.

Rendering jade into more sophisticated forms began in the Shang dynasty, and the craft continued to be refined until the start of the first millennium before waning in popularity. The craft was revived during the Ming dynasty, and many skilled craftsmen emerged. Creative technique peaked during the Qing dynasty.

Antique jadeware fetches high prices,

Chinese landscape paintings, such as "Green Mountains and White Clouds" by Wu Li (left), often have multiple focal points. Another Chinese art form, jade carving, reached its peak in the Qing era, exquisitely demonstrated in "Luohan Meditating in White Jade" (below).

during the Ming and Qing dynasties. This method involves coating a core of wood or tin with layers of lacquer. When the outer coat has dried, the artist carves decorations into the lacquer. The core is left untouched, serving as the background for the relief.

The use of lacquer was widespread by the first millennium A.D., when the substance coated musical instruments, eating and drinking utensils, weaponry, furniture, and funerary objects. In later centuries, artists added popular patterns, motifs, and themes to lacquered surfaces. During the Tang dynasty, artists found that iron filings soaked with vinegar would make lacquer sap turn black, instead of brown, as it dried. Adding cinnabar to the sap turned it red. These two colors became the standard for lacquerware.

PAINTING

Chinese painting is divided into two major schools. *Gongbi* is a meticulous style with strict rules of composition, close attention to detail, and fine brushwork. *Sieyi (Xieyi)* is a freehand style that generalizes shapes and uses a richer brushwork and ink technique.

Although Chinese painting dates to the

which vary greatly depending on age and style of the work and the status of the original owner. The cost of more recent pieces depends on the quality of the work and the reputation of the craftsperson who created it. Fake jadeware is prevalent throughout Asia; to the untrained eye it is impossible to distinguish from the real thing. Get professional assistance if you plan to buy.

LACQUERWARE

Lacquer comes from the sap of the lacquer tree *(Rhus verniciflua)*, found in central and southern China. Its use in the country dates back to the fifth millennium B.C., when it was used to coat eating utensils and ritual objects.

Once exposed to air, sap from the lacquer tree turns brown and solidifies. It is then refined and either applied to objects ready for carving or embellishment, or molded into forms. After the base coat is applied to an object, many thinner coats are added to form layers. When the lacquer is dry, it is smoothed and polished to give it its trademark sheen. For producing forms, fabric or paper is saturated in lacquer and then jammed into molds. Once the form has set, it is removed from the mold and more layers of lacquer are applied.

Lacquerware carving—which began during the Tang dynasty—reached its creative height

Neolithic period with painted pottery, other media such as silk and paper hanging scrolls, fans, and albums appeared much later during the Tang dynasty.

Traditionally, figures, landscapes, and flower-and-bird combinations have formed the subject matter of Chinese paintings. Landscapes are not restricted to a single focal point. A painting can have a shifting perspective and may encompass objects that are both near and far, based on the notion that people view things from a mobile perspective—for example, on a boat trip down the Yangzi River.

Most traditional Chinese painters have also been poets and calligraphers. To the Chinese, artists needed to incorporate "painting in poetry and poetry in painting." Inscriptions, seals, and poetic words helped to explain the painter's sentiments as well as add to a painting's beauty.

Color in Chinese painting is added after the basic brushwork is finished. Brushwork in shades of black ink creates the images, which are enriched by subtle, harmonious shades.

CONTEMPORARY ART

The Japanese influenced Taiwanese art in the period immediately before World War II. The Japanese were keenly interested in European art, and Taiwanese artists traveling to Japan to study art picked up European techniques. The Taiwanese then applied these techniques to homegrown subjects and themes, and a new style of Taiwanese art began to evolve.

After the Japanese were defeated and the Chinese Nationalist government moved to the island, this style fell away in favor of traditional Chinese artistic themes and techniques. The Nationalists offered encouragement through competitions and other events.

Styles swung back toward the Western again in the late 1950s and 1960s, as a new generation of Taiwanese artists embraced abstract and pop art. During the 1970s, after Taiwan lost its seat in the United Nations, artists (poets, novelists, and painters) began to explore Taiwan's identity through their work and started to emulate the work of artists during the Japanese occupation, employing more modern forms of European style and technique.

After the lifting of martial law in 1987, artists began to reflect Taiwan's newfound sense of freedom and identity in their art. The Taipei Fine Arts Museum (see pp. 78–79) is the best place to go for an introduction to Taiwanese contemporary art. The city also has a thriving art scene, with many private galleries displaying and selling the works of Taiwanese artists.

CINEMA

The early development of cinema in Taiwan coincided with the Japanese occupation (1895–1945), although early feature films and documentaries shot on the island were made without Taiwanese actors. The first true Taiwanese film using local funding and local actors was *Whose Fault Is It?* (1925). The Japanese, as expected, tightly controlled the content and subject matter of this and subsequent Taiwanese movies.

The outbreak of the Sino-Japanese War in 1937 put the industry on hold. A number of Shanghai filmmakers followed Nationalist leader Chiang Kai-shek from the mainland at the end of China's civil war in 1949, forming the nucleus of a revived film industry on Taiwan in the 1950s. Government funding helped support the fledgling industry, but only for films in Mandarin. Early attempts at making films in the Taiwanese language were discouraged by the government, received no funding, and petered out.

As Taiwan began its surge toward modernization in the 1960s, the government's Central Motion Picture Corporation introduced a quasi-propaganda genre called "health realism." These films were an attempt to persuade citizens to come to terms with all the fast-paced changes in Taiwanese society by using traditional Chinese values to solve modern social problems.

Toward the end of the 1970s, a low budget sub-genre called "social realism" emerged, featuring the winning formula of sex, violence, and gang subculture. Repetitive themes and plots and over-the-top violence soon led to these films losing their appeal.

By the late 1970s, Taiwanese moviegoers were growing tired of all this moral malaise and escapism. Combined with the emergence of slicker films from Hong Kong and cheap pirated videos of Hong Kong and Western movies, Taiwanese cinema was in trouble and screaming out for a change in direction.

Taiwanese director Ang Lee's film, *Crouching Tiger, Hidden Dragon*, won four Academy Awards in 2000. His *Brokeback Mountain* brought more Oscar honors in 2006.

The government began to support new, young directors. The groundbreaking film *In Our Time*—a social look at Taiwan since the takeover by the Nationalists in 1945—came out in 1982. It became the model for what was dubbed the New Cinema Movement. *The Sandwich Man* (1983) was directed by three young filmmakers, including one who later became Taiwan's most famous director, Hou Hsiao-hsien. The movie, which depicts U.S. economic aid to Taiwan during the darker days of the Cold War, is regarded as the foremost creative effort of the New Cinema Movement. It enjoyed both critical acclaim and commercial success.

New Cinema films generally portray rural people in Taiwan coming to terms with changes in society. Techniques of deep focus, long takes, a non-linear narrative, and a discontinuity of editing give New Cinema films a documentary feel.

While most New Cinema directors chose rural settings for their films, others, like Edward Yang, explored urban themes. His movies, including *Taipei Story* (1985), concern the social and personal problems that confront women, disaffected youth, the middle class, and the urban elite.

The most famous of the New Cinema films is Hou Hsiao-hsien's *City of Sadness* (1989), which picked up a Golden Lion award at the Venice Film Festival. The film explores the relationship between the Taiwanese and the oppressive Nationalist troops during the early years of the Nationalist government's iron-fisted rule.

The brooding and dour imagery of New Cinema began to lose its appeal in the 1990s, and a second generation of creative filmmakers started to arrive on the scene. Movie themes tended to be more exploratory and less menacing. Tsai Ming-liang's *Vive L'Amour* took the 1994 Golden Lion in Venice. Ang Lee, who has achieved fame in the U.S. with his

At contemporary artist Ju Ming's outdoor sculpture garden and gallery in northern Taiwan

Hollywood productions, *Crouching Tiger, Hidden Dragon* and *Brokeback Mountain,* first took on the sensitive subject of homosexuality in *The Wedding Banquet* (1993) and explored the Chinese obsession with food in *Eat Drink Man Woman* (1994).

With a few exceptions—and despite its acclaim—New Cinema never became popular with the mainstream movie audience. Taiwan's film market continues to be dominated by Hong Kong films, with their crowd-pleasing action, stylized violence, melodrama, slapstick comedy, and much-loved stars.

POP MUSIC

Slick numbers sung in Mandarin, collectively known as Mando pop, dominate the popular music scene in Taiwan. Artists from Hong Kong, who now record their songs in both Cantonese (Canto pop) and Mandarin, share the limelight with local entertainers. As in most pop music, substance is eschewed for simple lyrics and catchy tunes. Popular themes revolve around the causes of teen angst: love, lost love, and unrequited love. Performers are invariably good-looking and wholesomely sexy. Music and video production is polished and appealing.

Like Hong Kong's Canto pop, Taiwanese Mando pop has a big following among substantial Chinese communities in other countries in East and Southeast Asia, as well as among people in mainland China.

The diva of Mando pop was the much-loved Teresa Deng, who held pan-Asian appeal by singing lyrics in Mandarin, Taiwanese, Japanese, and English. Deng's untimely death in 1995, at the age of 43, was mourned throughout the region and the late singer has since attained legendary status.

The Taiwan music scene also has some vibrant alternatives. Folk and rock tunes, with lyrics attuned to social problems, have earned a number of artists commercial success.

Taiwan's alternative music scene has a big following, a somewhat unusual phenomenon in an Asian music scene largely dominated by saccharin banality. It kicked off around 1994 and has grown into a thriving industry. Alternative bands crank it out at crowded pubs and clubs all over Taipei, mostly on weekend nights. ■

The remarkable transformation of Taiwan into a modern, democratic, and vibrant society in just a few decades is best exemplified on the lively and sophisticated streets of Taipei, the island's capital.

Taipei

A uniformed guard lowers the flag in front of Chiang Kai-shek Memorial Hall.

Taipei

AS RECENTLY AS THE 1960s, TAIPEI WAS LITTLE MORE THAN A SLEEPY BACK-water with few paved roads and a handful of cars. But from the 1970s on, the city began to grow in the unbridled fashion that characterized many Asian cities during the period. Taipei is now a modern, vibrant city, home to about three million people.

In 1709 three farmers from Fujian province established a farm on the banks of the Danshuei (Danshui) River in what is now Taipei. More immigrants followed, settling around the Danshuei. One settlement became known as Manka, today's Wanhua and the most historic area in the city.

Because of their location on the bustling Danshuei River, Manka and the nearby area of Dadaocheng emerged as the most important

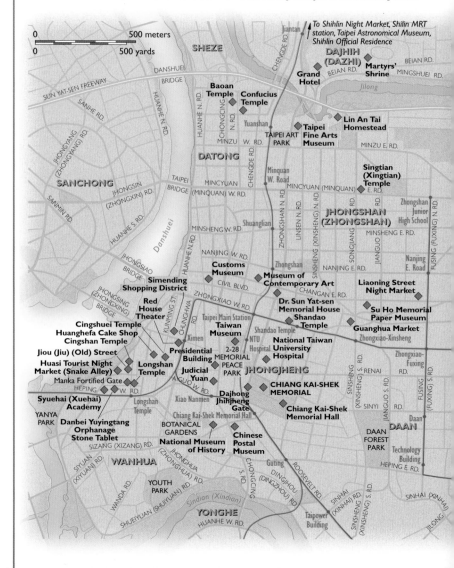

Taipei's excellent MRT trains zip along tracks both above and below the ground.

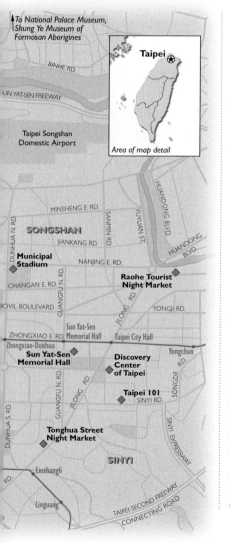

areas of the city. In 1875 prominent Qing dynasty official Shen Bao-jhen (Shen Bao-zhen) applied to establish the prefecture of Taipei in what is the present-day Jhongheng (Zhongzheng) District. Today Taipei is the island's largest city and its administrative, economic, and cultural center.

In the three-plus decades since the early 1970s, Taipei has developed the same problems as many Asian cities, where economic growth has taken priority over the environment and quality of life. But in the 1990s, city fathers took stock. Horrendous traffic jams led to the construction of an extensive mass rapid transit system, the MRT, considered the best in Asia. Bus lanes along widened city streets encouraged people to leave cars at home, and the city's notorious taxi drivers were made to clean up their act—and their cabs. New parks gave the city's population some breathing space.

Taipei's streets are laid out in grid fashion and signposted in English as well as Chinese. But confusion can arise. Streets are divided into sections according to compass direction; alleys are numbered and named according to the major streets they branch off of. Major north–south arteries are also numbered in English as boulevards, east–west arteries as avenues. A typical address, for example, could read No. 24, Lane 18, Jhongshan (Zhongshan) North Rd., Section 2. When heading out have someone write your destination in Chinese. Your hotel will supply you with a card for the hotel written in Chinese so you can find your way back.

Taipei residents are friendly to foreign visitors, but many do not speak English. For English-language directions, check with a hotel or police station. ∎

2-28 Memorial Peace Park & around

2-28 Memorial Peace Park

⬛ Map p. 56

🚇 MRT: National Taiwan University Hospital station

Taiwan Museum

www.tpm.gov.tw

⬛ Map p. 56

✉ 2 Siangyang (Xiangyang) Rd.

☎ 2382-2699

🚇 MRT: National Taiwan University Hospital station

THE NAME OF THIS PARK WAS CHANGED FROM TAIPEI NEW Park in 1996. It honors the Taiwanese who were killed in an uprising against Chinese Nationalist misrule that began on February 28, 1947 (see sidebar p. 59). The park's grounds are interesting for their memorial, museums, and some quirky contents. The park is lively in the morning, when residents take walks and do *tai ji quan* exercises.

Just inside the park's east gate is the **2-28 Memorial,** a rather ungainly postmodernist structure of huge concrete cubes supporting a steel spire. Beyond the structure, the **2-28 Memorial Museum** informs visitors about unsavory aspects of the Kuomintang's early years in power, illustrating them with unsettling photographs and artifacts. The park also houses an open-air theater, along with

The Shin Kong Life Tower rises above 2-28 Memorial Peace Park, which commemorates the thousands killed in the 1947 uprising against the Chinese Nationalist government.

oddities that include old cannon, two European-built steam locomotives dating back to the late 19th century, and a megalithic tomb.

At the northern end of the park is the **Taiwan Museum.** Built in 1915 in an eye-catching—if surprising—Greek Revival style, the recently renovated museum houses exhibits on natural history and a collection of aboriginal artifacts.

The **Presidential Building** (*122 Chongcing/Chongqing Rd., Sec. 1, www.president.gov.tw*) is just to the west of the park at the end of wide Ketagalan Boulevard. The Japanese constructed the bold red-brick building, finished in 1919, in the neo-Renaissance style they favored then. Its central tower was once the tallest structure in Taipei. In fact, in order to keep an eye on things, the Japanese ordered that no building in the city could be higher than the tower.

Next door is the **Judicial Yuan building** (*124 Chongcing Rd., Sec. 1*). Built in 1934, its design—again, highlighted by a broad brick facade, archway entrance, central tower, and carved ornaments—almost mirrors the design of the Presidential Building.

Back in front of the Taiwan Museum, head north along Guancian (Guanqian) Road toward Taipei Main Station and the 51-story, 804-foot (245 m) **Shin Kong Life Tower** (*66 Jhongsiao/Zhongxiao West Rd., Sec. 1, tel 2389-5858*). It was recently supplanted by Taipei 101 (see p. 87) as the tallest building in Taipei. From the 46th-floor viewing deck you get sweeping views of the city and mountains beyond.

Cross Jhongsiao West Road to Taipei Main Station and the **Taipei Underground Mall,** a collection of retail outlets that runs for 650 yards (600 m) to Zhongshan MRT station on the Danshui line, linking the commercial areas around Taipei Main Station and Nanjing West Road. While the shops sell nothing out of the ordinary—computers, clothing, souvenirs, books, and magazines—the place is certainly remarkable for its sheer length.

When you emerge from the mall at Zhongshan MRT station, head to the **Museum of Contemporary Art** (*39 Changan West Rd., tel 2552-3720, www.mocataipei .org.tw*), in part of another architectural legacy of Japanese occupation. This former government office building has been caringly renovated. Inside it, numerous galleries house temporary exhibits. ∎

White Terror

On February 27, 1947, the beating and arrest of a vendor for illegally peddling cigarettes ignited large-scale public protests the next day against the government repression and corruption that had existed since the Japanese surrendered in 1945. Chinese leader Chiang Kai-shek sent thousands of troops from the mainland to quell the protests. The army showed no mercy, rounding up and executing lawyers, academics, doctors, students, and local leaders. Reports of soldiers knocking on doors and shooting the person who answered were common. Between 18,000 and 28,000 people were murdered and thousands more imprisoned over the next decade in what has become known as the White Terror (white being the color of death for the Chinese). Some remained in prison until the 1980s. It took a new government in 1996 to finally acknowledge these horrors and memorialize those who died, at 2-28 Memorial Peace Park. ∎

Chiang Kai-shek Memorial

Chiang Kai-shek Memorial
www.cksmh.gov.tw

⚠ Map p. 56

✉ 21 Jhongshan (Zhongshan) South Rd.

☎ 2343-1100

🚇 MRT: Chiang Kai-shek Memorial Hall station

THE MASSIVE CHIANG KAI-SHEK MEMORIAL HALL AND surrounding park were built to memorialize the Nationalist leader and long-time president of the Republic of China. Work on the 250-foot (76 m) marble-clad edifice began in 1977, two years after the Generalissimo (as he liked to be called) died. It opened to the public in 1980, on the fifth anniversary of his demise. The massive monument was, in its early years, a place of pilgrimage for many Taiwanese.

These days, as Chiang's aura fades, the surrounding gardens, pavilions, and expansive plaza are still crowded, but more often with people enjoying the sense of open space in a busy city, rather than with visitors paying their respects to the late leader.

Although the memorial may have lost some of its relevance, you cannot help being impressed by its size and grand architectural style. The striking **Memorial Hall** is clad in gleaming white marble, with an octagonal step-pitched twin-eave roof of brilliant blue-glazed tiles topped with a golden dome. It sits amid 62 acres (25 ha) of immaculately tended gardens, hedges, carp ponds, and pavilions. Whitewashed walls topped with blue tiles form a long colonnade that wraps around the complex. Windows on the outer wall are shaped in Chinese motifs, such as plum flowers and open books.

The main entrance to the park is marked by the magnificent 98-foot (30 m) five-arched Ming-dynasty-style **Dajhong Jhihjheng (Dazhong Zhizheng) Gate** (the Gate of Great Centrality and Perfect Uprightness), on Jhongshan (Zhongshan) South Road. The marble facade and 11 roofs of blue-glazed tiles atop the gate reflect those of the main hall. The huge gate faces southwest toward the Kunlun Mountains in China, symbolizing Chiang's dream of one day retaking the mainland.

Beyond the gate, the complex opens to a vast paved plaza running 220 yards (200 m) to the Memorial Hall. Flanking the plaza are the National Theater on the right and the National Concert Hall at left, the buildings that make up the National Chiang Kai-shek Cultural Center.

The plaza narrows to become the **Boulevard of Homage,** flanked by beds of blazing red flowers, and continues on to the marble steps of the Memorial Hall. To gain entrance, you climb the steps—guarded by auspicious white stone lions—to a towering 46-foot (16 m) archway and mighty bronze doors, beyond which a bronze seated statue of Chiang gazes proudly over the plaza. Inscriptions on the wall behind and to the left and right of the statue are Chiang's descriptions of Sun Yat-sen's "Three Principles of the People" philosophy of ethics, democracy, and science. From there you descend into the bowels of the hall on one of two staircases, each with 89 steps, representing the age of Chiang when he died.

Inside the lower level are an audiovisual room, library, lecture hall, study center, and two small art galleries—the **Chiang Kai-shek Art Gallery** and the **Hua En Art Gallery**—which hold temporary exhibitions of local and international artists.

Much of the area is given over to the enormous 21,500-square-foot

(2,000 sq m) **Exhibition Hall,** which traces Chiang's life and achievements through documents, photographs, paintings, and memorabilia. The highlights of the exhibition are two gleaming black bulletproof limousines once used by the late president. The **Chiang Kaishek Memorial Office** contains the original 1950s furnishings from the Generalissimo's office, including his pens, writing brushes, desk, and cabinets. After visiting the memorial, take some time to stroll around the park and its well-tended gardens.

NATIONAL CHIANG KAI-SHEK CULTURAL CENTER

Contrasting with the solemnity of the memorial hall are the two almost identical buildings—the **National Theater** and the **National Concert Hall**—that face each other across the plaza.

These beautiful buildings, both important centers for the performing arts in Taiwan, are rendered in grand Chinese palace style. Sitting on white concrete bases, their thick red columns support bright multicolored eaves and furled bright yellow glazed-tiled roofs.

More than 800 performances are held in these two world-class performing-arts venues annually. If you'd like to attend, you can purchase tickets for the day's show at the reception desk on the first floor of the National Theater. ■

The graceful National Concert Hall hosts hundreds of performances a year.

Flanked by a peaceful lotus pond, the National Museum of History offers antiquities inside and tranquil walks outside (above and opposite).

National Museum of History and Botanical Garden

ALTHOUGH IT IS OVERSHADOWED BY THE LARGER National Palace Museum (see pp. 80–85), the National Museum of History is still an important repository of historical Chinese artifacts. The adjacent Botanical Garden makes for a pleasant amble after visiting the museum.

Most of the museum's 10,000 artifacts were brought in from mainland China or donated by private organizations, adding up to an impressive collection of bronzes, jades, pottery, porcelain, lacquerware, textiles, inscriptions, coins, carvings, paintings, and calligraphy spread over galleries on four floors. As is the case in most museums in Taiwan, English-language explanations are sporadic. The museum does conduct tours in English at 3 p.m. daily. Free English audio guides are also available.

Just inside the entrance is a corridor running the width of the museum with a collection of stone steles and carvings of Buddhist iconography from early Chinese dynasties. These include a magnifi-cent four-sided thousand-Buddha column from the Northern Qi dynasty (550–577) and the centerpiece of the collection, a 5-foot-high (1.53 m) Buddha tower from the Northern Wei dynasty (386–534). This complex pagoda-style stone carving incorporates depictions of hundreds of monks and nuns in acts of devotion.

The elevator to the **second floor** opens to a corridor of traditional Chinese landscape paintings and calligraphy. At the end of the corridor is a gallery housing temporary exhibitions. The remaining galleries on the floor are given over to a large collection of Tang dynasty (618–907) tricolor ceramics. The collection, notable for its high level of craftsmanship, typifies the elegance of the period.

Objects in the first part of the collection include utilitarian items of the time, such as tripod jars, incense burners, and glazed ornamental figures in the shape of oxen, hens, and other symbolic animals. You can also see horses and riders involved in the imperial pursuit of polo, a sport that was introduced from Persia during the Tang dynasty. The collection then moves on to more glazed figures of horses, this time without their mounts. These expressive figures, which were used as funerary objects, are magnificently crafted. After horses come camels, also funerary objects. All these saddled animals have similar expressions, heads held high and mouths agape as if screeching. The final phase of the collection presents figurines from the Tang dynasty: ladies of the Imperial Court, military and civil officers, and fierce-looking chimeras, celestial guardians.

On the **third floor** is the General History of Chinese Cultural Artifacts Exhibition, a superb, albeit eclectic, display of relics from various dynasties, although like other displays it lacks English-language captions. Among the objects here are ceramic pillows with floral inscriptions; porcelain plates, vases, and bronze and gold Buddha images; ceramic models of houses and bronze pagodas; bronze wine and cooking vessels; and landscapes carved from stone.

The **fourth-floor gallery** has displays of finely woven badges worn during the Qing dynasty (1644–1911) by military and civil officers to indicate rank. The floor also has an exhibition of traditional drinking vessels, including ceramic pots, clay bottles, and tiny wine cups. Along a corridor off the gallery, through a moon-shaped door, is a traditional teahouse with timber floors, simple wooden tables and chairs, and views of the Botanical Garden.

BOTANICAL GARDEN

These gardens sit next to the National Museum of History, with 20 acres (8 ha) divided into 17 sections of plant families, interlaced with shady paths, boardwalks, and meandering ponds. Their major attraction is the **Lotus Pond,** where, in summer, water lilies burst

into brilliant red, white, and yellow. The most picturesque entrance to the Botanical Garden is on Heping West Road. A small plaza inside has a map. Head along the path to the right to reach the Lotus Pond.

Other park highlights include a **Herbarium** (take the path straight ahead from the entrance plaza); a **Palm Garden** alongside the path to the Lotus Pond; and a **Fern Garden** in the northwestern corner of the gardens, where a boardwalk takes visitors through a Jurassic-park-like display of thick green foliage. ■

Chinese traditional medicine

Chinese traditional medicine is rooted in the ancient concept of yin and yang, or the balance of contrasting elements in nature, and in the belief in Qi, or vital energy. Chinese traditional doctors attempt to manipulate the balance of this theoretical vital energy using herbs, minerals, animal parts, acupuncture, massage, and other methods. By attempting to establish harmony among the organs and systems, physicians believe they can keep their patients in good health.

Certain streets in Taipei are lined with shops dispensing traditional medicines. Their exotic ingredients, tucked in row after row of drawers and displayed in jars on shelves, often resemble a small museum of natural history rather than a dispensary. Among the curiosities are cinnabar and amber to relax the nerves; peach pits and safflower to improve circulation; and ginseng to strengthen the heart. Snakes and lizards are often seen floating in large jars.

Throughout much of China's turbulent history, acupuncture and herbs were the primary health treatments. By the 20th century, Chinese doctors had mapped out 350 precise acupuncture points, grouped into systems of channels that were said to conduct vital energy, or Qi, through the body. Modern practitioners insert stainless steel needles into these points, twisting and moving the needles to achieve the desired effect. Scientists believe acupuncture may release endorphins, which block pain and cause mild euphoria.

More than 2,000 traditional remedies have been documented in Chinese literature, although only about 150 are commonly used these days. The Taiwanese have a high regard for traditional medicine, and millions swear by its efficacy, although most will visit both traditional practitioners and doctors trained in Western medicine to treat their health problems. Western visitors should exercise caution when it comes to traditional medicines; some herbal mixtures can be quite powerful or even dangerous.

The use of mixtures to treat ailments is the bedrock of Chinese traditional herbal prescriptions. On a visit to the doctor, the patient will answer questions about his or her state of health. After the diagnosis, and frequently after a traditional physical examination, the doctor will generally select, measure, and cut about four or five ingredients. The patient then takes the ingredients home to boil them with water into a thick brew. Adherents believe such curative blends can reduce fevers, cure diarrhea, eliminate headache, and in general promote good health.

Massage is another common traditional treatment. By restoring Qi, or unblocking clogged-up Qi channels, it is supposed to cure problems such as stiffness, back pain, fever, or painful joints. The massage can be strenuous, often breaking blood vessels and leading to bruises, which are said to appear where the imbalances existed.

Related to this is the practice of using glass or bamboo suction cups, thought to draw out evil energy and cure arthritis. The cups are heated with a wad of flaming, alcohol-soaked cotton to create a vacuum, and then placed on a vital point, where the flesh swells into the cup. Like massage, it

also leaves marks: It is common to see round circular bruises on the backs and legs of sunbathers in Taiwan.

Chinese traditional medicine is gaining popularity in the West. While adherents believe it shows some promise in treating chronic diseases, serious testing still needs to be done to prove its safety and efficacy. ∎

Opposite: A Chinese traditional-medicine pharmacist weighs ingredients carefully. Above: Drawers in a traditional-medicine shop may contain hundreds of herbs and exotic remedies, ready to be measured and mixed.

Taipei's night markets

Taipei's night markets

🅼 Map pp. 56–57

TAIPEI HAS A PROFUSION OF LIVELY NIGHT MARKETS throughout the city. Some serve up a familiar menu of snack foods, clothes, and knickknacks, while others offer more exotic fare. The markets usually open at around 6 p.m. and close around midnight.

Taipei's night markets, such as this one in Wanhua, are bustling spots where shoppers can buy anything from snack cakes to computers.

GUANGHUA MARKET

Taiwan is the world's biggest manufacturer of notebook computers, and it seems most of them are for sale in and around Guanghua Market. Hundreds of retailers sell laptop, notebook, and desktop computers, software and peripherals, digital cameras, mobile phones, and other electronic goods. Many of the polite shop attendants speak a little English, and there is no hard sell. It is perfectly acceptable to go from retailer to retailer comparing prices while attendants readily give you advice. Take the MRT to Zhongxiao-Xinsheng station.

HUASI (HUAXI) TOURIST NIGHT MARKET

The market—more famously known as **Snake Alley**—has been sanitized by the city fathers. Once notorious for its snake restaurants,

RAOHE TOURIST NIGHT MARKET

Raohe Tourist Night Market, in the area northeast of Bade Road, Section 4, and Fuyuan Street, is introduced by an archway and strings of hanging lamps. About 140 street vendors and 400 storefront stalls line the 1,640 feet (500 m) of narrow Raohe Street. Traditional Chinese opera and other performances are frequently held at the market. To get there, take any of the following buses: 28, 32, 51, 53, 54, 63, 203, 205, 256, 306, or 311.

SHIHLIN NIGHT MARKET

Shihlin is home to the largest night market in Taipei and is a great place to try delicious Taiwanese snack foods. The new multilevel structure that houses the sprawling market has 380 vendors offering plenty of mouthwatering fare (try the oyster omelets). The atmosphere is enlivened with lots of hubbub, blinking neon lights, and workers walking around with signs advertising specials at their food stalls.

Crowds throng the aisles and streets until late at night. Kids (and adults) shoot pellet guns at balloons to win prizes and fortune-tellers do brisk business. Vendors sell the usual market goods: cheap clothing, shoes, CDs, bags, and toys. Take the MRT to Jiantan station; the market lies just northwest near Yangming Theater on Wenlin Road.

TONGHUA STREET NIGHT MARKET

West of Jilong Road between Sinyi (Xinyi) Road, Section 4, and Heping East Road, Section 2, this is one of Taipei's smaller night markets, but what it lacks in size it makes up for in bustle. The market connects with the Linjiang Street Night Market, which offers snacks ranging from sausages and stuffed buns to steamed rice cakes. ∎

brothels, shady fortune-tellers, and assorted tricksters, the market has been transformed from a city embarrassment to a spot promoted by tourism authorities. A few snake restaurants still remain in this covered market street, and they are the main attraction for many visitors, who enjoy the entertaining, but sometimes cruel, antics of the snake handlers in front of these restaurants. Besides the snake restaurants, there are more conventional Chinese eateries that offer pancake soup, salty rice pudding, freshwater turtle, and other seafood. You'll also find shops selling luggage, books, clothes, fruit, and souvenirs. To reach the market, take the MRT to Longshan Temple station.

Longshan Temple

Longshan Temple

🅰 Map p. 56

✉ 211 Guangjhou (Guangzhou) St.

☎ 2302-5162

🚇 MRT: Longshan Temple station

LONGSHAN (DRAGON MOUNTAIN) TEMPLE IS ONE OF Taiwan's oldest and most important temples, and it has survived its share of disasters over the last 260-plus years. Originally built in 1738, the temple was leveled by an earthquake in 1815, rebuilt, and badly damaged again by a typhoon in 1867. It was fully reconstructed between 1919 and 1924, only to fall victim to a wayward Allied bomb in 1945, which destroyed its main hall but left the statue of the temple's main deity, Guanyin, the goddess of mercy, undamaged. The main hall was rebuilt and the temple restored once again in 1957.

Immigrants from three counties in China's Fujian Province who moved in the 18th century to Manka (now Wanhua), Taipei's oldest district, built the temple. The new arrivals modeled and named it after the sacred Dragon Mountain, where they had previously worshiped in China. It was originally intended to be a Buddhist temple, but has since incorporated many Taoist deities and other temple elements into its elaborate design.

The temple is famous for the exquisite detail of its stone sculp-

One of Longshan Temple's many altars, all a colorful feast for the senses

tures, woodcarvings, and bronzework. Its guardians employed one of Fujian's finest temple architects and builders, Wang Yi-syun (Yi-xun), to oversee its reconstruction in 1919. These days only Taiwan's most skilled temple craftsmen are employed to carry out maintenance and restoration work on the rich ornamentation at Longshan.

The 12 main support columns of the main hall, with their sculptures of writhing dragons hewn from solid stone, exemplify the temple's rich design. A more subtle example, at least to the Western eye, of Longshan's magnificent temple art are the inscriptions on the temple walls and pillars, exceptional for both their abundance and their literary and calligraphic attainment. People still come to Longshan simply to take rubbings of these beautiful writings.

The temple consists of three halls—front, middle, and rear— separated by courtyards. The main gates of the temple are open only during festivals or for the visits of important personages. Temple lore holds that you should enter through the small gate to the right of the main gate and exit through the small gate to the left. The stone-framed window to the left of the main entrance is carved with scenes from the classic Chinese novel, *Romance of the Three Kingdoms.* To the right of the entrance is an octagonal bamboo window on which is carved the Chinese characters for "firecrackers announce that all is well."

In the **courtyard** in front of the main hall, people take turns standing under a huge yellow lantern, holding joss sticks and bowing in prayer.

The small **front hall** is notable for its patterned bas-relief granite walls, inscribed pillars, and pair of dragon columns cast in bronze, the only two such columns in Taiwan. The prow-shaped roof ridge of the hall is edged with dragons and lined with brilliantly colorful porcelain figurines depicting various mythological scenes. This architectural approach, along with the painted patterns that embellish the underside of the hall's eaves and roof supports, is carried through to the other two halls.

To get to the **first courtyard** you can go through passageways on either side of the front hall. The eastern passageway leads you to the

A devotee prays to one of Longshan Temple's dozens of deities.

temple's **bell tower,** while the western passage takes you through to the **drum tower,** both with unusually shaped hexagonal two-tiered roofs.

Guanyin is enshrined in the center of the **main hall** amid a riot of color and ornate decoration. The goddess is attended by the bodhisattvas Manjursi to her left and Samantabhadra to the right, while images of 18 lesser attendants cluster around.

Taiwanese merchants originally built the **rear hall** at the end of the 18th century as the old Manka district grew in stature as a trading port. They enshrined the popular Taoist deity Mazu—(see sidebar p. 169)—here. The walls are richly embellished with intricate stone carvings and pillars. Two of the pillars here are unusual in that the carvings on them depict human figures. A number of images of lesser deities are enshrined in sections of the hall to the goddess's left and right. (Dozens of deities are worshiped to varying degrees at Longshan.)

The temple is almost always bustling with worshipers and tourists; the best time to visit is in the early evening when it is at its busiest and most colorful.

LONGSHAN TEMPLE

Built in 1738, often hailed as Taiwan's Forbidden City, the temple is the best preserved of its kind in Taiwan. It features a roof with multiple curling eaves and carved pillars and beams. What sets it apart is the exquisite detail of its stone sculptures, woodcarvings, and bronzework.

Main Hall

West Side Room

Drum Tower

Exit (Tiger)

Front Hall

Entrance (Dragon)

Rear Hall

East Side Room

Bell Tower

The main hall is for worship of the host deity, Guanyin, the Buddhist goddess of mercy; the rear hall is dedicated to Mazu, the Taoist goddess of the sea; while throughout you'll find altars devoted to a panoply of lesser deities from different religions. All were brought to Taiwan by immigrants from China and placed together here out of convenience. ■

The streets around Longshan Temple make up part of Taipei's oldest district.

A walk around Wanhua District

The first settlement in Taipei city, Wanhua by the early 19th century had become Taiwan's third largest city, thanks to booming trade with the mainland. Its decline began with the settlement of the Dansheui (Danshui) River downstream. Many remnants of Wanhua's colorful past still remain, and strolling the busy streets brings its share of entertainment.

Evenings are the best time for a walk: The temples and alleys come to life after dark.

Start at **Cingshuei (Qingshui) Temple ❶** (81 Kangding Rd., tel 2371-1517), which honors Song dynasty Taoist monk Chen Chao-ying, revered for providing medical care to the poor. Dragons, other mythical creatures, and fine patterned carvings enliven its roof and walls.

Exit the temple from the front and go straight, or west, down Gueiyang (Guiyang) Street, Section 2, for about 300 yards (270 m). Cross Siyuan (Xiyuan) Road and, after 10 more yards (10 m), on your left you'll spot **Cingshan (Qingshan) Temple ❷** (218 Gueiyang St., Sec. 2), wedged between two buildings. The narrow temple has magnificently carved beams and murals. The deity enshrined in the main hall fronted by the temple's courtyard is King Cingshan (Qingshan), who can dispel pestilence and dispense justice.

Backtrack to Siyuan Road and turn right, or south, for another 22 yards (20 m), until you come to **Yadong Tianbula ❸** (56 Siyuan Rd., Sec. 1), a clean, air-conditioned restaurant

specializing in Taiwanese snack food. Try a bowl of *mian sian (mian xian)*—vermicelli soup with oysters.

Continue in the same direction on Siyuan Road and turn right, or west, on Gueilin (Guilin) Street. In 110 yards (100 m) beckons the entrance to **Snake Alley ❹**, also called Huasi (Huaxi) Street. Wander past seafood restaurants, antique shops, and foot massage parlors—as well as the famous snake restaurants. Not everyone's cup of tea, but it does open a window to an older China, where snake is believed to have magical properties.

Exit Snake Alley at Guangjhou (Guangzhou) Street and turn left, or east. Walk 110 yards (100 m) and cross Siyuan Road. On the left is **Longshan Temple ❺** (see pp. 68–71), one of Taipei's most important places of worship. Running alongside the outer eastern wall of the temple, **Herb (Cingcao/Qingcao) Lane ❻** is a narrow covered alleyway piled with canvas sacks and display boxes full of different teas and

Orphanage Stone Tablet ⑦ (243 *Guangjhou St.*), in front of Renci (Renqi) Hospital. Inscriptions tell of the orphanage established by Wanhua residents in 1870.

Continue west along Guangjhou Street for 200 yards (183 m) to where it intersects with Huanhe South Road, Section 2, and turn right. Continue for another 330 yards (300 m), across Gueiyang Road, to a huge store, **Jia Jhen (Jia Zhen) ⑧** (183 Huanhe Rd.), on your right. This is the place to pick up both useful items and interesting souvenir gifts, including traditional cookware. ∎

🗺 See area map p. 56
▶ Cingshuei (Qingshui) Temple
↔ 0.8 mile (1.25 km)
🕒 3 hours
▶ Jia Jhen (Jia Zhen) kitchen store

NOT TO BE MISSED
- Cingshuei Temple
- Longshan Temple
- Herb Lane

---

herbs. Goods have been sold here since 1738.

Return to Guangjhou Street, turn right, go back across Siyuan Road, and continue west the way you came from Snake Alley. In about 100 yards (91 m)), on the left side of Guangjhou Street, awaits **Danbei Yuyingtang**

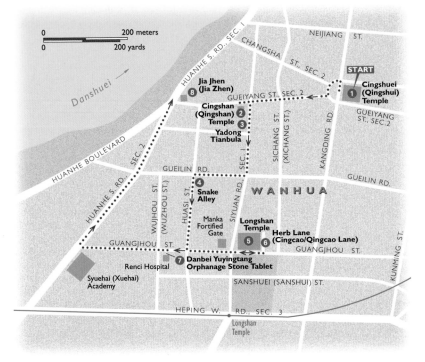

Lin An Tai Homestead

Lin An Tai Homestead

www.ca.taipei.gov.tw/civil/lin-an-tai/

🗺 Map p. 56

✉ 5 Binjiang St.

☎ 2598-1572

🕐 Closed Mon.

💲 $

🚇 MRT: Yuanshan station

THIS HOMESTEAD, BUILT BETWEEN 1783 AND 1785, IS THE oldest residential building in Taipei, with side-wing buildings added between 1822 and 1823. It was originally constructed in Taipei's Daan District, a mile (1.6 km) or so southeast of its present location. But under threat from urban development, it was dismantled brick by brick in 1978, warehoused, and rebuilt at its present site in 1983.

The homestead is an outstandingly preserved example of the southern Fujian style seen during the Ming (1368–1644) and Qing (1644–1911) dynasties. It sits at the rear of a substantial spread of lawn and hedges behind a small **crescent pond.** As well as being a concession to *fengshuei (fengshui),* the pond provided water for breeding fish and fighting fires.

Carvings of fruits and vases decorate the alcove main doors to the homestead and surrounding panels and eaves. Family seals and banners on the right-hand side of the door symbolize learning and power.

Just beyond the main doors, the gate hall has more carvings and adornments. On the ceiling, carvings of fruits denote longevity, many generations, and luck.

Mythical figures decorate the columns that support the ceiling.

From the gate hall you pass into the **inner court,** where you gain access to the inner buildings and main hall. The wooden doors of the inner rooms have patterned carvings topping delicate latticework.

The **main hall,** the most ornate of all the rooms, contains the wooden ancestral altar. The altar is carved with a legion of legendary figures and flanked by delicately crafted wooden latticework shaped into flowers and window frames fashioned with dragons.

Covered corridors connect the maze of inner and outer rooms, 34 in all, many of which have been given over to a small museum displaying imperial-era clothing, weapons, and other artifacts. ■

A crescent pond reflects the details of Taipei's oldest homestead.

Confucius & Baoan Temples

THESE TWO NEIGHBORING TEMPLES OFFER A CONTRAST IN architecture, from the subtle craft of the buildings and sweeping roofs of the Confucius Temple to the gaudy tribute to the god of medicine at the Baoan Temple. The architecture of the Confucius Temple is in tune with its meditative nature, while the ornate Baoan Temple reflects Taiwan's devotion to its plethora of deities.

Confucius Temple

🅰 Map p. 56
✉ 275 Dalong St.
☎ 2592-3924
🚍 Bus: 41, 246, 288

Inside and outside the structures of Taipei's **Confucius Temple** are bamboo groves and sculpted gardens, potted bonsai plants, ponds, and arching miniature bridges. Its temple buildings, while rich with detail, nonetheless hold back on ornamentation to a large degree, which is typical of most Confucius temples in Taiwan.

The annual celebrations on September 28, Confucius' birthday, (also celebrated as Teachers Day), are held at the temple's **Dacheng Hall,** where the tablet of Confucius is placed. The hall is a stunning example of temple architecture without the usual ornamental gloss. Its distinctive double-eave swallow-tail roof is topped by a ship-prow ridge, on the center of which a sits a pagoda to ward off evil. At each end of the prow are two cigar-shaped objects, replicas of bamboo cylinders once used to preserve manuscripts. Carved stone dragon columns support the lower-eave roof, while the heavy wooden doors feature superb latticework.

Inside the hall, look up toward the ceiling cavity at the intricate web of support beams and brackets. No nails were used in the construction of the hall.

The **Baoan Temple** (*61 Hami St., tel 2595-1676, www.baoan.org .tw*), over 200 years old, features dragon carvings on its support columns, as well as roof ridges that seem to groan under the weight of its many porcelain mythological figurines. The interior of the tem-

ple is crowded with gilded images of a multitude of deities, including an image of its main god—Baosheng Dadi, the god of medicine—which was brought to Taiwan from Fujian province in China by immigrants in 1805. ∎

Fairs at the Baoan Temple are as colorful as the temple itself.

Confucianism in Taiwan

Confucius (551–479 B.C.), from a poor but noble family, was the most notable sage of ancient China. His thoughts were official state canon until the end of the Qing dynasty in the early 20th century. Many of his philosophical tenets have endured and remain central to the Taiwanese character.

Confucius' teachings were recorded after his death in *The Analects,* a tome that later became required study for Chinese scholars. Confucius believed in harmony, and he taught that true pleasure could not be found in the pursuit of money or sensual delights, but in generosity to friends, frequent social interaction, and obedience to hierarchy. His primary concern was the creation of a moral human who observed *li* and *ren.* Li, or ritual, is the practice of following ceremony; rites help guide a person in daily life. Ren, or benevolence, is the force that binds people in a web of relationships and obligations.

For Confucius, relationships between people always involved a superior and inferior, such as a ruler and subject, father and son, husband and wife, or older friend and younger friend. Confucius taught that inferiors should always respect and obey their superiors, although those superiors in turn had responsibilities to those below them.

Modern Western thought, which holds that respect must be earned, has eroded the status of traditional Confucian ideals in modern Taiwan. Nonetheless, these ideas have survived and still play a central role in Taiwanese society. Hierarchy often determines family relationships and still dominates the Taiwanese educational system.

Family obedience remains strong; fathers rule the home. In Taiwan's political elections, entire families vote as instructed by their fathers. Other family members—mothers, eldest sons—do not hesitate to harangue "inferiors" on all manner of subjects, prescribing tough courses of action spiced with warnings of dire consequences. Many young Taiwanese chafe under this browbeating, even as they do as they're told.

The concept of ren can be seen where relationships are greatly valued, whether at work, at home, or among friends. Ren has also evolved into the modern term *guansi (guanxi),* which also deals with relationships and influences, but outside the concentric circles of family and friends. In daily life, some Taiwanese prefer to settle disputes and do business without resorting to outside authorities. It is common in Taipei to see traffic accidents resolved this way: An argument ensues, blame is apportioned, and money changes hands. Only as a last resort are police called in.

Li can be observed in the Taiwanese emphasis on education. The Confucian hierarchy is still in place in schools, and students are strictly ranked based on their test scores, which in turn determine which high schools and universities they attend. The government has moved to relax this educational hierarchy, but progress has been slow.

Confucian ideals will likely continue to loosen in modern Taiwan. As the country continues to modernize and internationalize, it will be increasingly influenced by Western culture and ideals. ∎

Ritual celebrations each September (right) mark the birthday of Confucius (above).

Taipei Fine Arts Museum & environs

THE TAIPEI FINE ARTS MUSEUM HOUSES LOCAL AND international collections of contemporary and modern art in more than 13,000 square yards (11,000 sq m) of exhibition space. It hosts both permanent and temporary exhibitions, including some enthralling electronic media in its catacomb of basement galleries.

Near the museum, the Grand Hotel, with its magnificent facade and lofty position, is a Taipei landmark.

The museum does its best to exemplify its modern nature in its architecture, with a whitewashed chunky design interrupted by full-length windows. Outside, bronze sculptures lead along a plaza to the main glass door of the museum.

Selections of the museum's modest but impressive permanent collection of 3,600 pieces are

housed in the second- and third-floor galleries, with exhibitions changing every six to twelve months. The two **second-floor galleries** are given over to highlights from the permanent collection, which present works from numerous Taiwanese artists. The art shows the development of modern art in Taiwan through a variety

of media, including sculpture, watercolor, oil, drawing, calligraphy, and ink painting.

The **third-floor galleries** present thematic exhibitions that also reflect Taiwan's history through contemporary art. Rotating exhibitions include "Taipei: The Tamsui," "Taipei: Historical Buildings," and "Taipei: The City." The exhibits attempt to present the changing face of Taipei from a fortified city during the Qing dynasty (1644–1911) to the modern metropolis. Paintings depict street scenes, popular temples, restaurants, hot springs, and other elements of Taipei life.

The **basement galleries** serve up works from young and experimental artists, mainly working in electronic media. These often

result in wonderfully bizarre encounters with over-the-edge video, film, photography, light, sound, and multimedia expression.

AROUND THE MUSEUM

Just south of the museum is **Taipei Art Park,** a broad expanse of landscaped gardens and modern sculptures, which is worth a stroll after visiting the museum.

On the north side of the museum is the Taipei Story House, long called **Yuanshan Villa** *(181-1 Jhongshan N. Rd., tel 2587-5565, www.storyhouse.com.tw),* an out-of-place, three-story mock-Tudor mansion built in 1914 by a local tea merchant. It houses a combination coffee shop/tea room.

Modeled after the imperial style of an ancient Chinese palace, the 490-room **Grand Hotel** (see p. 245; *1 Jhongshan/Zhongshan North Rd., Sec. 4, tel 2886-8888)* is a Taipei landmark, made more imposing by its lofty position atop a ridge at the northern end of the city. Huge red columns dominate the hotel's facade, helping to support its sweeping yellow-tiled roof—the largest classical Chinese-style roof in the world.

A quarter-mile (0.4 km) to the east is the **Martyrs' Shrine** *(139 Beian Rd., tel 2885-4162).* Like the Grand Hotel, the structures here are rendered in the ornate style of the Ming dynasty (1368–1644). The shrine is dedicated to fallen heroes of the Chinese revolution and the war against Japan (330,000 in all). Arched doors at the main gate lead to a vast courtyard; in the main shrine, huge brass-studded doors open to walls inscribed with the names of the heroes along with murals depicting their feats in battle. Of special note is the ceremonial changing of the guard, held like clockwork on the hour. ■

Taipei Fine Arts Museum
ww.tfam.gov.tw

🅰 Map p. 56

✉ 181 Jhongshan (Zhongshan) North Rd., Sec. 3

☎ 2595-7656

🕐 Closed Mon.

🚇 MRT: Yuanshan station

National Palace Museum

National Palace Museum

www.npm.gov.tw

- 🅰 Map p. 57
- ✉ 221 Jhihshan (Zhishan) Rd., Sec. 2
- ☎ 2881-2021
- 💲 $$
- 🚈 MRT: Shihlin (Shilin) station, then bus 225, 304, minibus 18 and 19 and Red 30

The National Palace Museum, with its vast collection of Chinese art and antiquities, is a must-see for a visitor to Taipei.

THE NATIONAL PALACE MUSEUM HOLDS THE WORLD'S largest collection of Chinese artifacts, nearly 650,000 items in all. But only a fraction of these, about 15,000, are on display at any one time. The rest of these treasures are stored in thousands of crates in air-conditioned vaults tunneled into the mountain that backs the imposing, Chinese-palace-style building.

HISTORY

This vast collection has its origins in the Song dynasty (960–1279), when Emperor Taizong began gathering treasures from all over China. The ever growing collection shuffled from emperor to emperor and palace to palace over the centuries before finding a permanent home in Beijing's Forbidden City.

The collection expanded considerably during the Qing dynasty (1644–1911), as the dynasty's succession of art-loving emperors scoured China in search of more treasures. While China's 1911 revolution ended China's dynastic rulers, the emperor at that time, Puyi, was a hard man to evict. When he was finally told to leave in 1924, the art collection found a new home in Beijing's National Palace Museum.

But this museum had a brief existence. By the time the museum's scholars had painstakingly identified and categorized the vast treasure trove some eight years later, the Japanese had invaded Manchuria and ensconced Puyi as its puppet head of state. By 1933, with war inevitable, the collection's caretakers feared the collection would fall into the hands of the Japanese, so they packed it up and hauled it by train to Nanjing. A month later it was transferred to a warehouse in Shanghai—until it was threatened again by the Japanese.

Over the ensuing years, the collection was divided up and crates spirited to different parts of China ahead of the advancing Japanese army. After the war, the collection returned to Nanjing, but it did not remain there for long. By fall 1948, Chiang Kai-shek's Nationalists were facing certain defeat by Mao Zedong's Communists. It was decided to begin shipping the most precious artifacts to Taiwan.

Because the Nationalists intended eventually to retake mainland China, they made no plans to establish a museum to display these treasures. A bomb-shelter warehouse was built in the west coast city of Taichung, and the collection was stored there. As the years wore on and a triumphant return to the mainland looked less and less likely, the Taiwanese government finally built the "temporary" National Palace Museum in Taipei. The museum opened in 1965.

THE MUSEUM

Only a fraction of the museum's vast collection is on display at any one time, presented in long-term and special exhibitions throughout the museum's 35 galleries. At the information desk in the lobby you can rent hand-held audio equipment on specific exhibitions to help you through a self-guided tour. Free English-language tours begin at 10 a.m. and 3 p.m.

LONG-TERM EXHIBITIONS

Displayed primarily according to chronology, in some galleries by thematic context, individual pieces within a long-term exhibition may be withdrawn and added at certain periods. The long-term exhibitions feature relics, artifacts, and statuary such as bronzes, jades, porcelains,

and carvings. Special exhibitions of paintings, calligraphy, books, documents, and embroideries are short due to the fragile nature of their form.

First-floor galleries

A good place to start is **Gallery 101,** with the exhibit on "Compassion and Wisdom: Religious Sculptural Arts." Through exquisite pieces of Buddhist sculpture one explores here both revelation of Buddhism's religious ideals and also the changing worldly concepts of beauty manifest through the imperial epochs.

The expansive **Gallery 103** is home to two cultural explorations, "Gems in the Rare Books Collection" and "Early Dwellers of Taiwan: Illustrated Historical Documents in the Collections of the NPM." The gems of the former are from the museum's priceless collection of 200,000 rare books, many inherited from leading Qing-dynasty imperial households. The artwork, the books' importance as windows into Chinese life, and the development of book-production technology are unveiled. The gems of the latter are painting scrolls, maps, ancient books, documents, and block prints that give insight into the culture, practices, and belief systems of Taiwan's aboriginal peoples in the 18th and 19th centuries.

Second-floor galleries

"Transitions and Convergences (221-960)" greets the cultural explorer in **Gallery 201.** These centuries saw great disturbances and lack of cohesion in China. One positive result was great independence of artistic exploration and expression. People of the steppe tribes to the north settled within China's borders, bringing a synthesis of their religious

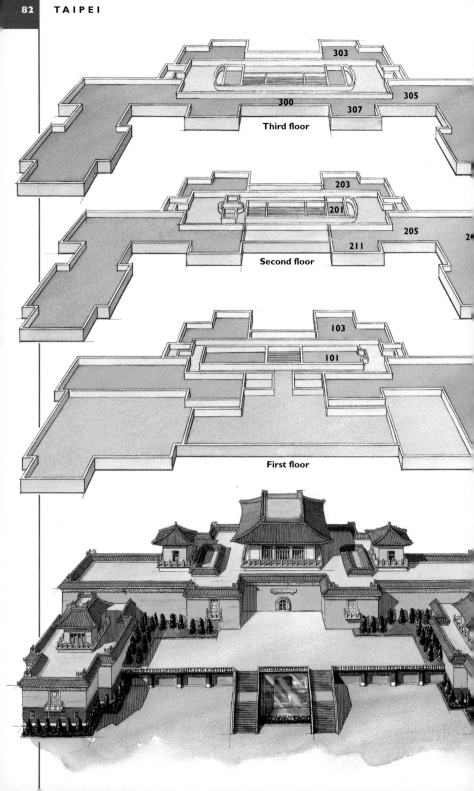

303

305

300

307

Third floor

203

201

205

2

211

Second floor

103

101

First floor

MAIN EXHIBITION BUILDING: Spread over three floors, the museum's galleries contain priceless collections of bronzes, ceramics, jades, paintings, calligraphy, and rare books, among other artworks and antiquities.

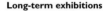

Long-term exhibitions

101 Compassion and Wisdom: Religious Sculptural Arts

103 Gems in the Rare Books Collection and Early Dwellers of Taiwan

201 Transitions and Convergences (221–960)

203 Prototypes of Modern Styles (960–1360)

205 The New Era of Ornamentation (1350–1521)

207 The Contest of Craft: Ming Dynasty's Chia-ching to Ch'ung-chen (1522–1644)

209 Treasures from an Age of Prosperity: The Reigns of Emperors K'ang-hsi, Yung-cheng, and Ch'ien-lung (1662–1795)

211 Toward Modernity: Late Ch'ing Dynasty (1796–1911)

300 The Mystery of Bronze

303 The Neolithic Age: The Beginning of Civilization (pre-1600 BCE)

305 Classical Civilization: The Bronze Age (1600–221 BCE)

307 From Classic to Tradition: Ch'in and Han Dynasties (221 BCE–220 CE)

customs and cultural practices. New paths were trod, and the greatest creative peaks attained, in the Sui (581-617) and Tang (618-907) dynasties. The museum's collection of Tang tri-color pottery is among the world's greatest.

In **Gallery 203** we find "Prototypes of Modern Styles (960-1360)," concentrated on the brilliant artistic heights achieved in the Song dynasty (960-1279). This, an age of cultural openness and experimentation, had as its base an appreciation of frugal esthetics in both high art and daily living. This was also an age of scientific innovation, with craftsmen using sophisticated techniques in making daily-use wares of high artistic merit—simple lines and natural grace emphasized. This preference continued during the Yuan dynasty (1271-1368).

"The New Era of Ornamentation (1350-1521)" graces **Gallery 205.** With the advent of the Ming dynasty the emphasis on simplicity and frugality of design in objets d'art was abandoned in favor of exuberant color and intricate pattern. This was especially true in the renowned Ming porcelain, as advances in technique enabled elaborate painting and glaze coloring. The NPM's collection of Ming porcelains is among the finest in existence.

By moving on to **Gallery 207** one moves on to "The Contest of Craft: Ming Dynasty's Chia-ching to Ch'ung-chen (1522-1644)." The late Ming period was one of turmoil and expanding freedoms, in terms of artistic production a period of relaxation of traditional rules and influence from external cultures. The status of craftsmen improved, production was expanded from the imperial house to the general educated public, and scholars themselves engaged in production, bringing heightened status.

A gilded bronze Buddha image, cast by an anonymous Qing dynasty artist in 1782, is part of the museum's collection of priceless religious relics.

In **Gallery 209,** in "Treasures from an Age of Prosperity: The Reigns of Emperors K'ang-hsi, Yung-cheng, and Ch'ien-lung (1662-1795)," we witness one of the high periods of Chinese civilization. There was peace in the empire, releasing intellect and energies for creative pursuits, and contact with the West was made while new trade routes were opened. New ideas flowed in as part of a "lively exchange between East and West."

Finally, in **Gallery 211,** we watch the decline of the Qing dynasty and the end of the imperial era in "Toward Modernity: Late Ch'ing Dynasty (1796-1911)." In this period external forces threatened to overwhelm a decaying sociopolitical fabric. In the arts, the impact of Western industrial technique forced fundamental changes in Chinese handicraft production. The result was works of sophisticated craftsmanship focused on intricate detail and, in terms of thematic approach, a move toward realism. The Jadeite Cabbage with Insects sculpture is one of the museum's signature pieces.

Third-floor galleries

In **Gallery 303** the visitor enters "The Neolithic Age: The Beginning of Civilization (pre-1600 BCE)." Found jade objects have been key guideposts to the spiritual culture of China's ancient denizens; the brilliant works are here approached in terms of use in religious worship, indicators of regional styles in East Asia, an area which had developed superior jadework craftsmanship by the late Neolithic era compared to the rest of the Eurasian continent, and as indicators of the distribution of influence of the three great clans that appear to have dominated China during this era.

In "Classical Civilization: The Bronze Age (1600-221 BCE)," housed in **Gallery 305,** featured are inscribed bronze vessels created at the peak of this artform, during the Shang (ca 1766-1122 B.C.) and Zhou—Western Zhou (ca 1122–771 B.C.), Eastern Zhou (ca 770–256 B.C.)—dynasties. Pieces are wrought in fine detail, and inscriptions demonstrate some of the earliest examples of calligraphy. One of the collection's most treasured pieces is the Moa Kung ting food vessel. Its 500-character inscription is the most unrestrained example of ancient calligraphy yet found.

The technological mysteries of Shang and Zhou bronze production are unveiled in **Gallery 300** via modern multimedia technology in "The Mystery of Bronze." The knowledge of the ancients is brought to life with virtual-reality and other appealing digital animation.

Moving on in chronological order, **Gallery 307** houses "From Classic to Tradition: Ch'in and Han Dynasties (221 BCE–220 CE)." This era marked the end of feudalism and the establishment of imperial rule. The use of bronzeware in ritual tapered off, with the beauties of artistic creation now brought to everyday objects, made from a wide range of materials, the decorative motifs reflecting the physical and ideological world swirling about and defining the Han people.

OTHER COLLECTIONS
Calligraphy
Calligraphic works created during the Tang, Ming (1368–1644), and Qing (1644–1911) dynasties are regularly exhibited in special short-term exhibitions. Watch for "Clearing After Snowfall" and "Sending Regards to a Friend," both by Yuan Huan Tieh, and "Three Passages of Calligraphy," by Ping An, Ho Ju, and Feng Chu Tieh.
Paintings
"Early Spring" by Kou Shi Hang—ink and color on silk mountain scenes on scroll— and the

similar but more landscape-expansive scenes of "Travelers Amid Mountains and Streams" by Fan Kuan are two Song dynasty masterpieces exhibited from time to time. Also keep an eye out for the classic "Bamboo" by Wen Tung, one of the most important pieces of calligraphic art; and "Portrait of a Consort of Emperor Jen-tsung Hou Tsuo Hsiang" (anonymous), painted on silk scroll and illustrated with a faithful rendition of his consort and ladies in waiting.

The museum's special exhibitions of Ming and Qing paintings are crowd favorites for their grand and highly decorative landscapes, along with bird-and-flower, and figurative paintings representing narrative themes from history or legend.

THE MUSEUM'S NEW LOOK
From 2002 through 2006, the National Palace Museum underwent extensive renovations. With the facelift complete, the museum is arranging its vast collection in a new exhibition format, much different from what formerly existed.

In some areas various pieces are grouped within their dynastic periods, rather than their art form. For example, much of the second floor encompasses artistic achievements in all forms from the Tang to the Qing dynasties, while a section of third floor galleries covers the artistry and craft of the earlier Shang and Zhou through Jin and Han dynasties.

The museum has also introduced a multimedia room, along with interactive and exploratory exhibits. ∎

Taiwan's Mona Lisa: The exquisite "Jadeite Cabbage with Insects," from the Qing dynasty (1655–1911), said to be part of a dowry. Bok choy, a metaphor for purity, symbolizes the bride's purity, while the insects, known for their ability to reproduce, are symbolic of fertility.

National Dr. Sun Yat-sen Memorial Hall

www.yatsen.gov.tw

🗺 Map p. 57
✉ 505 Renai Rd., Sec. 4
☎ 2758-8008
🚇 MRT: Sun Yat-sen Memorial Hall station

National Dr. Sun Yat-sen Memorial Hall & around

THE NATIONAL DR. SUN YAT-SEN MEMORIAL HALL IS A graceful tribute to the founder of modern China, a man revered in both China and Taiwan as the "National Father." Taipei residents come here to honor the man who helped to end China's dynasties, visit the memorial's exhibits and art galleries, fly kites, exercise, and relax in the plaza and gardens that surround the hall.

A bronze statue of the Father of Modern China sits in thoughtful repose outside National Dr. Sun Yat-sen Memorial Hall.

Viewed from the main entrance, the massive memorial hall—which boasts a magnificent sweeping roof of yellow-glazed tiles—sits at the end of an expansive plaza awash with red and yellow flowers bordered by neatly trimmed hedges. A bronze 20-foot (6 m) statue of a seated Sun dominates the grand entrance gallery. On each side of the statue, on small pedestals, are two immaculately uniformed guards, bearing arms and standing so still they could be mistaken for statues themselves.

To the right of Sun's statue is a gift shop selling Sun-related souvenirs. Beyond it is a gallery with photographs and paintings of Sun over the years, his books, and narrations of the numerous uprisings he led against the Qing dynasty (1644–1911) rulers in China. Photographs of revolutionary "martyrs" cover the gallery walls, and Sun memorabilia, including his watches, clothes, and walking sticks, fills glass cases. None of these exhibits has captions in English.

Next to the gallery is a public library, where visitors browse through some of the 300,000 volumes pertaining to Sun's political philosophy.

The hall also contains a number of well-presented art galleries given over to long-term and temporary exhibitions of Chinese art. The excellent artworks have no English captions.

The **Jhongshan (Zhongshan) National Gallery** on the hall's second floor holds significant international and national exhibitions; the third-floor **Yat-sen Gallery** displays Chinese paintings and calligraphy; while the other gallery on the third floor, the

Deming Gallery, is given over to exhibitions of Taiwanese artists.

TAIPEI 101

Looming beyond the memorial to the southwest on Songjhih (Songzhi) Road is the world's tallest building (for the time being at least), the 101-floor Taipei 101. The recently constructed building's design is meant to symbolize the growth of bamboo, with each shoot unfolding from the one below. The effect—eight tapered tiers emerging from a pyramid base and topped with a circular column and radio tower—is eye-catching, to say the least. The building's spectacular 140-foot-high (42 m) glass-domed enclosure covers an indoor plaza 31,000 square feet (2,865 sq m) in size. Elevators shoot visitors to observation decks on the 89th and 91st floors. Views from these decks are outstanding.

DISCOVERY CENTER OF TAIPEI

This is one of the city's newest museums, showing different stages of Taipei's development through four floors of artifacts, scale mod-els, photographs, topographical maps, and video displays. Many of the displays are interactive. One of the more interesting exhibits is an interactive topographical map of Taipei, which has a touch-screen that highlights different areas of the city and their development.

You can also experience the smells of old Taipei by sniffing exhibits of lemongrass, tea, and camphor that were once among the major exports carried on the Taipei Basin's Danshuei (Danshui) River.

The first floor incorporates scenes of modern Taipei and records people's impressions of the changing city. The second floor features temporary exhibi-tions, while the third-floor gallery contains exhibits about Taipei's modern era, including the rapid transformation of the Sinyi (Xinyi) District from a rural area of rice paddies into the city's commercial district. The fourth floor explores the old walled city, with attractive scale models and cutaways. If you are in a group, ask for an English-speaking guide; a self-guided text tour is also available for a deposit. ■

The National Dr. Sun Yat-sen Memorial Hall houses photographs and memorabilia of the revered revolutionary leader.

Taipei 101 (Taipei Financial Center)
www.tapei-101.com.tw
🚇 Map p. 57
✉ 8 Songjhih (Songzhi) Rd., Sinyi (Xinyi) District
☎ 8101-8899 (Observ-atory reservations)

Discovery Center of Taipei
www.discovery.taipei.gov.tw
🚇 Map p. 57
✉ Taipei City Hall, 1 Shihfu (Shifu) Rd.
☎ 2757-4547
🕐 Closed Mon. & national holidays
🚇 MRT: Taipei City Hall station

More places to visit in Taipei

CHINESE POSTAL MUSEUM

With its staggering collection of more than 500,000 Chinese and foreign postage stamps, 20,000 postal-related items, 6,000 documents, and 20,000 books related to postal systems, this museum rates as once of the largest museums of its type in the world. On weekends, vendors set up stalls outside the museum selling stamps; they are usually crowded with Taipei's sizable community of avid philatelists. 🄼 Map p. 56 ✉ 45 Chongcing (Chongqing) South Rd., Sec. 2 ☎ 2394-5185, ext. 851 ⊕ Closed Mon. 🅂 $ 🚍 Bus: 3, 243, 248, 262, 268, 304

CUSTOMS MUSEUM

The outstanding feature of this intriguing museum is its Preventative Operation Section, which holds displays of contraband nabbed from smugglers over the years. Exhibits here range from the mundane to the truly extraordinary. You can't miss an amazing 10-foot-high (3 m) ivory pagoda carved in astonishing detail, or the museum's sizable collection of guns, including a gold-plated German Luger with the name of one Heinrick Kriegnoff and the date 3/15/37 inscribed on it. There are also exhibits on the not-so-foolproof methods drug traffickers use to conceal goods, including shampoo bottles, hollowed-out Buddha images, and phony incense sticks. 🄼 Map p. 56 ✉ Directorate General of Customs Building, 13 Dacheng St. ☎ 2550-5500, ext. 2212-2214 ⊕ Closed Sat.–Sun., reservations required 🚍 Bus: 9, 12, 52, 206, 223, 250, 274, 304, 601

DR. SUN YAT-SEN MEMORIAL HOUSE

This lovely Japanese-style complex, set among tranquil gardens of bonsai plants, carp ponds, pavilions, and arching bridges, was once a luxury inn where Sun stayed in 1913. The house possesses a modest collection of Sun memorabilia, including photographs and documents. 🄼 Map p. 56 ✉ 46 Jhongshan (Zhongshan) North Rd., Sec. 1 ☎ 2381-3359 ⊕ Closed Mon. 🅂 $

NATIONAL TAIWAN UNIVERSITY HOSPITAL

Opposite the Gongyuan Road entrance to

2-28 Memorial Peace Park is a striking neo-Renaissance-style building, one of two that make up the old hospital. Built in 1916, it forms the larger component of what was once the biggest hospital in the Far East. Its pilaster, supported by four sets of Roman columns, and generous windows surrounded by decorative plasterwork enliven its redbrick facade. The second, earlier-built hospital (1907) has a more muted appearance, but its first-floor entrances, colonnaded second-floor veranda, double-pitched roof, and powder gray color give it a classical look. 🄼 Map p. 56 ✉ 1 Changde St. 🚇 MRT: NTU Hospital station

RED HOUSE THEATER

This oddly shaped edifice sits in the midst of Simending. The octagonal building was constructed in 1908 as a market and became a theater for Beijing opera, and then for movies, after the Japanese occupation. Renovated in 1999, the two-story building includes a second-floor theater that hosts performances of puppetry and children's theater under a beautiful domed ceiling. On the first floor is a coffee shop and gift shop decorated with memorabilia from Taiwan's movie industry. 🄼 Map p. 56 ✉ 10 Chengdu Rd. ☎ 2311-9380 ⊕ Closed Mon. 🚇 MRT: Ximen station

SHANDAO TEMPLE

This is one of seven major temples built by Japanese Buddhists during the country's occupation of Taiwan. Constructed in 1933, it little resembles other Buddhist temples in Taiwan; from a distance it looks more like an apartment building with an imposing four-columned entrance gate attached. The nine-floor temple has its own museum, which has an excellent collection of Buddhist art, with works covering Chinese dynasties as far back as the Northern Wei (386–534). The most outstanding relic is an exquisitely carved wooden image of Guanyin from the Song dynasty (960–1279). 🄼 Map p. 56 ✉ 23 Jhongsiao (Zhongxiao) East Rd., Sec. 1 ☎ 2341-5758 ⊕ Closed Mon. 🚇 MRT: Shandao Temple

SHIHLIN OFFICIAL RESIDENCE

This expansive estate of former President

Chiang Kai-shek was turned into a park and opened to the public in 1996. After entering via the very long entrance driveway befitting a presidential residence, you can follow park pathways through a number of gardens, pagodas, pavilions, and an experimental greenhouse. The parklands include gardens in front of the president's residence, where Chiang and his wife, Soong Mayling, sought respite from affairs of state. You'll also encounter a fountain in a garden full of statues; a lovely orchid pavilion with classically sculpted wooden walls and

section of the museum devoted to its history and culture. Exhibits include arts and crafts, scale models of dwellings, weapons, day-to-day utensils, farming and fishing implements, costumes, and ornaments. The spiritual side of the cultures is explored through funerary objects and items used for sacrifice, divination, and exorcism. A basement cinema shows short films (in Chinese) on various aboriginal cultures. www.museum.org.tw ⚠ Map p. 57 ✉ 282 Jhihshan (Zhishan) Rd., Sec. 2. ☎ 2841-2611 ⏲ Closed Mon. 💲 $$

The beautiful grounds of Chiang Kai-shek's estate, known as the Shihlin (Shilin) Official Residence, opened as a public park in 1996.

decorated eaves; and a Chinese garden with winding pathways, carp ponds, and a sturdy red-columned pavilion. ⚠ Map p. 56 ✉ 1, Lane 460, Jhongshan North Rd., Sec. 5 ☎ 2881-2512 🚇 MRT: Shilin station

SHUNG YE MUSEUM OF FORMOSAN ABORIGINES

Five floors of exhibits describe Taiwan's recognized aboriginal groups. A topographical map of Taiwan in the lobby shows the territories and villages of the tribes, and each tribe has a

🚇 MRT: Shihlin (Shilin) station, then bus 213, 255, 304, minibus 18, 19.

SIMENDING (XIMENDING) SHOPPING DISTRICT

This trendy area is Taipei's answer to Tokyo's Shinjuku District. The collection of department stores, cinemas, pedestrian malls, boutiques, secondhand clothing stores, and restaurants attracts throngs of young people during the evenings and on weekends in an entertaining display of youth fashion and

The Taipei Astronomical Museum takes the visitor on a tour of stargazing history from ancient to modern times.

attitude. Many local streets are closed to vehicles on evenings and weekends. 🗺 Map p. 56 🚇 MRT: Ximen station

SINGTIAN (XINGTIAN) TEMPLE

This bustling temple is dedicated to Guangong, the red-faced, black-bearded god of war and patron saint of merchants. It is an outstanding example of Taoist temple architecture, which eschews much of the over-the-top ornateness of other temples. Multilevel roofs have carved ship-prow ridges and are adorned with large colorful dragons at their edges. A huge brass incense pot with a gilded dragon handle sits in front of the main hall. Here, nuns and priests in blue robes bless people with incense sticks as part of the practice of *shoujing,* touching various places on their bodies to invite back souls who have received a fright and left the body. In the covered courtyard before the main hall—notable for its beautifully carved dragon columns—rows of trestle tables groan under the weight of offerings of fruit and flowers. The temple differs from many others in that it has no donation box, prohibits the burning of paper money, and discourages raucous religious ceremonies. It also runs a charitable foundation. www.ht.org.tw 🗺 Map p. 56 ✉ 109 Mincyuan (Minquan) East Rd., Sec. 2 ☎ 2502-7924 🚍 Bus 5, 49, 63, 214, 225, 277, 285

SU HO MEMORIAL PAPER MUSEUM

Who would have thought paper was so interesting? The first floor of this delightful museum has displays of handmade paper from all over the world; create your own souvenir pieces of paper using the museum's equipment (extra fee). The second-floor exhibit takes you through the history, materials, and process of paper manufacture; the third floor has exhibits tracing the his-tory of paper manufacture in Taiwan. On the fourth floor is a mock-up of a handmade-paper factory. www.suhopaper .org.tw 🗺 Map p. 56 ✉ 68 Changan East Rd., Sec. 2 ☎ 2507-5539 🕐 Closed Sun., major festival days 💲 $ 🚇 MRT: Zhongxiao-Xinsheng station

TAIPEI ASTRONOMICAL MUSEUM

This museum's four floors of exhibition halls take you through the themes of ancient astronomy, planet Earth, space science and technology, stars and galaxies, and the universe, using models, images, photographs, computer animation, and video. The museum has a number of telescopes that allow visitors to take a closer look at the heavens. (Viewing times are between 10 a.m. and noon, and 2 p.m. to 4 p.m.) The museum's IMAX Dome Theater has spectacular hourly shows from 9 a.m. to 4 p.m. (with extra shows on weekends) featuring human exploration of space, while its Iwerks 3D Theater gives viewers a different experience with the aid of polarized glasses. www.tam.gov.tw 🗺 Map p. 56 ✉ 363 Jihe Rd. ☎ 2831-4551, ext. 703 for English 🕐 Closed Mon. 💲 $; $ for IMAX & Iwerks shows 🚇 MRT: Shilin station ∎

Many of Taiwan's most attractive destinations—ranging from colorful gold-mining towns to spectacular coastal scenery—are just a short drive from Taipei.

Around Taipei & the North

A simple clay teapot.

Using bottle tops as playing pieces, dedicated board gamers attract onlookers in Wenchang Park, Taoyuan.

Around Taipei & the North

TAIPEI CAN BE USED AS A BASE FROM WHICH TO EXPLORE AREAS around the city as well as the island's north. Most of the attractions are within easy reach (in most instances, not much more than an hour's drive away), making for quick excursions from the sometimes hectic capital. Because they are close to the capital, however, many of these destinations get crowded on weekends.

To the city's north, just 40 minutes from central Taipei, the mountains of Yangmingshan National Park offer a delightful escape from Taipei. Within the park's boundaries, roads and hiking trails climb to some truly spectacular vistas of the Taipei Basin and northern Taiwan, while the park's hot springs, fumaroles, lakes, and mountain meadows provide scenic diversity.

To the west of Yangmingshan, and easily accessible by MRT from Taipei, is the rustic hot-springs resort of Beitou, Taiwan's oldest. Here you can stay in a tranquil Japanese-style inn for a taste of hot-springs bathing in your own room. You can also reach another historic town, Danshuei (Danshui), by MRT from

Taipei. Here you can take in remnants of the island's European colonial history, along with the story of one of its most famous foreign residents, Canadian missionary and benefactor George Leslie Mackay (1844–1901). Most of the compact town's attractions are close together, making it ideal for a walking tour.

A more rambunctious side to

Toufen•
Jhunan
(Zhunan
•Houlong
Miaoli
Shihtan•

Sanyi• Dahu•

Huoyanshan
(Fire Mountain)
Nature Reserve
Shengsing
Station
Houli•

CENTRAL WEST
p. 207

Taiwan's recent history is found at Jioufen (Jiufen), which grew from a tiny mountainside settlement to a raucous town of prospectors, merchants, prostitutes, and wine houses after the discovery of gold in the 1890s. The town's laddered streets and charming old buildings bedecked with balconied teahouses draw many nostalgic visitors from the city.

From Danshuei, the North Coast Highway follows a weathered coastline of craggy cliffs and rock formations east to Keelung, Taiwan's second biggest port. Just to the southeast of that city, the Northeast Coast National Scenic Area hugs the narrow corridor between the mountains and Pacific Ocean. Visitors along this route are treated to rugged coastal scenery, sandy beaches, and sweeping ocean vistas.

The east end of the Northern Cross Island Highway begins in Ilan County, cutting through the central mountains and some beautiful scenery. Some of the sections traversed are given over to peaceful forest recreation areas laced with mountain trails.

Southwest of Taipei, you will find the town of Yingge, famed for its pottery factories and shops. The Sansia (Sanxia) Zushih (Zushi) Temple in nearby Sansia is recognized as an outstanding example of a traditional temple restored using modern techniques.

West and southwest of Taipei in the counties of Taoyuan and Hsinchu, attractions are more of the man-made variety, with a number of theme parks, including the quirky Window on China, with its miniature replicas of famous structures including the Forbidden City, the Sphinx, and the Eiffel Tower. ■

Mujha's (Muzha's) teahouses

**Mujha (Muzha)
Tea Plantation
circular route**

- Map p. 93
- Bus: 236, 237, 282 to Jhengjhih (Zhengzhi) University, then minibus 10 from the university

Yaoyue Teahouse

- Map p. 93
- 6 Lane 40, Jhihnan Rd., Sec. 3
- 2939-2025

**Taipei Tea
Promotion
Center**

- Map p. 93
- 8-2 Lane 40, Jhihnan Rd., Sec. 3
- 2939-1473
- Closed Mon.; experimental plantation open 10 a.m.–11 a.m. & 2 p.m.–3 p.m.

**Big Teapot
Teahouse**

- Map p. 93
- 37-1 Lane 38, Jhihnan Rd., Sec. 3
- 2939-5615

MUJHA'S (MUZHA'S) TEA PLANTATIONS CLING TO THE sloping hills above the narrow, 2-mile-long (3.2 km) Maokong (Cat's Paw) Valley in the southeast section of Taipei. The area is a favorite of many city residents, who head here in the cool of the evening to drink tea at one of the numerous teahouses perched on the hillsides, while enjoying views of Taipei's twinkling lights below. A daytime trip to the teahouses in the valley, which gets its name from the eroded, cat's-paw-shaped rocks that line the banks of the valley's Jhihnan (Zhinan) Stream, is just as rewarding.

The teahouses are found along Jhihnan Road, Section 3, a 4-mile-long (6 km) loop that heads south for 2 miles (3 km) from Jhengjhih (Zhengzhi) (Political) University to the head of the valley. The road heads west across Jhihnan Stream and then north again, twisting for 1.5 miles though Lane 40, Lane 38, and Lane 34 to a junction one-half mile (1 km) above Jheng-jhih University.

Here the road meanders through idyllic plantations before reaching a cluster of picturesque teahouses, set among the terraced hillsides, where you can sip tea and watch farmers at work.

About 350 yards (320 m) north of the Jhihnan Stream along Lane 40, the **Yaoyue (Inviting the Moon) Teahouse** sits amid wooden pavilions and picnic tables surrounded by topiary gardens. Here you can drink tea while taking in some splendid views of the teahouses and temples on the other side of the valley. The teahouse is encircled by forest, with sections cleared to allow for daytime panoramas and views of the distant lights of Mujha in the evening.

About 400 yards (365 m) north on Lane 40 is the **Taipei Tea Promotion Center,** a two-story, redbrick building with whitewashed cement trim. The inside—which houses artifacts related to tea farming and brewing—is awash with light from latticed windows that stretch from floor to ceiling.

Permanent displays show how teas are classified; they include free tea tastings and lessons on brewing. The center also has displays of

machinery used in the fermentation and curing process and pottery tea sets with information on how they are made. Spectacular views of downtown Taipei can be enjoyed from the experimental tea plantation on the slopes behind the center; the acrid but appealing smell of maturing tea leaves adds to the atmosphere. English-language tours of the center and plantation need to be arranged by phone at least two days in advance.

On Lane 38, about 300 yards from the display center, **Big Teapot Teahouse** juts out on pillars over the tiered plantation slopes. The building is covered in bright red bricks, while dark latticed railings stand between patrons and the hillside plantations. The interior is lined with dark lacquered wood in imperial style. Views sweep across hillside plantations to Taipei city.

The **Big Teapot Teahouse** is one of the best places in Mujha to try "tea cuisine." Most local teahouses serve up dishes using locally raised free-range chicken. The Big Teapot's "Three Cup Range Chicken" (*San Bei Yeji*), a traditional rural recipe, is delicious and a superb match for the plantation's Iron Goddess and Baojhong (Baozhong) teas. A new cable-car service glides visitors from Taipei Zoo to Jhihnan Temple and on to the tea plantations (*$*). ■

Northern Taiwan's high altitudes and mild climate create ideal conditions for growing tea.

The preparation and drinking of tea can be a highly ritualized affair in Taiwan.

Taiwanese tea

With its high mountain slopes, Taiwan is ideal for growing tea, and it produces some of the world's best brews. Differences in flavors depend on the type of plant, the altitude at which it is grown, the climatic conditions in the area, the timing of the harvest, and the methods used to cure the leaves.

Probably the most famous tea in Taiwan is Dongding Oolong, which comes from around the town of Lugu in Nantou County. This region of high foothills bordering the Central Mountain Range is home to some of the best tea in Taiwan. Tea was first planted in Nantou about 150 years ago, and the moist hills, cool climate, and leached soil have turned out to be perfect for tea growing.

Like all quality teas, Dongding Oolong undergoes lengthy curing. The leaves are softened in the sun for two hours, then rolled for 20 minutes. This bruises them and brings the juice to the surface. The juice oxidizes when it makes contact with the air, a process known as fermentation. This lasts three hours, after which the leaves are heated again to stop the fermentation. It is this partial fermentation that distinguishes Oolong from green tea,

which is not fermented, and black tea, which is fully fermented.

Next, farmers pack the leaves into bags and roll them vigorously until they are pressed into hard little kernels. The kernels dry overnight and then cook over a charcoal fire for 40 minutes. This imparts a smoky aftertaste that is one of the tea's hallmarks.

A more curious type of tea is Dongfang Mei Ren, or Oriental Beauty, from the border region of Hsinchu and Miaoli Counties. This is no ordinary brew; its flavor derives from insects that live and breed in the tea leaves. The bugs deposit their egg sacks in a sticky paste, which is harvested and brewed with the leaves. The tea picks up an unusual scented flavor, like an Earl Grey, but earthier and more robust. All Oriental Beauty is organically grown—otherwise the insects would die, and the unique tea would lose its signature flavor.

Oriental Beauty is famous and costly—90 U.S. dollars for 600 grams (21 oz)—but it is not Taiwan's most expensive tea. That title belongs to Lishan Oolong, which can cost 200 U.S. dollars or more for 600 grams (21 oz). Lishan Oolong grows on the slopes of Lishan (Pear Mountain) at altitudes above 7,200 feet

(2,200 m). At that height, a sudden mountain freeze can wipe out an entire crop. Lishan tea is picked just twice a year, compared with five harvests for Dongding Oolong, and the flavor is so concentrated that it can be brewed up to ten times. It is one of the world's finest teas, a pale gold liquid that is subtle and refined.

Many other popular varieties of tea are grown in Taiwan, notably the lightly fermented Baojhong (Baozhong) and the more heavily fermented Iron Goddess or Tieguanyin tea (sometimes also called Iron Buddha), which has a tan color, a full, mature flavor, and a

slightly sweet aftertaste. Like wine, tea varieties are almost endless, and the tea one chooses to drink depends on the time of day, the guests, and one's general mood.

The preparation of tea follows a standard ritual. Allow freshly boiled water to cool slightly, then pour it over the leaves in the pot to wash them. Swirl this water around, pour it into the assorted mugs and cups, and then drain them. For the second brew—the best— steep the leaves for a few seconds, then pour the brew into a pitcher to stop contact with the leaves. Serve it to guests in small cups. Subsequent steepings take more time, and the better the quality of the tea leaves, the more times they can be brewed. ■

After tea pickers finish their work (top), the leaves are cured (middle) and packaged. Sometimes tea leaves are incorporated into dishes (above).

Yangmingshan

Yangmingshan National Park

www.ymsnp.gov.tw

⚑ Map p. 93

✉ 1-20 Jhuzihhu (Zhuzihu) Rd., Yangmingshan, Taipei

☎ 2861-8744

🚌 Bus: 230, 260 to Yangming Park, 15-minute walk up pathway to visitor center

FROM TAIPEI'S SHIHLIN DISTRICT, YANGDE BOULEVARD winds high into the mountains north of the city to the entrance of Yangmingshan National Park. Along the way its passes the luxury villas of Taipei's moneyed classes, who prefer the area's cooler climes, cleaner air, and panoramas. Once inside Yangmingshan National Park, trails lead hikers up the mountainsides. The less energetic can drive along roads leading closer to the summits, following well-marked signs to the park's main attractions along the way.

It is best to visit Yangmingshan during the week. On weekends and holidays, the park can become intolerably crowded. Private vehicle access is strictly controlled

A road sign in Yangmingshan warns motorists about low-flying owls (above). The park's azaleas light up hillsides each year (opposite).

at these times, to encourage use of frequent buses.

The crowds come to Yangmingshan National Park for the varied landscape, ranging from craggy cliff faces, sulfur-ravaged mountainsides, and steamy hot springs to tranquil lakes and expansive alpine meadows. The

Yangmingshan National Park Headquarters and Visitor Center in the midst of the park beside Yangde Boulevard has displays on the park's geology, flora, and fauna. You can also pick up maps and other information.

Just before the visitor center along hilly and winding pathways, **Yangming Park** (*$*) presents a pleasant collection of landscaped gardens with ponds, grottoes, waterfalls, stands of forests, and various artifices, including its famous flower clock. The park is an easy and relaxing place to spend a few hours. It blazes with color from the middle of February to the end of March, when cherry blossoms open and gardens of rhododendrons and azaleas splash the park with color. Wildflowers also bloom in other areas of the national park. This is a particularly beautiful but busy time of year in Yangmingshan, as people head up from Taipei to enjoy the park's springtime color and atmosphere.

By car, you can backtrack one mile (1.6 km) along Yangde Boulevard, then turn east (left) onto Cingshan (Qingshan) Road and follow signs to the park's sights. Along this road you'll come across a particularly fine example of the weird workings of Mother Nature at the **Lengshueikeng (Lengshuikeng) Fumarole Nature Preserve,** where sulfurous clouds billow out of a bowl-shaped vent to waft above thick bamboo groves. Here you will also find **Milk Lake,** surrounded by rocks covered in thick foliage and named for the yellowish white color of its water. The water's unusual pallor comes from its high sulfur content. Elsewhere in the park at Dayoukeng, Macao, and Sihuangping (Sihuangping), you can find similar hollows belching steam and corrosive gases. These have caved in the Earth's surface and turned the surrounding areas into a lunar landscape of yellow sulfur and crumbling rocks.

Yangmingshan was first used for growing wet rice and grazing water buffalo during the late Qing period, and a number of pasturelands perched atop plateaus can still be found in the park. Some, including **Cingtiangang (Qingtiangang)** (*$ per car on access road*)—a luxuriant meadow covered by a blanket of deep green grass at the end of an access road just to the east of Lengshueikeng—even have a few small herds of cattle grazing contentedly on their slopes. Cingtiangang is popular for family picnics, boisterous student outings, and kite flying.

Go back and continue along Cingshan Road. You'll soon come to the entry point for **Menghuan Pond** on the left. The pond's waters are blanketed by a layer of plants, mostly Taiwan *isoetes*, a rare type of water fern native to Yangmingshan. A scenic trail encircles the pond.

Continue north along Cingshan Road until it meets a T-junction and follow the signs east to **Siaoyoukeng (Xiaoyoukeng) Recreation Area** along the northern saddle of Cisingshan (Seven Stars Mountain)— Yangmingshan's highest peak, which rises to 3,739 feet (1,120 m). This takes you to one of the park's

major geological sites. Here, strong acidic hot springs and sulfur gases rising through the Siaoyoukeng fault have eroded the rock face, causing it to crumble and collapse. The result is a huge, steaming, barren scar shoveled out of the side of the mountain, one of Yangmingshan's more unusual sites. A terrace above the visitor center at Siaoyoukeng offers startling views of the phenomenon. Inside the center is a scale model of the mountain and

Birding is a favorite pastime at Yangmingshan, revealing such colorful species as the black-capped kingfisher.

surrounding area, with lots of geological information.

You can climb Cisingshan from **Siaoyoukeng Visitor Center** (69 Jhuzihhu/Zhuzihu Rd., tel (02) 2861-7024, closed Mon.). The climb covers about one mile (1.6 km) and takes about 40 minutes. The 360-degree views from the top are breathtaking.

DATUN NATURE PARK

From just south of Siaoyoukeng, turn west (left) on Bailaka Highway (County Route 101A) to the northwestern section of Yangmingshan and Datun Nature Park. The park stands in the shadow of 3,543-foot-high (1,080 m) **Datunshan,** the second

highest mountain in Yangmingshan park after nearby Cisingshan. The entrance to the park is opposite the entrance to the Butterfly Corridor. The park opens to a valley locked between towering mountains, where meadows are cut with a meandering pond and crisscrossed by raised wooden walkways.

You can continue toward Datunshan's peak along Bailaka Highway or climb the trail from Datun Nature Park. The trail takes you through stands of bamboo and pampas grass to the summit.

The views from the observation pavilion on the mountain's windswept peak are magnificent. You see startling panoramas of mountains and rivers, Taipei's urban sprawl, and the Pacific Ocean dotted with ships and fishing boats. To the northwest, you can see the Danshuei (Danshui) River, whose wide mouth turns a brilliant orange in the late afternoon sun. In the south, mountains fade into the distance.

Lying under the layer of haze that fills the Taipei Basin, Taipei and its suburbs are in full view in the early morning from Datun. During the day, this urban panorama is impressive for its sheer size, but after dark it becomes beautiful, changing into a vast sea of twinkling lights. At each observation platform along the trail there is a map giving the names of the peaks in front of you. Cisingshan is among the most impressive, with one slope dominated by a smoldering crater.

TRAILS

May is when Yangmingshan's 151 species of butterflies are at their peak on the mountaintops, but at other times of the year you will still be able to spot plenty of them, especially along the shady **Butterfly Corridor,** a 1.8-mile (3 km) trail that winds from the eastern slopes of Datunshan to the Erzihping (Erziping) area. You can pick up the trail opposite the entrance to Datun Nature Park; it takes about two hours to walk.

From Erzihping, you can join up with the forested **Bird Watching Trail,** where you may spot up to 20 different species of birds, including the Taiwan blue magpie and the colorful Muller's barbet, with its emerald green chest. To catch the birds at their most active, it is best to go at dawn or dusk. The trail ends at Cisingshan camping area, near the administrative offices of Yangmingshan National Park. ■

People flock to Yangming Park in spring, when the cherry blossoms burst into bloom.

Beitou

Beitou
△ Map p. 93

**Beitou Hot
Springs Museum**
http://peitoumuseum.culture
.gov.tw
- ✉ 2 Jhongshan
  (Zhongshan) Rd.
- ☎ 2893-9981
- 🕐 Closed Mon.
- 💲 No charge
- 🚇 Xin Beitou MRT
  station, or taxi

**Taiwan Folk Art
Museum**
www.fulu.com.tw
- ✉ 32 Youya Rd.
- ☎ 2891-2318
- 🕐 Closed Mon.
- 💲 $
- 🚇 Xin Beitou MRT
  station or taxi

**Opposite:
Beitou's hot-
springs hotels
rely on a supply
of piping hot
water that
bubbles to the
surface through
faults.**

THE JAPANESE OPENED THE FIRST HOT-SPRINGS HOTEL
here in 1896, making Beitou Taiwan's oldest such resort. Beitou
reached its peak during World War II, when it became popular with
Japanese troops on R&R. Locals say that kamikaze pilots used to
spend their last few days at the resort, "marrying" Beitou girls before
flying off to meet their fate.

In the ensuing years, Beitou's
popularity gradually waned. But a
hot-springs boom and the arrival
of an MRT line in the late 1990s
revived the town. Beitou is now the
most convenient place in which to
experience hot-springs bathing
close to Taipei. (See pp. 42–43 for a
discussion of hot-spring geology.)

A snapshot of Beitou's history
and Taiwan's hot-springs culture
can be found at the **Beitou Hot
Springs Museum,** a 10-minute
walk up Jhongshan (Zhongshan)
Road from the Xin Beitou MRT
station. The restored Victorian-style
brick-and-wood building, originally
built by the Japanese in 1913, once
served as a public bathhouse. The
50-by-20-foot (15 by 6 m)
Romanesque **indoor bathing
pool** on the first floor gives some
idea of how seriously the Japanese
took hot-springs bathing. Columns
supporting a recessed ceiling frame
the pool, while romantic motifs of
gliding swans, sailboats, and snow-
capped mountains are embossed on
stained-glass windows.

The beautifully restored
Tatami Room, enclosed by
sliding rice-paper screen doors,
dominates the second floor. Other
rooms in the museum are given
over to exhibits on such subjects
as hot-springs geology and
the history of the Beitou area. The
**Hollywood of Taiwan Film
Gallery** traces the flourishing
local filmmaking industry of the
1950s and '60s, when many films
were shot in the area.

A little farther east along
Jhongshan Road, the thick clouds
of steam hanging over a bubbling
sulfur pit at **Hell Valley** (Closed
Mon., tel 2893-9981) evoke the
apocalyptic atmosphere that earns
the area its name. This haunting
natural phenomenon is one of
Beitou's most famous attractions.

According to its curators, the
Taiwan Folk Art Museum
(on Youya Road, farther up hilly
Jhongshan Road from Hell Valley)
was once a club and inn for
kamikaze pilots. The traditional
Japanese-style building is now a
museum and garden housing a
wildly eclectic private collection of
artifacts on Taiwanese and
aboriginal culture. One of the
more interesting is an **exhibition
on foot-binding** on the second
floor. It takes you through this
traditional process with explanations, photographs, and displays
of the tiny slippers worn by the
women who suffered this fate.

A loftier, more expansive view
of the steamy phenomenon that
occurs in Hell Valley can be found
at **Longfeng Valley** along
Cyuanyuan (Quanyuan) Road,
where wooden observation decks
overlook a former sulfur mine, one
of 27 that once existed in Beitou.
Cracks in the Earth emit plumes of
steam that waft high over an area
made barren by toxic sulfur gasses.

At the height of its popularity
Beitou had over 70 inns and hotels.
These days only a dozen or so
remain (see p. 252). ■

Beitou Hot Springs Museum (built 1913), the former public bathhouse

Typical volcanic terrain

Steam

Steam rises from heated water.

Mineral deposits collect around the edge of pools.

Water is forced toward the surface through cracks.

Underground water course and reservoir of water, heated by subterranean hot rocks

Heated rocks beneath the Earth's surface

A walk around Danshuei (Danshui)

In the historic port town of Danshuei (Danshui), you can find evidence of Taiwan's colonial past, reminders of the work of respected Canadian Presbyterian missionary George Leslie Mackay, and bustling streets along the Danshuei River.

From the Danshui MRT station catch Red Bus No. 26 along Jhongjheng (Zhongzheng) Road to the Aletheia University bus stop, about 1.25 miles (2 km) from the MRT station. From the bus stop, after paying an entrance fee, walk up a garden path to a hill overlooking the mouth of the Danshuei River and the Pacific Ocean. You will find the red concrete fortifications of **Fort San Domingo** ❶. *(1, Lane 28, Jhongzheng Rd., Danshuei, tel 2623-1001, closed Mon.).*

This small, sturdy fort neatly encapsulates much of Taiwan's history. It was built by the Spanish in 1629 and later occupied by the Dutch, Chinese, and British, who turned it into a consulate. After Britain recognized mainland China in 1972, the British vacated the consulate compound and returned it to the Taiwanese government in 1980.

Danshuei's distinctive Fort San Domingo dates back to 1629.

The fort's first floor has four prison cells opening onto a small, high-walled exercise yard, as well as a scale model of the fort and information about its history. On the walls of the two second-floor rooms are replicas of maps from the period and a wonderfully crafted scale model of a 17th-century Dutch warship, the *Prins Willem*.

A footpath runs alongside the fort to the former **British Consulate** ❷, a redbrick Victorian building constructed in 1871, which provides river views from its wide verandas and bay windows. The rooms are filled with late 19th- and early 20th-century furniture, which tends to clash with such latter-day additions as wall-to-wall carpeting and linoleum. Return to the entrance of the fort and turn right toward **Aletheia University** (also known as Oxford University College), passing an imposing neo-Gothic-style church on the left.

Across a spread of lawn and gardens is the original college building, now housing the **Aletheia University Museum** ❸ *(32 Jhenli/Zhenli St., Danshuei, tel 2621-2121)*. The small museum building, which is also the original Oxford College that Mackay built in 1882, is a delightful amalgam of British colonial design and Chinese architectural flourishes, including a traditional tiled roof crowned with a steeple shaped like a Buddhist *chedi* and topped with a crucifix. The museum is dedicated to the memory of missionary Mackay, who was greatly respected in Taiwan for his benevolence. Inside are photos, diaries, historical information, and other memorabilia.

Return to the entrance to the university and head left down narrow Jhenli (Zhenli) Street. After about 150 yards (140 m), small eateries and food kiosks line the left-hand side of the street. A few doors down on the left is an **open-fronted restaurant** ❹ at 6-1 Jhenli Street *(no English signage, tel 2621-1785, closes 3 p.m.)*; sample some of its famous homemade soy milk and *a-gei*, a Japanese dish of vermicelli noodles inside tofu.

Continue down Jhenli Street toward the

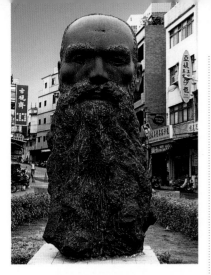

Locals call this long-bearded bust of missionary Mackay "the cuttlefish statue."

river for about 110 yards (100 m) to the intersection at Jhongshan (Zhongshan) Road. Turn right at the intersection and walk down the hill for 110 yards (100 m). Here, in a tiny park in the middle of the street, is a large **granite bust of Mackay ⑤**, whose features have taken on a distinctly Chinese appearance. Directly to the

left as you face the statue is a small lane that leads 33 yards (30 m) to the **Mackay Hospital ⑥** (*open Sun. 2:30 p.m. to 4:30 p.m.*), which now houses a small museum dedicated to the missionary. Built by Mackay, it was the first Western hospital in Taiwan. Next door is **Danshuei Church,** also built by Mackay, although there is not much left of the original structure. Proceed to Jhongshan Road and turn right, or southeast, toward the MRT line. About 275 yards (250 m) along the road is a Bank of Taiwan building at the head of Lane 95. Turn right into this narrow lane, and after 55 yards (50 m) you will come to the **Longshan Temple ⑦**, dedicated to the goddess Guanyin. This venerable temple was built in 1796 and is among the oldest in Taiwan. Retrace your steps up Lane 95 to Jhongshan Road and turn right; down the road you will see the MRT station from which you started. ∎

⊠ See area map p. 93
► Fort San Domingo
⟳ 0.62 mile (1 km)
⏱ 90 minutes
► Danshui MRT station

NOT TO BE MISSED
- Fort San Domingo
- British Consulate
- Aletheia University Museum
- Longshan Temple

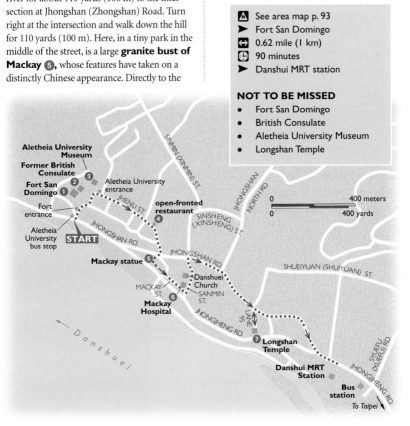

Aletheia University Museum
Former British Consulate
Fort San Domingo ①
Aletheia University entrance
Fort entrance
Aletheia University bus stop
START
JHONGSHAN RD.
JHENLI ST.
SANMIN (XINMIN) ST.
open-fronted restaurant ④
SINSHENG (XINSHENG) ST.
JHONGSHAN
NORTH RD.
Mackay statue ⑤
JHONGSHAN RD.
Danshuei Church
SANMIN ST.
MACKAY ST.
Mackay Hospital ⑥
SHUEIYUAN (SHUIYUAN) ST.
JHONGJHENG RD.
LANE 95
Longshan Temple ⑦
Danshui MRT Station
SYUEFU (XUEFU) RD.
JHONGJHENG RD.
Bus station
To Taipei

Danshuei

0   400 meters
0   400 yards

North Coast

North Coast

◭ Map p. 93

Visitor information

www.northguan-nsa.gov.tw

✉ North Coast & Guanyinshan National Scenic Area Tourist Center, 164-2, Putoukeng, Puping Village, Sanjhih (Sanzhi) Township, Taipei County

☎ 2636-4503, ext. 190

Ju Ming Museum

www.juming.org.tw

✉ 2 Sishih (Xishi) Lake, Jinshan Township, Taipei County

☎ 2498-9940

🕒 Closed Mon., & Tues. if Mon. is a holiday

💲 $$

FROM DANSHUEI (DANSHUI), THE NORTH COAST Highway (Provincial Highway 2) skirts the coastline east to the port city of Keelung. The area is known for its wide sandy beaches and rocky coastline, which sprouts numerous eye-catching rock formations. The 40-mile (64 km) route can easily be covered in a day.

About 15 miles (25 km) east of Danshuei is one of the most popular beaches along the north coast: **Baisha (White Sand) Bay** *(closed dusk–8 a.m., $)*, a generous sweep of white sand locked between rocky promontories. The beach can get so crowded on summer weekends that it's hard to see the sand for all the umbrellas and bodies. The half-mile (0.8 km) stretch is markedly quieter during the week and during the winter.

Expansive sea views open up along **Cape Fuguei (Fugui),** where the Taiwan Strait, East China Sea, and Pacific Ocean meet. The cape is noted for its rocky outcroppings and lush greenery.

About 2 miles (3 km) farther east at **Shihmen (Shimen)** (Stone Gate), a stone arch stands by the coastal side of the highway. Climb to the top of the 26-foot (8 m) arch, relax on remnants of gun emplacements, and take in the views.

Legend holds that during the Qing dynasty, 17 merchants drowned after their boat sank on a rough crossing of the Taiwan Strait. One merchant's dog vainly attempted to rescue his master before swimming ashore, where it sat on the beach and eventually pined away. The **18 Kings Temple** memorializes these unfortunate souls as well as the dog, whose statue takes pride of place in the main shrine overlooking the ocean just to the east of Shihmen. Worshipers at the crowded temple light cigarettes and place them in stands, just as they would incense, believing the merchants

were fond of smoking. You reach the temple on a side road at the highway's 19-mile (31 km) mark.

Just before the town of Jinshan, about 24 miles (39 km) along the highway, another side road heads inland to the **Ju Ming Museum,** which celebrates the works of one of

Taiwan's foremost artists. The museum contains about 500 sculptures and 500 paintings by the prolific Ju, many placed outdoors on 26 acres (10.4 ha) of undulating parkland. The grounds also display sculptures by other artists.

Back on the highway, at Jinbaoli Street in the center of Jinshan, you can see excellent examples of Qing dynasty buildings. A viewing platform in the town looks out over the rocky Candlestick Islets, 500 yards (460 m) offshore.

Taiwan's north coast reaches its most dramatic point at the 1-mile-long (1.6 km) promontory at **Yeliou (Yeliu),** about 3 miles (5 km) east of Jinshan. The Yeliou Geological Park's amazing rock formations, etched into almost recognizable shapes, sprout from a desolate sandstone landscape. A stone bridge leads over a tidal pool to the tip of the promontory and spectacular views.

Just beyond Yeliou is **Ocean World** *(tel 2492-1111, $$$),* worth a stop if you enjoy aquariums and dolphins. The 1-mile (1.6 km) stretch of sand at **Green Bay,** just south of Yeliou, has been developed into a seaside resort called Green Bay Seashore Recreation Club. It costs a hefty NT$500 to enter. ■

A wooden walkway leads to a lookout on Mount Keelung, between Jioufen (Jiufen) and the sea. Lofty ocean vistas are common along the north coast.

Jioufen (Jiufen)

Jioufen (Jiufen)
 Map p. 93

**Jioufen (Jiufen)
Folk Art Gallery**
✉ 131 Cingbian
   (Qingbian) Rd.
☎ (02) 2497-9400

**Jioufen (Jiufen)
Gold Mining
Museum**
✉ 66 Shibei Alley
☎ (02) 2496-6379
💲 $

ISOLATED JIOUFEN, PERCHED HIGH ON A MOUNTAIN behind Shenao Bay, about 45 minutes east of Taipei, sprang to life in the 1890s with the discovery of gold. Over the years, thousands of prospectors poured into the town to seek their fortunes. At the peak of the gold rush in the 1930s, the town became so rambunctious it earned the nickname "Little Shanghai." After World War II, the gold ran out and the town's gilded prosperity faded.

But good times returned after the release of the Taiwanese film classic *City of Sadness* by director Hou Hsiao-Hsien in 1989. The film uses Jioufen as a stand-in for Taipei as it details the period between the end of Japanese occupation and 1949, when Nationalist forces established a government-in-exile.

After the release of *City of Sadness,* the town's narrow streets and antique architecture captured the fancy of Taiwan's artists, who moved there for both inspiration and cheap studio rentals. Visitors, wanting a little of the past in an island bent on progress, followed.

Jioufen has a charm hard to find anywhere else in Taiwan. It's a pleasure to wander its laddered streets and narrow alleys, lined with homes and art and souvenir shops, and to relax in teahouses and cafés with stunning views of the mountains and the Pacific Ocean.

Most people come to the hillside village along County Route 102, which becomes Ciche (Qiche) or

"Car" Road along the town's eastern edge. The junction of Ciche and Jishan Roads is a good place to start exploring the village on foot, as most of the attractions are either on level ground or downhill from here.

The first section of **Jishan Road** is densely packed with gold and jewelry shops, eateries, boutiques, art galleries, and handicraft and souvenir shops, along with numerous small restaurants and cafés. About 110 yards (100 m) along Jishan Road, near its end, is the junction with **Shuci (Shuchi) Road,** a steep, 362-step pathway running north–south. This street provided most of the shooting locations for *City of Sadness*. The old buildings bordering the stone steps are almost all three stories high, with uninterrupted views to the sea. Here you'll find more teahouses, galleries, and restaurants, but with food and decor of a higher caliber than those of Jishan Road.

At the corner of Shuci and Cingbian (Qingbian) Roads, **Jioufen Folk Art Gallery** has exhibits on local history. A second-floor café offers coffee and tea with great views. Opposite the gallery, also on the corner of Shuci and Cingbian, is the **City of Sadness** restaurant *(294-2 Cingbian Rd., tel (02) 2406-2289),* where scenes from the movie were filmed.

From the restaurant, turn left and head west along Cingbian Road for about 15 yards (13 m), then turn right at Shibei Alley to the **Jioufen Gold Mining Museum.** The small museum houses a collection of gold-mining implements, antique lamps and tools, and plenty of rock samples, but it lacks English-language captions and information. However, the curator, who gives demonstrations of gold mining, keeps visitors entertained. ■

Once a raffish gold-mining town, Jioufen (Jiufen) is now a nostalgic flash from the past for its throngs of visitors.

Keelung

Keelung
🗺 Map p. 93
Visitor information
http://tour.klcg.gov.tw
✉ Tourist Information Center, Keelung City Govt., 1 Yi 1st Rd, Keelung City
☎ (02) 2427-4830

THIS CITY OF 400,000, REACHED BY BOTH THE NORTH Coast and Northeast Coast Highways, is Taiwan's second biggest seaport. Like the island's other ports, it was a gateway for foreign occupiers, missionaries, traders, and merchants. Although today's Keelung has little to show for this in terms of historical sites, it makes an interesting stopover along the north and northeastern coastal routes.

You can start your tour of the city at the huge statue of the goddess of mercy, Guanyin, located on a hill in **Jhongjheng (Zhongzheng) Park** (*daily 9 a.m.–5 p.m.*), close to the city center. The 74-foot (22.5 m) statue serenely overlooks the city and its harbor; behind it is a Buddhist temple.

Climb farther up the hill to **Ershawan Fort,** a fortification that once guarded the entrance to Keelung Harbor. All that is left of the original fort, built in 1840, is the renovated medieval-style fortress gate. Once through the gate, you can amble along shaded paths and view the reproduction cannon that mark

the fort's former gun emplacements.

For views of the strange, weathered rock formations that define much of the north coast, head to **Heping (Peace) Island,** an islet protecting the south side of Keelung Harbor. On the 163-acre (66 ha) island's north shore is a large amusement park (*tel (02) 2462-8714, $*).

Among local tourists, Keelung is most famous for lively **Miaokou Yeshih (Yeshi)** (Temple Mouth Night Market), which runs past Dianji Temple on Rensan Road. This stretch of restaurants and food stalls is a good place to try Taiwanese snack foods and soak up the bustling atmosphere. ■

Odd rock formations dot the shoreline around Keelung.

Northeast Coast National Scenic Area

Cliffs and inlets mark the northeast coast (above). The area also has historic attractions such as this temple on the Caoling Historic Trail (below).

THE NORTHEAST COAST NATIONAL SCENIC AREA HUGS THE narrow corridor between Taiwan's eastern mountains and the Pacific Ocean, running from Nanya, just east of Keelung, almost to the town of Toucheng, 41 miles (66 km) to the south. Coastal scenery, sandy beaches, and ocean vistas characterize the area, which can get crowded on weekends and holidays; choose a weekday for a calmer visit.

Most of the sights can be reached easily by traveling along the Northeast Coast Highway (Provincial Highway 2), although to get to some attractions you will need to park off the highway and walk a short distance. Not all directions to attractions are signposted in English, so it may be best if you take a guide along.

Nanya is the northern gateway to the Northeast Coast National Scenic Area. It is known for the sea- and wind-eroded rock formations and outcroppings scattered along the coast. The area's small, picturesque fishing villages set against

Northeast Coast National Scenic Area

www.necoast-nsa.gov.tw

🏔 Map p. 93

✉ Fulong Visitor Center, 6 Singlong (Xinglong) St., Fulong Village, Gongliao Township, Taipei County

☎ (02) 2499-1115, ext. 221

a backdrop of lush green mountains add to the effect.

Just over a mile (1.6 km) farther at **Bitou Cape,** wind and wave erosion has created an array of cliff and rock formations, including sea caves, platforms, undercuts, bluffs, and knolls. The platforms at the bottom of the cape are weathered into patterns of honeycomb and tofu. A trail leads from the Bitou Elementary School onto the cape and to sweeping panoramas. It ends at the towering, brilliantly white **Bitou Lighthouse,** standing 390 feet (120 m) above the crashing surf; the lighthouse itself is 40 feet high (12.3 m). Coastal views here are spectacular.

The sandstone cliffs rising from the sea at **Longdong (Dragon Hole) Cape** make it the premier rock-climbing destination in Taiwan. The 100-foot (30 m) cliffs are popular for their surface variety, and they are a good place to learn the sport. From the top of the cape, there are stunning views to Bitou Cape to the north and Sandiao Cape to the south.

You can take a trail down to **Longdong Bay Park** (tel (02) 2490-9445, $), site of the northeast coast's largest bay. With its surprisingly clear water flush with marine life, it's a popular spot for diving and snorkeling, and for fishermen who cast their lines from the rock platforms at the water's edge.

On the bay's south side is **Longdong South Ocean Park,** which combines a marina, seawater pools, and marine-ecology exhibitions in its visitor center (tel (02) 2490-2112, $). The entrance to the park is at the 60-mile (96 km) mark along the highway. Its seawater pools are converted abalone ponds, where water rises from knee-deep to 10 feet (3 m) depending on the tide. Because the pools are connected to the sea, you can

often find yourself swimming among shoals of fish, sea anemones, sea stars, shrimp, and crabs. The visitor center has displays explaining the area's interesting geology and marine life. Along the shoreline, you will see even more cliffs, odd rock formations, and sea terraces.

Jinshawan (Golden Sand Bay) Beach Park—just south of Longdong—is a pleasant sweep of sandy beaches. It stands out from other beaches along the coast primarily because of the lack of crowds and amenities. No entry fee because, for environmental reasons, no swimming.

In contrast, 200-acre (80 ha) **Yanliao Seaside Park** (tel (02) 2490-2991, $$) is the largest beachside park on the northeast coast. You'll find it at the 65-mile (104 km) mark of the highway. Its network of walkways and pavilions lends a Chinese character to the area. The park's sandy beach (the longest in Taiwan) stretches south for about 2 miles (3 km). This length made it the ideal landing spot for the Japanese when they first arrived in 1895. A monument in Taiwantemple style near the beach honors those who fought against the occupation. The park also incorporates terraced rice fields and rolling hills, where you can catch some ocean panoramas. On the beach you can rent sailing, surfing, and fishing gear or snack in a number of cafés.

About 2 miles (3 km) south is Taiwan's largest camping area at **Longmen (Dragon Gate) Riverside Camping Resort** (tel (02) 2499-1791, $). The campgrounds are found in the national scenic area—a surprisingly picturesque area given that part of it used to be a quarry—near where the northeast's largest river, the Shuangsi (Shuangxi), meets the Pacific. There are more than 230 campsites near

the river, so don't expect solitude.

Campers pitch tents in a grassy meadow or on wooden platforms. The area also has roofed wooden platforms and places where camper vans can be parked and hooked up to power sources. You can hire paddleboats, rowboats, and canoes for jaunts upstream through lush vegetation. From the campground, campers and visitors can get to nearby Yanliao Seaside Park via a suspension bridge.

By Longmen on the south side of the Shuangsi River's wide estuary is **Fulong Beach** (*tel (02) 2499-1211, $*). The beach is another wide, long sweeping stretch of sand and

Nanya is famous for its striated, weathered sandstone formations.

the area's most popular, mainly because of the estuary, which is ideal for the more sedate types of water sports. No end of water-sport devices can be hired here. Walkways, interspersed with shady pavilions, take you along the coast and river.

The **Fulong Visitor Center** *(tel (02) 2499-1115, ext. 221)*, the official visitor center for the national scenic area, provides plenty of tourist information and has displays of local geology, geography, culture, and flora and fauna. It also has a couple of theaters showing short films about the area. Best of all is the delightful driftwood exhibition, where local artists have created pieces using driftwood washed up along northeast coast beaches during typhoons. A cultural display introduces the lives of local farmers and fishermen, and an art gallery hosts temporary exhibitions of works from local artists.

Maoao Fishing Village, tucked into the north side of Sandiao Cape, is the best example of a traditional fishing village along the coast. Three streams, rimmed by luxuriant banyan trees, run down from the mountainside and through the village, adding an appealing flavor to the many simple, traditional stone houses that dot the village.

At **Sandiao Cape**—the easternmost point of Taiwan—panoramas open to the Pacific Ocean, the rugged coastline north to Bitou Cape and south to Honeymoon Bay. At the tip of the cape you can see the whitewashed **Sandiao Cape Lighthouse** *(tel (02) 2499-1300, closed Mon.)*.

Two miles (3.2 km) farther south at Lailai, troops of anglers balance on slippery stone platforms and brace themselves against the crashing waves. This part of the coast supports a rich growth of plankton and algae, which attracts an abundance of available fish and,

in turn, an abundance of anglers.

South from the nearby village of **Dali,** coastal rock formations take the shape of tofu (rock sectioned into squares, similar to bean curd) and *cuesta* (rocks gently sloping to a peak on one side, with a sheer face on the other), all of which adds up to some splendid scenery.

Behind the town's Tiangong Temple is the southern end of the **Caoling Historic Trail,** which heads north to the small town of Fulong. The trail is the remaining section of a renovated Qing dynasty trail, built in the early 19th century to provide a trade link between the Taipei Basin and the Lanyang Plain and to encourage more settlers to move to the plain. The 6-mile (10 km) historic trail takes you up to some outstanding views of the coast, ending at the Shuangsi River, just to the west of Fulong.

About 3 miles (4 km) south of Dali you'll find the village of Dasi (Daxi), which faces **Honeymoon Bay.** The bay gets its name from its heart-shaped shoreline, although unromantic viewers might say it more closely resembles a horseshoe. The beach is notable for its wide spread of sand, which at low tide extends about 330 feet (100 m) out from the shoreline and reveals legions of tiny scurrying crabs. In the right conditions, waves can reach a formidable 6 feet (2 m), making the bay a popular destination for Taiwan's surfers.

Stone paths interspersed with lookout pavilions and lined with shady banyan trees follow the shoreline at **Beiguan Tidal Park** *(tel (03) 978-0727)*. From them you can look out over coastal rock formations (consisting mainly of pointy cuestas and patterned tofu rock) that jut into the Pacific. One such path leads to the top of one of the largest cuestas for wide-ranging ocean and coastal views. ∎

Opposite: A rock climber takes on a challenge at Longdong (Dragon Hole) Cape, one of the northeast coast's most popular climbing destinations.

Sansia (Sanxia) Zushih (Zushi) Temple

Sansia Zushih Temple

- ⛰ Map p. 93
- ✉ 1 Changfu St., Sansia (Sanxia), Taipei County
- ☎ (02) 2671-1031
- 💲 $ (donation)

Li Mei-shu Memorial Gallery

www.limeishu.org

- ⛰ Map p. 93
- ✉ 10 Lane 43, Jhonghua (Zhonghua) Rd., Sansia, Taipei County
- ☎ (02) 2673-2333
- 🕐 Sat. & Sun., and groups by appt.
- 💲 $

The ornately decorated Sansia (Sanxia) temple is one of Taiwan's finest examples of temple architecture.

SANSIA (SANXIA) ZUSHIH (ZUSHI) TEMPLE IS AN OUTSTANDing example of modern restoration techniques applied to traditional Taiwanese temple architecture. Originally built in 1769, the temple has been rebuilt three times, the last time beginning in 1947. Restoration is still underway, and visitors can watch the restoration crew at work. The temple's architecture and adornments represent the highest standards of Taiwanese temple art.

Each beam in the tiered roofs of the temple's buildings is opulently decorated, and few parts of the interior and exterior walls have escaped painting or carving. The beams that support the temple's roofs are carved with lifelike human figures and gilded. Interior walls have shallow engravings and bas-reliefs illustrating a wealth of Chinese legends. In addition to themes from Chinese mythology, the temple's carvings depict bears, Pekingese dogs, turkeys, squid, and crab—elements rarely seen in Taiwanese religious buildings.

The complex contains an abundance of doors, panels, pillars, and statues cast in bronze. Camphor and cypress, after being carved into mythological characters and scenes, have been covered in gold leaf.

Enter the complex via the first courtyard to Sanchuan Hall through the heavy bronze **Sanchuan doorway.** Walls and window frames flanking the doorway are adorned with stone carvings. Two stone lions, carved boldly to epitomize their vigilance, guard the entrance. The male lion holds a pearl in its mouth, while the lioness plays with a cub.

The ceiling of **Sanchuan Hall** is a superb example of the structural complexity employed in Chinese temple architecture. Layers of stacked brackets climb to the ridges of the roof, using an ancient and ingenious technique that allows them to hold the immense weight of the tiled roof while eliminating the use of nails in construction.

Dragon Door Hall (to the right) and **Tiger Door Hall**

flank Sanchuan Hall. Carvings of coiled dragons, lion cubs, and flowers cover the stone drums on each side of the doors. The drums, like the stone lions that guard the Sanchuan doorway, are there to protect against evil spirits.

The two halls take you to the second courtyard in front of the main shrine. Here, three pairs of **stone pillars** are adorned with intricate three-dimensional figures. One of the pairs of columns features flowers and birds; each pillar sports 50 birds—each with its own distinctive posture—perching on the branches of plum trees.

A pair of bronze lions guard the steps leading up to the **Main Shrine,** where the icon of the Divine Progenitor is enshrined on a high altar in the central hall. At the entrance to the hall are extraordinarily detailed stone columns, with decorative figures carved three to four layers deep. The Divine Progenitor sits under a spiraling wooden ceiling embellished with gilded ridges and relief patterns. The carvings that enliven the roof

ridges are cut from Chinese cypress.

The **Drum Tower** (to the left) and the **Bell Tower** flank the main shrine. Each has a hexagonal, three-tiered roof topped by six wildly posing mosaic-tile dragons strung along the ridges.

The sun god presides in the **East Shrine** behind the Bell Tower, while the moon god sits in the **West Shrine,** behind the Drum Tower. These gods are guardian deity images cast from bronze and positioned to maintain a favorable balance of the opposing principles of yin and yang.

LI MEI-SHU MEMORIAL GALLERY

Li Mei-shu is regarded as one of Taiwan's most influential post-World War II artists and is the man responsible for the magnificence of Sansia Zushih Temple. Li began to restore the then-dilapidated temple in 1947, and he was still working on it shortly before his death 36 years later. The memorial gallery houses many of Li's paintings and chronicles his life's work. ∎

A stone carving at Sansia (Sanxia) Zushih (Zushi) Temple

Jiaosi (Jiaoxi) & Ilan County

JIAOSI (JIAOXI) IN ILAN COUNTY IS A POPULAR HOT-springs town with more than a hundred hotels and inns clustered within a mile's (1.2 km) radius of the town's railway station. Bathing at the hot springs dates back to the Qing dynasty, when locals built walls around the pools to protect the modesty of the bathers. After the Japanese occupiers arrived in 1895, they further improved on the situation, constructing bathhouses and inns.

Crowds enjoy Ilan's International Folklore and Folk Game Festival.

These days water is pumped from the hot springs directly into hotel guestrooms. Most hotels also have outdoor bathing pools for daytime visitors. The water is colorless and odorless, and some drink it for its health-giving properties.

About 550 yards (500 m) north of the railway station at the junction of Jhongshan (Zhongshan) and Gongyuan Roads is **Jiaosi Park,** often called Yuanshan Park, a pleasant area of landscaped gardens dotted with carp ponds.

Follow Jhongshan Road south from the railway station for just over half a mile (1 km) to the richly adorned **Sietian (Xietian) Temple** (*51 Jhongshan Rd., Sec. 1, tel (03) 988-2621*). The temple, built in 1804, is one the largest in northern Taiwan devoted to the god of war, Guangong.

About 2 miles (3.5 km) west of the railway station along Wufeng Road, **Wufengci (Wufengqi) Waterfall** tumbles down from the surrounding mountains. A pathway leads into the hills to this three-tiered spectacle. Climb the trail to the more dramatic second section. The trail then continues to the top of the falls, where you can watch water pour over rocks to pools 330 feet (100 m) below.

South of Jiaosi in the city of Ilan, the **Taiwanese Opera Museum** (*101 Fusing/Fuxing Rd., Sec. 2, Ilan City, tel (03) 932-2440, closed Mon. & national holidays, $*) has an interesting and colorful collection of Taiwanese opera paraphernalia, musical instruments, and costumes, as well as puppet-theater artifacts. Displays illustrate the evolution of Taiwanese folk opera using mock-ups of traditional opera stages. The puppet theater has a collection of brightly clad marionettes along with their tiny props.

FOREST RECREATION AREAS

Ilan marks the eastern terminus of the Northern Cross Island Highway (Provincial Highway 7), which cuts across Taiwan's central mountains. Look for the **Cilan (Qilan) Forest Recreation Area** *(6 Taiya Rd., Sec. 4, Taiping Village, Datong Township, Ilan County, tel (03) 980-9606, $)* 26.5 miles (38 km) southwest of the city of Ilan on a branch of Highway 7 that leads to Lishan. This beautiful area in the Lanyang Valley has superb views to the mountains.

About 7.5 miles (12 km) inside the recreation area you'll find the **Chinese Historic Men Arboretum,** a haunting primeval forest featuring 51 huge, ancient cypress trees. Each is named after a famous person from Chinese history whose time period supposedly corresponds to the age of the tree.

About 10.5 miles (17 km) west of the town of Cilan along the Northern Cross Island Highway,

the frequently fog-shrouded **Mingchih (Mingchi) Lake** nestles amid soaring mountains at the **Mingchih Forest Recreation Area** *(41 Mingchih Ln., Yingshih Village, Datong Township, Ilan County, tel (03) 989-4106).* A trail dotted with lookout pavilions meanders through the old-growth cypress trees around the lake.

Just south of Cilan, the mineral waters at **Renze Hot Springs** seep from the earth at a scalding 203°-plus F (95° C). The resort's hotels add cool water to the spring water to make soaking bearable.

From Renze Hot Springs, the road climbs to **Taipingshan Forest Recreation Area** *(58-1 Taiping Ln., Taiping Village, Datong Township, Ilan County, tel (03) 954-5114, http://recreate.forest .gov.tw, $).* The area has gardens, a forest park, and mountain views. A narrow branch road twists another 11 miles (18 km) to the crystal-clear waters of little **Cueifeng (Cuifeng) Lake.** ∎

The Cilan (Qilan) Forest Recreation Area offers fine mountain and valley views.

Jiaosi (Jiaoxi) & Ilan County
⚅ Map p. 93
Visitor information
http://tourism.e-land.gov.tw
✉ Tourism section, Ilan County government, 451 Heping Rd., Kaisuan (Kaixuan) Ward, Ilan County
☎ (03) 925-1000, ext. 1361
🕐 Closed Sun.

Wulai

Wulai

 Map p. 93

Wulai Aboriginal Culture Village

✉ 31, Pubu Rd., Wulai Township

☎ 2661-6635

💲 $

Visitors have spectacular views of Wulai Falls from the cable car that climbs up the gorge.

THE MOUNTAIN RETREAT AND HOT-SPRINGS RESORT OF Wulai is within easy reach of Taipei, just 40 minutes south by car or bus. Although Wulai village is little more than a jumble of souvenir shops, hotels, and eateries, the area serves up some spectacular scenery. The Wulai region has a sizable population of Atayal aborigines, who put on shows at various venues.

No traffic is allowed into Wulai; vehicles park at the tollgate at the northern end of the town. From there a small bridge crosses the Nanshih (Nanshi) River into the village. It only takes about five minutes to walk through **Wulai village.** Where the village stops, another bridge crosses back over the Nanshih. From here you can

reach **Wulai Falls,** the area's major scenic attraction. They are a magnificent sight, especially after it rains, which is often. Water plunges from a vertical cliff face laced with lush green foliage and pummels the Nanshih River 262 feet (80 m) below.

Just left of the bridge, on the banks of the Nanshih River, people commune with nature at Wulai's **outdoor bathing pool.** Pool walls built from riverbank rocks regulate the amount of cool water that mixes with the hot-springs water, creating different temperatures for each of the three pools.

Beyond the bridge, a mini electric railway ($) regularly heads south about 1.25 miles (2 km) to **Wulai Aboriginal Culture Village,** directly across the river from Wulai Falls. You can also reach the falls on foot in about 20 minutes via a paved one-lane road that moves through the gorge alongside the Nanshih River. The Wulai Aboriginal Culture Village is a cultural center owned and operated by local Atayal residents. The village has handicrafts and Atayal food for sale and holds regular song and dance performances. A ticket to the **Aboriginal Culture Center** includes a show.

From Wulai village, a cable car ($) climbs steeply and spectacularly to the top of Wulai Falls. A dated amusement park called Dreamland is located here. It has a lake where you can hire rowboats, a number of tame rides, and a small zoo. ■

Yingge

YINGGE IS FAMED FOR ITS POTTERY FACTORIES AND FOR the shops that produce and sell a wide variety of ceramics—all of which has led tourism authorities to label it the City of Pottery. It's worth a visit to see how lumps of clay are expertly transformed into fine pieces by the town's legions of artisans.

An artisan carefully shapes a clay pot at one of Yingge's many potteries.

The **Yingge Ceramics Museum,** a striking, modern building combining curved and linear glass curtains with exposed concrete and steel, is a good place to get an introduction to contemporary and historic ceramic techniques and works of art.

The front entrance—a large opening in the wall—is connected to the main building by a bridge over a layered pool; it takes you past cascading water and installation artworks. The ceramics museum is made up of three interlocking buildings. In the north building are the principal display rooms as well as administrative offices. The middle building—the lobby—uses its open spaces and glass walls to allow in a flood of natural light. On the south side of the museum, the facade of the most striking of the museum's buildings is a smooth, gently curving wall of glass.

Inside, more than 2,000 pieces of pottery, both ancient and contemporary, fill the museum in displays based on four themes: Development & Techniques of Ceramics in Taiwan; History of Yingge Town; Prehistoric, Aboriginal, and Taiwanese Works of Ceramics; and High-Tech Ceramics. You will find plenty of background material in English on the history and significance of the pieces on display and on pottery in general. Audio guides are also available in English.

The museum also offers a 250-acre (10 ha) ceramics park with outdoor displays.

Yingge's streets are lined with pottery shops, many with factories on the premises, selling what seems like an endless array of ceramics. They range from toilet bowls and simple earthenware teapots to musical instruments, copies of Ming and Qing dynasty pieces, and exquisite glazed porcelains. The town's historical production core, and main draw with visitors, is cobblestoned, 300-meter-long **Old Pottery Street.** This pedestrian-only section of Jianshanpu St. sports 105 shops. English is widely spoken, and overseas shipments handled. ∎

Yingge
🅰 Map p. 93

Yingge Ceramics Museum
www.ceramics.tpc.gov.tw
✉ 200 Wenhau Rd., Yingge, Taipei County
☎ (02) 8677-2727
🕐 Closed Mon.
💲 $

Taoyuan & Hsinchu Counties

Taoyuan & Hsinchu Counties

🅰 Map p. 92

Cihhu (Cihu)

✉ Dasi Township, Taoyuan County

☎ (03) 332-2101, (03) 388-3552 (guide services); phone at least one day in advance

💲 $

Window on China

www.woc.com.tw

✉ 60-2 Henggangsia (Henggangxia), Gaoyuan Village, Longtan Township, Taoyuan County

☎ (03) 471-7211

💲 $$$$

Shihmen (Shimen) Reservoir Scenic Area

✉ 34 Erping, Daping, Longtan Township, Taoyuan County

☎ (03) 471-3740

💲 $

Leofoo Village

www.leofoo.com.tw

✉ 60 Gongzihgou, Renan Ward, Guansi Township, Hsinchu County

☎ (03) 547-5665

MOST VISITORS TO TAIWAN COME TO TAOYUAN COUNTY without knowing it when they fly into Taiwan Taoyuan International Airport, about 30 miles (50 km) southwest of downtown Taipei. Taoyuan's easy access from Taipei means that many city-dwellers travel there on weekends, so it is wise to avoid those times because of crowds. Farther southwest, the city of Hsinchu is notable for being the birthplace of Taiwan's huge computer and electronics industry.

At **Cihhu (Cihu),** near the town of Dasi (Daxi), 30 miles (50 km) southwest of Taipei on Provincial Highway 7, Chiang Kai-shek lies entombed above ground in a granite and marble coffin in one of his former country villas. The gravesite is "temporary," as before his death Chiang had requested his body be returned to his native province of Zhejiang in mainland China. The number of visitors coming to pay their respects has dwindled in recent years as Chiang's myth continues to unravel. But visitors still come to the simple, heavily guarded tomb, bowing before the sarcophagus of the former R.O.C. leader.

Spread over 67.5 acres (25 ha) near the town of Longtan, the quirky, run-down, but nevertheless entertaining **Window on China** theme park presents the globe's most famous structures on a scale of 1:25. Here you can wander around Beijing's Forbidden City, the Great Wall of China, and Taipei's Longshan Temple in a lot less time than if you were taking on the real deal. Nor has the park forgotten the rest of the world, from the Statue of Liberty to the Leaning Tower of Pisa. The models are meticulously executed. Hundreds of to-scale bonsai trees and human figurines surround the miniature structures. You can travel around the park—suitably enough—in a miniature railway.

The western section of the Northern Cross Island Highway starts

in Taoyuan County before climbing into the hills near **Shihmen (Shimen) Reservoir Scenic Area,** which contains one of Taiwan's largest lakes. The dam was completed in 1964 and now serves not only as a water storage area and hydroelectric power station, but also as a weekend refuge for harried

Taipei residents. The shimmering emerald waters of the lake amid verdant mountainsides make it an engaging spot. You can hire a boat for a paddle or a cruise or follow the trails around the lake.

Farther along the highway, the aboriginal town of **Fusing (Fuxing)** nestles beautifully amid the central mountains. The highway continues to wind its way east–southeast through some of the most spectacular scenery in Taiwan before reaching the city of Ilan near the northeast coast.

HSINCHU

The city of Hsinchu, the capital of Hsinchu County, is known for two things: its wet and windy weather and the Hsinchu Science Park, the center of Taiwan's huge computer and electronics industry (see pp. 124–125). The city does not have a lot to offer visitors aside from bars and clubs.

In the south of Hsinchu County, just south of Window on China, is **Leofoo Village,** a large theme and safari park. The theme park is divided into sections, including the American West, Southeast Asia, Arabia, and the South Pacific. The park's **Flume Ride** crawls up to the top of a mock-up of a volcano before dropping back to earth at a hair-raising 45-degree angle. Minibuses haul tourists through the safari park to view lions, giraffes, zebras, and other African animals. ∎

Kitschy but fun: Replicas of the Jefferson Memorial and other famous structures enthrall schoolchildren at Taoyuan's Window on China.

Taiwan's Silicon Valley

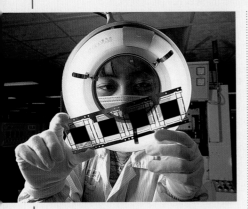

Taiwan has long been a strong exporting country, but until the 1980s the economy was powered by low-tech, high-volume exports such as toys, T-shirts, shoes, textiles, tennis rackets, and other inexpensive goods. Then, in the 1980s and '90s, producers of these low-cost items began to abandon Taiwan and set up their factories in China, Southeast Asia, and elsewhere, where land was plentiful and labor was cheaper. The exodus left a large hole in the island's industrial heartland, and Taiwan's days of making and exporting cheap goods were gone. In its place, Taiwan has found another kind of commerce: electronics, a potent industry that separates it from Asia's economic also-rans.

The island, quite simply, is a world-beater in electronics. It makes more computer monitors, mouses, motherboards, compact disk drives, digital cameras, and scanners than any other country in the world, and turns out more than one-quarter of the world's desktop computers as well as more than half of its notebook and laptop computers—more than 10 million per year.

Taiwan also excels in the manufacture of computer chips. Taiwan Semiconductor Manufacturing Corporation and United Microelectronics Corporation are the world's top producers of built-to-order integrated-circuit chips, devices that drive the world's computers, cell phones, and video games.

Taiwan's high-tech success is no accident. The government kick-started the industry in 1980 when it established the Hsinchu Science Park. Companies investing in the Hsinchu park were given tax breaks, research and development money, training, and technical assistance. The science park has been a runaway success, and today much of Taiwan's electronics output comes from Hsinchu, a one-stop high-tech shop 90 minutes south of Taipei by car. Currently, the Hsinchu complex is overflowing; some 400 companies operate there, and dozens are on the waiting list. Total investment is approaching 32 billion U.S. dollars and annual revenue generated by the park exceeds 30 billion dollars. More than 80 percent of the companies in Hsinchu are high-tech, producing semiconductors, telecom products, computer components, and related hardware.

Several other Asian countries that have since jumped on the high-tech bandwagon have been unable to reproduce Taiwan's success. Hsinchu's size and organization gives it a key competitive advantage over latecomers to the electronics game: When all related companies are near each other, they can work easily together. A producer of integrated circuits, for example, need only look next door to find companies that specialize in complicated tasks like making the masks used to produce the chips, testing the chips, and packaging them.

With the Hsinchu Science Park filled to overflowing, the government opened a second science park near Tainan in 1996, where it offered the same perks as at Hsinchu. The Tainan park enjoyed so much initial success that a third park has been opened near the central city of Taichung.

High-tech products now account for more than half of Taiwan's exports, and the little island has become the world's 13th largest exporting country. Not surprisingly, the people of Taiwan are enthusiastic converts to the world of electronics, and their per-capita use of computers, cell phones, and the Internet is among the highest in the world. ∎

Taiwanese workers turn out a sizable percentage of the world's silicon chips (opposite), laptop computers (above), and other high-tech devices. Since the 1980s, hundreds of companies have invested billions of dollars in making Taiwan one of the world's greatest exporters of electronics.

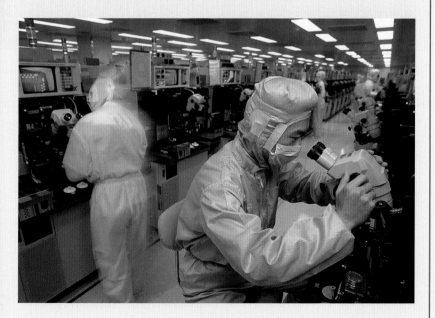

Miaoli County

MIAOLI COUNTY EXTENDS SOUTH FROM NEAR HSINCHU to the northern border of Taichung County in Taiwan's Central West region. It's a little out of the way if you are using Taipei as a base for travel in northern Taiwan, but if you are traveling from Taipei down the arterial Sun Yat-sen Freeway to Taichung or Kaohsuing, the journey could profitably be broken by some stopovers in the area.

One of these stopovers should be **Shihtoushan (Shitoushan)** (Lion's Head Mountain), just inside Miaoli's northern border. When viewed from a distance (and with sufficient imagination), 1,627-foot (496 m) Shihtoushan does resemble the head of a lion. But more significance lies in the mountain's attachment to Buddhism. Shihtoushan's mountainsides are dotted with Buddhist temples, some built into caves and set amid beautiful forest scenery. If you are

BORDERS.

BORDERS
BOOKS MUSIC AND CAFE
8705 N. Port Washington Rd.
Fox Point, WI 53217
(414) 540-1427

STORE: 0336   REG: 03/96 TRAN#: 1173
SALE   07/24/2010 EMP: 00334

NATL GEO TRAVELER TAIWAN-E02
        8900480   QP T   13.77
  22.95 40% BR PROMO
COUPON 159046770000000000

            Subtotal   13.77
BR: 8317731852

            Subtotal   13.77
            WISCONSIN 5.6%   .77
  1 Item   Total   14.54
            AMEX   14.54
ACCT # /S XXXXXXXXXXXX3000
            AUTH: 586216
NAME: CHIAPPETTI/THOMAS M

You Saved $9.18

    07/24/2010 01:17PM

within 60 days of purchase and the purchase price will be refunded in the form of a return gift card.

Exchanges of opened audio books, music, videos, video games, software and electronics will be permitted subject to the same time periods and receipt requirements as above and can be made for the same item only. Periodicals, newspapers, comic books, food and drink, digital downloads, gift cards, return gift cards, items marked "non-returnable," "final sale" or the like and out-of-print, collectible or pre-owned items cannot be returned or exchanged.

Returns and exchanges to a Borders, Borders Express or Waldenbooks retail store of merchandise purchased from Borders.com may be permitted in certain circumstances. See Borders.com for details.

BORDERS®

Returns

Returns of merchandise purchased from a Borders, Borders Express or Waldenbooks retail store will be permitted only if presented in saleable condition accompanied by the original sales receipt or Borders gift receipt within the time periods specified below. Returns accompanied by the original sales receipt must be made within 30 days of purchase (or within 60 days of purchase for Borders Rewards members) and the purchase price will be refunded in the same form as the original purchase. Returns accompanied by the original Borders gift receipt must be made within 60 days of purchase and the purchase price will be refunded in the form of a return gift card.

Exchanges of opened audio books, music, videos, video games, software and electronics will be permitted subject to the same time periods and receipt requirements as above and can be made for the same item only. Periodicals, newspapers, comic books, food and drink, digital downloads, gift cards, return gift cards, items marked "non-returnable," "final sale" or the like and out-of-print, collectible or pre-owned items cannot be returned or exchanged.

Returns and exchanges to a Borders, Borders Express or

after a few days of peace and solitude, some of the monasteries have rooms and dormitories and welcome visitors.

From the gate above the parking lot, stone steps take you toward the mountaintop, passing many temples, shrines, and other attractions along the way. They then descend gently past more of these structures. The last section of the trail, through forest and bamboo groves, is particularly appealing. The hike takes about three hours; along the way are small, traditional eateries.

The steps will bring you first to the temple called **Cyuanhua (Quanhua) Hall** *(tel (03) 782-2020)*. At Cuanhua's main hall, **Kaishan Monastery,** you can see nuns and monks going about their business in serene surroundings. Below the hall, nuns serve vegetarian meals at the temple's cafeteria. The temple provides overnight accommodation.

At the peak of the trail you reach at **Wangue (Viewing the Moon) Pavilion,** where you can linger and enjoy the expansive mountain vistas before heading back down past more temples, cave shrines, and pavilions.

SANYI

Located off the Sun Yat-sen Freeway in southern Miaoli, Sanyi is known as Taiwan's woodcarving center. **Jhongjheng (Zhongsheng) Road,** the town's main street, is lined with stores and workshops. On nearby Shueimei (Shuimei) Street, you'll find a staggering 200 shops selling woodcarvings and other wooden items. Follow the signs to **Guangsheng Village,** where many of Taiwan's wood sculptors have set up workshops and don't seem to mind visitors watching them work.

Also in Guangsheng Village, the

Sanyi Woodcarving Museum houses exhibits of fine wood sculptures, along with information on the history, techniques, and styles of woodcarving, but unfortunately for Western visitors, mostly in Chinese.

South of Sanyi, tectonic forces, wind, and rain have weathered the mountains at **Huoyanshan (Fire Mountain) Nature Reserve** *(Forestry Bureau, 2 Jhongshan/*

Zhongshan Rd., Hsinchu City, tel (03) 522-4163), creating jagged peaks and rock-strewn slopes. The best views of the mountain are from the south, and they are at their most impressive at sunset, when the mountain gives off a fiery red and orange aura.

A 10-mile (16 km) stretch of railway between Sanyi and Houli to the south will thrill train buffs. Trains twist through tunnels and over bridges straddling deep river gorges into the mountains. The delightfully restored **Shengsing (Shengxing) Station** sits at the railway's highest point, 1,320 feet (402.326 m) above sea level. ∎

Sanyi Woodcarving Museum

✉ 88 Guangsheng Village, Sanyi Township, Miaoli County

☎ (03) 787-6009

🕐 Closed Mon.

💲 $

Misty forests in Miaoli County (opposite). At the Sanyi Woodcarving Museum (above), visitors admire relief work on a traditional door.

Sanyi

🅰 Map p. 92

Visitor information

www.sanyi.gov.tw

☎ Sanyi Township Administration, (03) 787-2801

Visitors can wade through shallow waters in Donghsan River Water Park.

More places to visit around Taipei & the North

DONGSHAN RIVER WATER PARK

The park, often called Cingshuei (Qingshui) Park, is located next to the Dongshan River in Ilan County, east of Luodong. It is full of ponds, pools, spouting fountains, pavilions, and jetties; visitors can wade in the shallow pools or hire boats to row around the deeper areas. Ceramic dragons guard the riverbank, which is lined with colorful mosaics. Map p. 93 2036 Siehe (Xiehe) Rd., Wujie Township, Ilan County (03) 950-2097

JINBAOSHAN CEMETERY & TERESA DENG'S GRAVE

The grand views to the valley below, the town of Jinshan, and the north coast from this manicured cemetery on a mountain slope are stunning. But most people come to Jinbaoshan to pay homage to Taiwan's most famous musical export, Teresa Deng, whose untimely death in 1995 at the age of 43 sent the island into mourning. Deng's pop music—variously sung in Taiwanese, Mandarin, English, and Japanese—reached millions throughout East and Southeast Asia. A sound system set up at her grave sight plays recordings of her most famous songs. Map p. 93 18 Sishih (Xishi) Lake, Jinshan Township, Taipei County

SHIHSANHANG MUSEUM OF ARCHEOLOGY

Located west of the mouth of the Danshuei River, at the foot of Mt. Guanyin across from Danshuei port, this young, expansive facility was built right over a major archaeological site, which itself is one of the exhibits, that dates back some 500 to 1800 years. The museum was opened in 1998 to showcase the finds here and elsewhere in the area. The Shihsanhang people, unlike other pre-modern Taiwan dwellers, had metal-making know-how, perhaps acquired from China traders. On display are silver, copperware, gold jewelry, and coins. Visit the Bridge of Time, which enables visitors to travel through the Shihsanhang culture.

Try to leave time to ride rented bikes along the meandering paths that stretch from the museum upriver to the Bali-Danshuei ferry, about 4 km. Rental booths are at the ferry dock. The pathways move through a mangrove conservation area. Museum tickets ($) can be purchased at the museum itself, both ferry terminals, and the Danshui MRT station; the price includes museum entry, to/fro ferry rides, and shuttle-bus to/fro the museum. www.sshm .tpc.gov.tw 200 Bowuguan Road, Bali Township, Taipei County (02) 2619-1313 ■

The East Coast is the most undeveloped and unspoiled region of Taiwan. It is a place of great natural beauty, defined by spectacular gorges and coastlines, and bucolic hinterlands.

East Coast

Along the Mystery Valley (Shenmigu) Trail, Taroko Gorge

Relative isolation gives the east coast a special appeal, one enhanced by coastal panoramas.

East Coast

LOCKED BETWEEN TAIWAN'S CENTRAL MOUNTAIN RANGE AND THE PACIFIC Ocean, the island's rugged and largely unspoiled east coast presents the island's most beautiful river and coastal scenery. Here steep, towering sea cliffs drop perpendicular into the sea, and raging rivers cut deep and spectacular chasms into the mountains. Inland, charming rustic backdrops of hamlets idling on rolling hills, tea plantations, hot springs, and sweeping valley views offer a soothing respite from the coastline's drama.

One advantage to touring the east coast is the ease of accessibility to its highlights. Most are laid out before you as you drive down its coastal highway, which for most of the journey between Hualien, the region's biggest city, and Taitung to the south hugs the contours of the coastline.

At Cingshuei (Qingshui) Cliff, between the port cities of Suao and Hualien, sheer rock walls drop straight into the sea from towering mountains reaching 3,000 feet (1,000 m). The occupying Japanese managed to carve a road along the edge of the cliff face in the 1920s.

An equally spectacular engineering feat is the road that runs the length of stunning Taroko Gorge, just to the north of Hualien, and the easternmost section of the Central Cross Island Highway. Taroko is one of Taiwan's major tourist attractions (avoid weekends unless you like crowds), and the scenery is arguably the best you will find on the island. It was during the construction of the highway between 1956 and 1960 that easy access was gained to the vast marble deposits in the gorge, setting off a mining boom and earning nearby Hualien the moniker of Marble City.

The East Coast National Scenic Area stretches a little over 100 miles (160 km) south of Hualien to Taitung and is well suited to a scenic drive. Green and Orchid Islands, a boat ride away from Taitung, offer remote tropical splendor with a dash of history and culture, while inland from Taitung, in the East Rift Valley National Scenic Area, the scenery switches to bucolic. ■

AROUND TAIPEI
& THE NORTH
p. 91

TAROKO
NATIONAL
PARK

**Wenshan
Hot Springs**

To
Suao

9

Taroko

**Swallow
Grotto**

**Chingshuei
(Qingshui) Cliff**

Dayuling

8

Tiansiang
(Tianxiang)

Gorge

Sincheng (Xincheng)
Sioulin (Xiulin)

CENTRAL
CROSS ISLAND
HIGHWAY

**Tunnel of
Nine Turns**

Meilyuen (Meilun) R.

9

Tianchih
(Tianchi)

14

Jian

Hualien

Dongmen

Ami Culture Village

Carp L.

Shoufong

HUALIEN

9

Hualien Ocean Park

EAST

Fonglin

11

Fanshuliao

16

Wanrong
Guangfu

11曲

CENTRAL
WEST
p. 207

RIFT

Fongbin

**Rueisuei (Ruisui)
Hot Springs**

VALLEY

Rueisuei (Ruisui)

Cimei (Qimei)

9

Dagangkou

NATIONAL

11

Jhuosi (Zhuoxi)

*Siouguluan
(Xiuguluan)*

Yuli
Antong

Changbin

SCENIC

Dongli

**Antong
Hot
Springs**

20

AREA

SOUTH
CROSS ISLAND
HIGHWAY

Chihshang

East

Rift

TAITUNG

23

Chenggong

Guanshan

Beinan

**Bunun Cultural and
Educational Foundation**

9

Donghe

Yanping

11

Hongye Hot Springs

Luye

Chulu

Chulu Pasture

**National Museum
of Prehistory**

Beinan Culture Park

Beinan

THE SOUTH
p. 157

9

**Jhihben (Zhiben)
Hot Springs**

11

Taitung

**Green Island
Visitor Center**

Gongguan

Green I. Human Rights Memorial Park

24

Jhihben
(Zhiben)

Nanliao

Haishenping

**Jhihben (Zhiben)
Forest Recreation
Area**

Taimali

*Green Island
(Lyudao/Ludao)*

9

Dawu

9

Central Mountain Range

PACIFIC

OCEAN

*Orchid Island
(Lanyu)*

Langdao

Dongcing (Dongqing)
Village

Yeyou

Area of map detail

Taipei

**THE EAST
COAST**

0   20 kilometers

0   20 miles

Hualien

KNOWN AS MARBLE CITY BECAUSE OF LARGE DEPOSITS OF marble mined from nearby Taroko Gorge, Hualien is the largest city on the east coast. It's a tidy and busy place sitting in the shadow of the Central Mountain Range. The city serves as a jumping-off point for trips to spectacular Taroko Gorge and down the rugged east coast to Taitung, but it is not without its attractions, both within the compact city center and nearby areas.

Riverside Park follows the narrow flow of the Meilyuan (Meilun) River, which cuts through the city. You can get to the park from a pathway just before a bridge at the northern end of Jhongjheng (Zhongzheng) Road. Follow the park north for about 550 yards (500 m) and cross another bridge to reach Hualien's **Martyrs' Shrine,** built into the hillside of Mount Meilun. The shrine memorializes Chinese heroes important to the history of Taiwan. Steep steps introduce this stately and tranquil place, done in the classical Chinese architectural style of sweeping, swallow-tailed roofs supported by imposing red columns, and adorned with colorful eave paintings.

Farther up the hill, the park—which also has a playground and meandering pathways—affords some fine views of Hualien City.

Near the western end of Jhonghua (Zhonghua) Road, just before it crosses a small canal on the way to Carp Lake, is Hualien's most renowned temple, **Cihhueitang (Cihuitang),** the Hall of Motherly Love. On the left side of the temple complex is the ornate **Regal Mother of the West Temple** (Wangmu Niangniang Miao).

Extensive use of Hualien's marble is on display next door at the **Palace of the Jade Emperor** (Yuhuang Dadi Tian), a pilgrimage site that holds up to 2,000 devotees in its dormitories. The temple's dormitories are full during festivals, especially on the 18th day of the second lunar month (about six weeks after the lunar New Year), when pilgrims from all over Taiwan and other parts of East Asia arrive

Washed marble: Hualien is famous for its marble, most of which comes from nearby Taroko Gorge.

here to receive the blessings of priests in an attempt to rid themselves of their chronic ills.

On the outskirts of Hualien, **Carp Lake** (Liyutan), one of Taiwan's largest natural lakes, makes for a pleasant half-day excursion. The lake is set amid pineapple and other tropical fruit plantations in the foothills of the dominant Central Mountain Range. You can take your choice from the hundreds of rowboats and paddleboats clustered on the shoreline and head out onto the lake, or amble around the 3-mile (4 km) road that encircles the lake. A number of well-marked hiking trails lead from the lake up into nearby hills to some calming views of the lake and surrounding countryside.

Just south of Hualien, the **Ami Culture Village** celebrates the culture and traditions of the local Ami aboriginal tribe—Taiwan's largest aboriginal ethnic minority, numbering about 150,000—with displays of arts and handicrafts, and regular daily cultural shows.

Six miles south of the city center on Highway 11, adjacent to the East Coast National Scenic Area Visitor Center (see pp. 140–144), is the world-class **Hualien Ocean Park.** Spread over 126 acres

(51 ha), the park has themed areas that include a dolphin aquarium, a water park, a sea lion and seal habitat park and theater, plus plenty of rides. Hotel shuttle buses will take you there from Hualien. ∎

Betel nut beauties

Along roadsides outside major cities, you are bound to notice young, scantily clad girls perched on stools inside glass booths, most times looking extremely bored. These girls are purveyors of betel nut, or *binlang,* the fruit of the areca palm that give users a mild stimulating buzz when chewed. It also leaves the teeth and gums of users with permanent deep red stains. The betel nut beauties' uniform usually consists of a clinging blouse worn with a mini skirt, often enhanced with side slits—and sometimes less than that. The girls' main customers are truckers and taxi drivers, who once they pull up in front of the booths are attended by the girls, who give the drivers titillating views while filling the orders. ∎

The Hualien Aboriginal Dancers, an Ami troupe, perform predominantly in Taipei and at the Ami Culture Village south of Hualien.

Taroko Gorge

Taroko Gorge
Map p. 131

TAROKO GORGE IS SIMPLY A SPECTACULAR PLACE, A wonderland of natural beauty that would leave even the most jaded visitor impressed. Its deep marble canyons, rushing white water, and towering cliffs put it in league with the world's best scenic attractions. The main route through the gorge, the Central Cross Island Highway—a marvel of engineering in itself—runs along the bottom of the main gorge, taking in much of its splendor along the way.

Taroko's deep marble canyons, rushing white water, and precipitous cliffs place it at the top of Taiwan's scenic attractions.

Construction of the Central Cross Island Highway through Taroko Gorge was thought near impossible. In 1956 road crews, mainly decommissioned military personnel who had come over from mainland China with the Kuomintang government, started blasting and bulldozing their way through cliffs of solid marble. By 1960, at the cost of more than 450 lives, a 48-mile (78 km) road had been carved, completing the connection between the east and west coasts of the island.

The gorge is part of **Taroko National Park,** which encompasses 92,000 acres (37,000 ha) of the island's Central Mountain Range. The origins of this stunning place lay in the formation of the island of Taiwan some 12 million years ago, when the Philippine tectonic plate collided with the Eurasian landmass, buckling the Earth's crust and heaving land upward—twisting and folding it in the process—to form Taiwan's central mountains. Huge slabs of marble emerged at Taroko and, over time, were slowly etched by the Liwu River, eventually forming a deep, boulder-strewn gorge embraced by cliffs of solid marble.

Spectacular views are almost immediate as you follow the **Central Cross Island Highway** from the national park's entrance up into the gorge. You snake along a road carved out from the looming cliff side, often disappearing into tunnels and emerging to more staggering views of the canyon, the rushing Liwu River, and soaring cliffs. These views become even more dramatic as you climb farther into the gorge toward the main settlement of **Tiansiang (Tianxiang),** nestling between green mountains 14 miles (22.5 km) west of the park entrance.

About 100 yards (91 m) west of Tiansiang, you can climb across a pedestrian suspension bridge to the lofty **Siangde (Xiangde) Temple,** a collection of pagodas, ornate prayer halls, and bodhisattva statues—including a gilded 36-foot (11 m) Avalokitesvara bodhisattva image. Next to the image is the six-level **Heavenly Summit Pagoda.** Climb to the top for even loftier vistas of Tiansiang and the surrounding countryside.

About 2 miles (3 km) north of Tiansiang, at the mouth of the third tunnel along this section of the highway, steep steps carved from the mountainside take you down into the magnificence of the gorge and **Wenshan Hot Springs** (*closed indefinitely due to instability caused by typhoon and tectonic activity*). Here a large, heated natural pool, embraced by curving walls of marble, sits adjacent to the Dasha River, a tributary of the Liwu.

Despite the heavy concentrations of sulfur, the pool water is crystal clear. A bubbling spring lets hot water seep through a crack in the marble wall into the pool, while a drainhole spills the pool water into the river. Enjoy both hot spring water—125° F (48° C)—and cold river water rushing off your body.

Cycling or walking along the Central Cross Island Highway from the park entrance to Tiansiang brings you more in touch with Taroko's majesty, but you will need to be on constant lookout for passing traffic. This section is barely wide enough for two lanes of cars, and there are no dedicated bike lanes. If you do cycle or walk, start from Tiansiang and head east to the park entrance—it's downhill all the way. There are several sections, including the **Tunnel of Nine Turns** (see p. 137), that are vehicle-free, perfect for a stroll. Another option might be to get off the road to hike along designated trails (see pp. 138–139). ■

Catch of the day at tranquil Lotus Lake

Visitor information
www.taroko.gov.tw
✉ Taroko National Park Headquarters and Visitor Center, 291 Fushih (Fushi) Village, Sioulin (Xiulin) Township, Hualian County
☎ (03) 862-1100
🕐 Closed Mon. of 2nd week of each month

A tumbling waterfall at Taroko's Eternal Spring (Changchun) Shrine

Driving Taroko Gorge

This drive, along the Central Cross Island Highway from the entrance of Taroko Gorge National Park to the park's main settlement of Tiansiang (Tianxiang), measures only 14 miles (22.5 km), but allow plenty of time for parking and taking in the sights. The route, which follows the lip of the gorge, twists and turns most of the way.

On the north side of the Liwu River, opposite the arched entrance to the national park, is the **Taroko National Park Headquarters and Visitor Center ①** *(tel (03) 862-1100).* Here you can pick up brochures and maps. Park rangers also post notices of weather conditions and places to avoid.

A signposted side trail that takes you to the **Eternal Spring (Changchun) Shrine ②** starts 1.4 miles (2.3 km) west of the entrance. Its mountainous backdrop, classical Chinese design, and 45-foot-high (14 m) fronting waterfall make for a picturesque sight. A steep trail behind the shrine (see p. 139) leads up into the mountains for stunning views of the peaks of the Central Mountain Range.

From the Eternal Spring Shrine the road climbs alongside the steep walls of the gorge for 4.8 miles (7.7 km) to a turnoff to **Buluowan Recreation Area ③** *(tel (03) 861-2528, closed 1st, 3rd Mon. of month).* A short but steep road leads to a local Atayal community that has become a dolled-up tourist village. Set in the foothills, enclosed on three sides by precipitous mountains, the setting is spectacular.

The recreation area is the best place to take in some of what is left of the historic **Houhan Old Trail ④.** Before the opening of the highway, this trail was the main cross-island route, blazed by the Atayal centuries ago.

Back on the main road, go west for 2.5 miles (3.6 km) to **Swallow Grotto ⑤,** a section of the highway where a long tunnel has been blasted through the cliff face. The lower marble sections on the opposite cliff are pockmarked with hundreds of small grottoes, etched out of the rock by underground streams long dried up. Thousands of swallows once made their nests here, but increasing traffic over the years has scared them off. They may soon start returning, however, as park authorities have closed this dramatic section of the highway to traffic (a bypass has been built) to allow visitors more time to admire the scenery without worrying about traffic.

The grotto continues for 500 yards (457 m) to a café and souvenir shop.

Farther along is Jinheng Bridge and, on the Liwu River's north side, the brooding presence of **Yindianren (Indian) Rock** ❻. The huge rock, weathered into a shape resembling the profile of a Native American chief, is one of Taroko's most famous sights.

Another pedestrians-only section awaits 2.2 miles (3.6 km) on from Yindianren, the twisting **Tunnel of Nine Turns** ❼ (Jyucyudong/Jiuqudong), a series of short tunnels cut through sheer marble. The drama of Taroko reaches its peak here. The gorge squeezes between cliffs, and tiered waterfalls tumble down along the Liwu River, which rages down this narrow section of the gorge. You gain some perspective of the gorge's sheer size near the end of the Tunnel of Nine Turns when it opens to more extensive vistas. From the viewpoint at **Lioufang (Liufang) Bridge** ❽, you get a clear look at the tunnel and can see how it was cut through the mountains.

A mile and a quarter (2 km) farther into the gorge you reach the **Bridge of Motherly**

Devotion ❾ (Cihmu/Cimu Bridge). Stop for a look at the riverbed with its scattering of huge boulders thrown down from the mountains.

Heading west along the highway for another 1.25 miles (2 km) brings you to **Tiansiang (Tianxiang)** ❿, Taroko's largest settlement. This resort town is attractively set on the edge of the gorge and backed by verdant mountains, and it is where you'll find most of the accommodations available in Taroko, from guest houses to a luxury hotel. Just before Tiansiang, a suspension bridge leads over the river to a six-story pagoda perched on a mountain ridge. You can climb to the top for some outstanding views. The pagoda is part of the lofty Siangde (Xiangde) Temple complex (see p. 135). ■

🅜 See area map p. 131
► Taroko National Park Headquarters and Visitor Center
⟷ 14 miles (22.5 km)
⏱ 3.5 hours
► Tiansiang (Tianxiang)

NOT TO BE MISSED
- Swallow Grotto
- Yindianren (Indian) Rock
- Tunnel of Nine Turns
- Lioufang (Liufang) Bridge

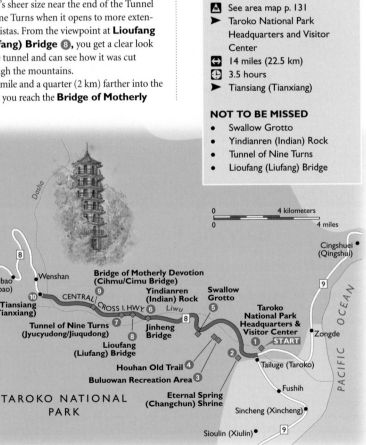

Baiyang Falls & other trails

Baiyang Falls & other trails

Map p. 131

See Taroko National Park Headquarters and Visitor Center, p. 135.

MANY OF TAROKO'S TRAILS ARE HUNTING AND INTER-village routes carved by the Atayal aboriginals, who once inhabited much of the gorge. Nearly all of the villages have disappeared, but a number of the trails have been turned into hiking paths. Some are little more than a stroll, others more difficult. All are spectacular.

Water Curtain Tunnel, located along Taroko's magnificent Baiyang Falls Trail

BAIYANG FALLS TRAIL
This delightful amble along a branch gorge takes in the most awesome scenery of all of Taroko's trails. The trailhead is a 1,000-foot-long (300 m) tunnel, half a mile (1 km) north of Tiansiang (Tianxiang) on the Central Cross Island Highway. The

end of the tunnel opens to cliff faces and a narrow gorge formed by a fast-flowing branch of the Liwu River. Here is a map board (in Chinese) and a viewing platform. You then cross a small bridge, which hugs the contours of the gorge for most of the way. Initially, the trail rises gradually to another lookout with views down to the gorge's rapids, before leveling out and winding along the side of the gorge and through numerous tunnels to reach the thundering **Baiyang Falls.** Here, water pours between huge bleached boulders and crashes into an emerald lagoon. The best views of the 50-foot-high (15 m) waterfall and the patterned-marble face of the gorge can be had by crossing a wood-planked suspension bridge to a lookout.

Cross back over the suspension bridge and follow the trail another 220 yards (200 m) to **Water Curtain Tunnel** (Shueiliandong/ Shuiliandong). Park authorities closed the tunnel after the September 21, 1999, earthquake (see sidebar p. 218), calling it too dangerous to enter. But if you shine a flashlight past the padlocked gate, you see the "water curtain" formed by water pouring through the roof of the cave. You return along the same route. The 1.3-mile trail (2.1 km) takes 90 minutes to walk. Bring a flashlight because of the tunnels; there are a grand total of eight, some quite long.

ETERNAL SPRING (CHANGCHUN) SHRINE TRAIL

Climbers of the short but strenuous Eternal Spring Shrine Trail are rewarded with vistas of the Central Mountain Range. The trailhead begins a few hundred yards off the Central Cross Island Highway, 1.4 miles (2.3 km) west of the entrance to Taroko National Park. From the temple, you begin a steep climb as it zigzags up to stunning views of the peaks of the Central Mountain Range. A **bell tower** and the nearby **Kuanyin cave temple** mark the trail's highest point. The trail then drops back down to the Central Cross Island Highway, about 2 miles (3 km) east of the temple.

The 0.85-mile (1.35 km) trail takes about 25 minutes to walk.

LOTUS POND TRAIL

This 4-mile (6.8 km) trail climbs to Lotus Lake, which at 4,000 feet (1,200 m) above sea level is Taroko's highest natural body of water. The trail begins at Hueitouwan, about 4 miles (6 km) west of Tiansiang, at a hairpin turn on the Central Cross Island Highway. The first section, which runs for 1.6 miles (2.5 km), is not much more than a leisurely stroll, taking about 30 minutes. After crossing a rickety suspension bridge to the right, the trail zigzags its way up the mountain, climbing 1,640 feet in 2.7 miles (500 m in 4.3 km) before reaching Lotus Lake. The second section of the hike takes about two hours and can be grueling. You return via the same route. There is a small hostel at the lake.

MYSTERY VALLEY (SHENMIGU) TRAIL

Following a hunting trail originally blazed by aborigines, you follow the **Shakatang River—**a tributary of the Liwu River—for 2.75 miles (4.4 km), passing through forest areas thick with giant ferns and by crystal-clear ponds, huge white boulders, and layered marble cliffs. Begin at Shenmigu Bridge just beyond the national park head-quarters near the park's eastern entrance. Cross the bridge and head left down the iron stair-way to the trail. The trail, noted for its numerous river crossings, continuously opens to stunning views of the gorge and surrounding mountain peaks. Timber-decked lookouts are placed along the trail to enhance the vistas. You return the way you came; the round-trip takes about four hours. ■

The delightfully scalloped footbridge at Sansiantai (Sanxiantai) was built to resemble a dragon. It reaches to a rocky islet with an encircling timber-decked walkway.

Driving down the east coast

This drive starts in the city of Hualien and hugs the isolated and relatively unspoiled eastern coastline before reaching Taitung, 106 miles (170 km) south. It takes you through the East Coast National Scenic Area.

Begin at the **Hualien Visitor Center** ❶ *(tel (03) 867-1326)*, located on Highway 11 about 6 miles (10 km) south of Hualien's city center, at the entrance to the East Coast National Scenic Area. The staff will provide you with area maps and brochures. The center also has an exhibition hall with environmental displays and aboriginal handicrafts. Along the sides of the exhibit room is a scale model of the coastline. Push the button on the wall and a funky model of a VW Kombi van appears and slowly rumbles along the route.

Three miles (4 km) farther on is the **Henan Temple** ❷, with its 50-foot (15 m) honey-colored statue of the goddess of mercy, Guanyin, standing on the side of a hill and overlooking the Pacific Ocean.

From Henan Temple, the highway narrows to two lanes and climbs higher along the base of the mountains that line the Coastal Mountain Range, offering broad ocean vistas. It then briefly turns inland, serving up a rustic feel of rolling hills, farmhouses, and rice fields at Shueilian (Shuilian), until you reach a bridge at **Fanshuliao** ❸, 9 miles (14 km) on from Henan Temple. Once you drive over the bridge—which spans the Fanshuliao River—park, cross the highway, and walk a short distance to the old, abandoned bridge that sits adjacent to the one you have just crossed. From here, you can get stunning views if you peer over the precipice down the narrow, deep gorge that cuts through the mountains to the nearby Pacific Ocean. Local legend has it that the Ami aborigines living here so revered courage that anyone who could vault across the gorge—which measured a good 40 feet (12 m) wide—using bamboo poles would become their leader. The bamboo groves in the 200-foot-deep (60 m) gorge are said to have flourished from the poles that the young men used in their attempts.

Highway 11 climbs farther up the side of the mountains to even more lofty ocean views, before dropping to **Baci (Baqi) Recreation Area ❹**, which lies 3 miles (4 km) farther on. From the lookout are sweeping vistas of the gray-black sands at **Jici (Jiqi) Bay,** and the mountains running

strung out along the coast and jutting into the Pacific Ocean.

The highway then winds down to the bay and the graceful 1.5-mile (2.5 km) sweep of **Jici (Jiqi) Seaside Resort ❺** *(visitor center, tel (03) 871-1251, closed Oct.–April),* which lies locked between verdant headlands and backed by steep foothills. The beach here is popular with locals despite the unappealing color of its sand. At the northern end of the beach, 3 miles (5 km) from the Baci (Baqi) lookout, you can park near the visitor center and have a stroll.

Highway 11 begins to follow the contours of what has now become a rugged coastline as the verdant mountains of the Coastal Mountain Range clash with the Pacific, offering some of the drive's best scenery. The highway then loops inland briefly and winds through the town of **Fongbin,** before turning back to the coast and more ocean and mountain views and onto the rocky coastline at **Shihmen (Shimen),** 39 miles (62 km) from Hualien and 15.5 miles (25 km) from Jici Bay.

Just beyond, a "tourist" sign announces your arrival in **Shihmen.** Park at the first building on the coastal side (the left) of the highway. The two-level, open-concept building here is **JOKI ❻** *(3 Shihmen/Shimen, Fongbin Township, Hualien County, tel (038) 781-616, www.joki.com.tw).* The fascinating coffee shop and art gallery, overlooking the rocky coast, features some wildly imaginative furniture and sculptures made from timber, steel piping, and smooth, veined rocks collected from the shore.

Just over a mile (2 km) farther down Highway 11, a road to the left leads to

---

▲ See area map p. 131
► Hualien Visitor Center
⟷ 95 miles (152 km)
⏱ 5 hours
► Taitung

NOT TO BE MISSED
- Fanshuliao
- Jhuo Er Ci (Zhuo Er Qi)
- Sansiantai (Sanxiantai)
- Donghe Bridge

Shihtiping (Shitiping) ⑦ (Stone Steps Terrace), named for volcanic rock that has been worn into terraced slabs along the coast for about half a mile (1 km). The visitor center *(tel (03) 878-1452)* has illustrations and explanations of the local topography, marine life, and vegetation, but they are written only in Chinese. The area has been landscaped into a park, and a wood-plank walkway takes you to observation decks to view the breakers thumping into this unusual coastline.

The **Siougulyuan (Xiuguluan) River** (see p. 145) empties into the Pacific Ocean at the 68-kilometer mark of Highway 11. The river is spanned by the graceful, 131-yard-long (120 m) **Changhong (Rainbow) Bridge,** with commanding views of the Coastal Mountain Range and the river's exit into the Pacific. About 100 yards (91 m) beyond the bridge a sleek, tall obelisk marks the Tropic of Cancer. You are now officially in the tropics.

Six miles (10 km) farther along the highway, you come to the **Basian (Baxian) Caves** ⑧ (Caves of the Eight Immortals). Evidence of human habitation during the Paleolithic Age has been discovered in these caves, and the visitor center *(tel (089) 88-1418, closed noon–1:30 p.m.)*—which has been fashioned to resemble the inside of a cave—carries out this theme, displaying some stone relics dating from the period, geological information, and life-size figures of the first inhabitants spearing deer and cooking fish; little of the information is in English. Behind the visitor center, pathways lead to a dozen small caves, which are now crammed with gilded Buddha and bodhisattva images, worshippers, and tourists; gift stalls do a brisk business selling religious paraphernalia.

After the Basian Caves, the coastal plain widens and the Coastal Mountain Range becomes more distant, but no less imposing. **Shihyusan (Shiyusan),** or Stone Umbrella, is a narrow though very large spit of rock that projects about 1,000 yards (914 m) into the sea at the 106-kilometer mark of Highway 11; it's worth a brief stop to check out its rock formations and some splendid views. Four miles (6 km) south, veer left off Highway 11 for 1.5 miles (2 km) to reach **Sansiantai (Sanxiantai)** ⑨ (Platform of the Three Immortals; *visitor center, tel (089) 850-785, closed noon–1:00 p.m.),* where a neck of land reaches out to a small island, connected by a lovely scalloped footbridge designed to resemble a dragon. Wood-plank pathways wind around the windswept island, which is crowned by three huge black-faced rocks said to resemble the three immortals, Chinese legendary figures who visited the area. The walk takes about 90 minutes. The wave-bashed beach at Sansiantai, made up of smooth black pebbles, attracts a lot of interest from tourists.

Backtrack to Highway 11 and continue south for 15 miles (24 km) through the town of **Chenggong** to the **East Coast National Scenic Area Visitor Center** *(tel (089) 841-520).* While the center has

Eight Immortals

Frequently featured in Chinese art, the Eight Immortals lived during the Tang and Song dynasties. They all attained immortality through chance. After an out-of-body experience, mystic Li Tie Guai found his body had been cremated, so he moved into a lame beggar's body; he carries a crutch and is a patron of the disabled. Alchemist Jhong Li Cyuan found a container holding the elixir of life; he carries a fan and is the patron of the military. Musician Lan Cai nursed beggar Li back to health, carries a flower basket, and is a patron of florists. Senior citizen Jhang Guo Lao, who refused to die, is seen with a donkey and is a patron of old men. He Sian Gu ground a magical stone and drank it with water. Depicted with a flower basket, she is a patron of housekeepers. Han Siang Zih dreamed his violent death before turning to Taoism and befriending immortal Jhong. He carries a fly-whisker and is a patron of barbers. Flautist Han Siang Zih grabbed a sacred tree branch. He carries a flute and is the patron of musicians. Fed up with a corrupt royal court, Cao Guo Jiou was meditating on a mountain when he chanced upon the other immortals. He is the patron of actors. ■

Buddha images enshrined in the Basian (Baxian) Caves

displays of aboriginal artifacts, illustrations, and models of east coast topography, flora, and fauna, plus a section devoted to outdoor activities, little is labeled in English. There are good views of the Pacific and **Green Island** (see pp. 152–153) from the plaza in front of the center. The adjacent **Ami Folk Center** *(tel (089) 841-751),* set against a generous sweep of landscaping, features traditional aboriginal dwellings and ceremonial houses.

Turn right just before the **Donghe Bridge** ⑩—at the 140-kilometer mark—and head west for about 200 yards (182 m) to a parking lot, where you can look down to spectacular views of the **Mawuku River.** The river's water rushes through a deep gorge littered with giant white boulders, set against a stunning mountain backdrop. Head back to the bridge and cross it to the small fishing village of **Jinzun.** Just before the village, on the left, is a small coffee shop (no Chinese or English name). Here you can relax in a convivial atmosphere while enjoying lofty hilltop views of black-sand beaches and rolling surf from its terrace. A trail from the coffee shop leads to the beach.

Six miles (10 km) farther south, just past the town of **Dulan,** the scenery opens to long beaches and palm groves. Just over a mile past town you come to an intriguing tourist road sign: **Water Flowing Upwards** ⑪. Turn right just past the sign, drive past the souvenir shops immediately on the left, then park and check out the wide irrigation channel next to the road where the water appears to run uphill—at least when there is water, after heavier rainfalls. No detailed scientific explanation needed, however; it's an optical illusion.

The last stop before Taitung, 7.5 miles km) past Water Flowing Upwards, is **Siaoyehliou (Xiaoyeliu)** ⑫. Behind the visitor center *(tel (089) 281-136)*—which features some tropical fish tanks and geographical information about the area—is a lovely shady garden of lawn, palms, and pathways winding down to the coastline. Here sandstone rock formations, different from the volcanic rock that defines much of the east coast, inspire names such as tofu rock, honeycomb rock, and fungus rock. ■

Siaoyehliou (Xiaoyeliu) is another spot on the east coast to view sculptured rock formations.

Siougulyuan (Xiuguluan) River

EMERGING FROM ITS SOURCE 10,200 FEET (3,200 M) IN THE
Central Mountain Range, the Siougulyuan River—the east coast's
longest—snakes downstream for 67 miles (108 km) before emptying
into the Pacific Ocean halfway between Hualien and Taitung.

The river's lower section initially
slices through high cliffs near
Rueisuei (Ruisui) before reaching
Cimei (Qimei), about 6 miles (10
km) from the coast. It then gushes
through a steep-walled gorge, flows
under Changhong (Rainbow)
Bridge near Dagangkou, and opens
up broadly to the sea. In all, there are
23 sets of rapids from start to finish.

The premier way to enjoy this
spectacular course is, of course, by
raft; indeed, the river draws some
100,000 people every year. The trip
takes three to four hours and can
vary from leisurely to downright
invigorating. The best times are
during the April to October monsoon season.

You can join a group for a
white-water-rafting trip at Rueisuei.
For more information and to
book a trip, visit the Rueisuei
Rafting Service Center *(215
Jhongshan/Zhongshan Rd., Sec. 3,
Rueisuei Township, tel (03) 887-
5400);* you can also arrange a trip
through your hotel in Hualien.
All gear is provided, but bring a
change of clothing, as you will
likely get soaked. If you make your
own way to Rueisuei, get there
before noon, as few, if any, rafts
leave after that time.

You can also drive 18 miles along
the lower river via the Rueigang
(Ruigang) Highway, which begins
near Dagangkou at the 68-kilometer
mark of Highway 11. This is also
an ideal cycling route.

In June the river comes alive
with 200 six-person rafts in a
world-class race that draws spectators all along its banks. ■

**Siougulyuan
(Xiuguluan)
River**
 Map p. 131
**Visitor
information**
www.eastcoast-nsa.gov.tw
☎ East Coast National
Scenic Area Visitor
Center (089) 841-
520

**Fierce white
waters and
spectacular
scenery
account for
the Siougulyuan
(Xiuguluan)
River's year-
round popularity.**

East Rift Valley

East Rift Valley

🅰 Map p. 131

**Visitor
information**

www.erv-nsa.gov.tw

✉ East Rift Valley
National Scenic
Area Visitor Center,
215 Jhongshan
(Zhongshan) Rd.,
Sec. 3, Rueilian
(Ruiliang) Village,
Rueisuei (Ruisui)
Township, Hualien
County

☎ (03) 887-5306

**Gentle breezes
and lofty launch
pads make the
rustic and
tranquil East Rift
Valley one of
Taiwan's favorite
parasailing areas.**

THE SLEEPY SEASIDE CITY OF TAITUNG IS THE SPRING-
board for a trip into the nearby East Rift Valley. Splicing the Coastal
Mountain Range from just below Hualien in the north to Taitung in
the south, this area provides a rural respite from the drama of Taroko
Gorge and the ruggedness of the east coast. Highway 9 follows the
valley floor past tranquil scenes of green rolling hills, pasturelands,
tea farms, forest recreation areas, hot springs, and plantations
embraced by towering mountains, perfect for a meandering drive.

A web of side roads and lack of
English road signs can make exploration difficult without some local
knowledge. The best way to tour
the area is to have your hotel
arrange a private driver or contact a
qualified local travel agency.

Although a dairy farm would
seem like an unusual tourist attraction, locals flock to **Chulu
Pasture** *(1 Muchang, Mingfeng
Village, Beinan Township, Taitung
County, tel (089) 571-002, $)* to
check out cows wandering in lush
meadows and being milked in
sheds. They pose for photographs
in front of fiberglass bovines and

gulp down the farm's famous milk
in its snack bar/souvenir shop.
Most tourist buses arrive in the
afternoon to watch the herds being
led out to pasture.

Leaving Chulu, Highway 9
winds through some lovely valley
scenery to the **Bunun Foundation Village** *(tel (089) 561-
211),* one of the few self-sufficient
aboriginal communities in Taiwan.
The community is home to 150 people who have successfully turned
their hand to tourism, while maintaining their communal culture.
The well-run cooperative has an
arts and handicrafts center, stores, a

restaurant serving up Bunun food, accommodations for visitors, and a theater with cultural programs twice daily. The shows are noncommercial and nonexploitative.

Also in Yanping Township, in tiny Hongye Village, is Taiwan's own "Field of Dreams" at Hongye Primary School (1 Honggu Rd., tel (089) 561-015). Students of the school, mainly Bunun aborigines, became the unlikely heroes of Taiwan in 1968, when they beat the Japanese Little League World Series champions while the latter team was on a goodwill tour of Taiwan

freeform pools and Jacuzzis sit under thatched shelters. A timber decked, open-air restaurant overlooks the scene, while the surrounding mountains add to the peaceful nature of the place.

Highway 9 continues to wind north through the valley over a series of bright red steel-arched bridges fronting river gorges, past plantations of pineapple and palm trees, and through hamlets nestled on mountainsides. Climb up Luye Scenic Drive through tea plantations to **Luye Tea Farm,** on Luye Plateau. Its two-story pavilion and

Bunun Cultural and Educational Foundation
www.bunun.org.tw
🗺 Map p. 131
✉ 191 Ward 11, Taoyuan Village, Yanping Township, Taitung County
☎ (089) 561-211

Sisters of the Bunun tribe

(see pp. 148–149). The school's modest main hall has been turned into the intriguing **Little League Memorial Hall** with pictures and paraphernalia of the school's proud baseball past, including photographs of the joyous, victorious 1968 team.

Nearby **Hongye Hot Spring Resort** (120 Honggu Rd., tel (089) 561-311, $) is an open-air complex of hot-spring pools owned and operated by the Bunun tribe. The resort's numerous circular and

teahouse offer startling views down into the valley formed by the Beinan River. Pastures and pineapple and palm plantations form patchworks in the valley across to the Dulan Mountain. The place is a favorite for parasail pilots, who launch themselves from the plateau from two ramps in front of the teahouse.

The teahouse has an open-air gallery on its second floor. Downstairs you can sample the variety of teas and sweets on sale. ■

Luye Tea Farm
🗺 Map p. 131
✉ 145 Lane 42, Gaotai Rd., Yongan Village, Luye Township, Taitung County
☎ (089) 550-797 or (089) 552-127

Baseball in Taiwan

On a calm summer evening in Sinjhuang (Xinzhuang), a suburb of Taipei, kites fly in the blue sky, children play, smoke rises from barbecues. But inside Sinjhuang (Xinzhuang) Baseball Stadium, it's more like a madhouse. Attention is riveted on the field, where the yellow-clad Brother Elephants are losing 6–0 to the Chinatrust Whales. Soon the Elephants score two runs, and two innings later, in a flurry of base hits, they score five more times, sending their fans into a deafening crescendo of flag-waving, drum-pounding, trumpet-blowing support. The Elephants beat the Whales 8–6. It's a dramatic comeback for the Elephants, and their fans walk happily away into the night. The presence of so many supporters, sitting in a great new ballpark and cheering with synchronized gusto, is an equally dramatic comeback for baseball in Taiwan.

Baseball has a long history in Taiwan. The Japanese taught the game to the Taiwanese in the early 1900s, and the locals then turned around and beat their colonial masters in a landmark tournament in 1930. The game surged in popularity in the 1960s, when Taiwan's Little League team won the first of an eventual 17 world titles. The Chinese Professional Baseball League (CPBL) was launched in 1990, and two years later, Taiwan's national team won a silver medal at the Barcelona Olympics.

Baseball fever in Taiwan peaked in 1996. That year, more than 1.3 million fans poured into the nation's ballparks; television ratings soared. A high-profile gambling scandal in the late 1990s caused the eventual collapse of several teams, and attendance began dropping. But by 2002, the game had regained its former popularity. Three new baseball parks opened, two on the outskirts of Taipei and a third in Kaohsiung.

Baseball in Taiwan is not the gentle pastime that American fans are familiar with—it is a loud, raucous affair. There are no "home" teams in the CPBL (the teams are owned by large Taiwan corporations). The six teams wander the island, playing in ten stadiums. This means that fans of both teams attend each game. Armed with drums, firecrackers, and noisemakers, they greet every pitch with lots of noise.

The sport has recently gotten another boost from the United States. A number of Taiwanese players have been signed by Major League teams, and hopes are high that one of them can be like Ichiro, the Japanese player who has been such a huge success in America. Pitcher Wang Chien-ming is giving it a good shot with the New York Yankees. Made a starter in 2005, he went 19-6 in 2006 and came in second in voting for the American League Cy Young award. ∎

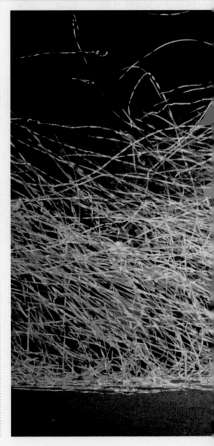

Baseball was introduced to Taiwan by Japanese colonists, and the two now are fierce rivals (above right). Pregame streamers greet players (right).

National Museum of Prehistory & Beinan Culture Park

National Museum of Prehistory
www.nmp.gov.tw
⚠ Map p. 131
✉ 1 Museum Rd., Taidong
☎ (089) 381-166
💲 $$

IN 1980, WORKERS BUILDING THE TAITUNG RAILWAY Station uncovered a major prehistoric culture archaeological site. Excavations revealed the most complete settlement found to date in Taiwan. The site has since been preserved and developed into an archaeological park, Beinan Culture Park, while the nearby National Museum of Prehistory, completed in 2001, displays the finds. The museum takes you on a fascinating chronological journey through the lives and times of Taiwan's ancient and modern native peoples.

NATIONAL MUSEUM OF PREHISTORY

The museum building is a hodge-podge design of multilevel roofs of different shapes, randomly placed square and porthole-shaped windows, and multicolored walls in green-tint concrete and redbrick

veneer, all rendered to evoke concepts that are found inside the museum. In the **main plaza** is a circular fountain, centered with a bronze sundial sitting on a columned pedestal.

Follow the stairs from the ground-floor lobby to the second floor and a glass-walled corridor looking down on Shan (Mountain) Square. The **second-floor permanent galleries** present an overview of Taiwan's natural history and Austronesian peoples, showing chronologically the geographic and geological changes of Taiwan, and the different eras of habitation by early peoples, with a timeline to the present aboriginal tribes.

From the galleries a sign leads to a winding ramp—symbolizing the descent into an archaeological dig—that takes you to a myriad of **small themed galleries** that follow Taiwan's natural and ancient histories. First is Taiwan's earliest known culture—the cave-dwelling Changbin people—presented in a life-size diorama. The walls and displays around the diorama include ancient relics dating back some 30,000 years. Subsequent **basement galleries** follow a similar layout.

The museum houses thousands of priceless antiquities, including

jade spearheads and carved jade ornaments from the Stone Age; tools and ornaments from the Iron Age; decorated pottery from the Neolithic Age; ritual, ornamental, and funerary objects made from jade, bronze, and iron; plus stone figures and coffins, rock wheels, and richly carved megaliths.

From the basement galleries, an escalator takes you back to the second floor and more modern times to explore galleries tracing the history and cultural development of Taiwan's different groups of indigenous peoples through tools, farming and fishing implements, icons, dwellings, musical instruments, clothing, art, and handicrafts.

BEINAN CULTURE PARK

The expansive, undulating, 328,000-square-yard (300,000 sq m) park at the foot of Mount Beinan (Beinanshan) is the site of a prehistoric Beinan settlement dating back 2,000 to 3,000 years. The park is designed to give visitors a firsthand view of the ongoing work of archaeologists who are uncovering it. A plaza marks the entrance to the park, with a path leading to the **amphitheater,** which is centered with circular marble patterned with jade earring motifs, symbolic of the Beinan people. Another path leads from the amphitheater to the **visitor center,** in the western area of the park. Behind the visitor center is the two-level **Observation Platform,** with a map board and sweeping views of the park and the city of Taitung in the distance.

Another path from the amphitheater winds to the **Excavation Area** on the park's eastern edge. Here you can occasionally observe archaeologists at the canopied dig and learn more from the adjacent exhibit booth. ∎

Watch archaeologists uncover secrets of Taiwan's ancient peoples at Beinan Culture Park (opposite), and see their finds at the excellent National Museum of Prehistory (above).

Beinan Culture Park

🅰 Map p. 131

✉ 200 Culture Park Rd., Nanwang, Taitung

☎ (089) 233-466

🕐 Closed Mon.

💲 $

🚉 Taitung Railway Station

Green Island

Green Island (Lyudao/Ludao)
🅰 Map p. 131

Getting there by ferry
Many departures daily from Fugang Harbor, 10 minutes north of Taitung City on Provincial Highway 11. See pp. 238–239 for more information.

GREEN ISLAND (LYUDAO/LUDAO) IS BECOMING INCREASINGLY popular with visitors, most of whom visit for its beaches, dazzling offshore coral, and scenery. But it also has a darker past. The island has a number of prisons, including one that incarcerated political prisoners until as late as the 1980s. The prison is now part of a park dedicated to human rights and the suffering of those opposed to the dictatorial rule clamped on Taiwan for nearly 40 years.

Jhaorih (Zhaori) Hot Springs is one of only a few in the world to be fed by seawater.

An 11-mile-long (17 km) road encircles the island. Start your trip at the **Green Island Visitor Center** *(tel (089) 672-026),* opposite the airport in Jhongliao (Zhongliao) Village. Inside are geological and flora and fauna displays, fish tanks, and photographs of the island's coral reefs and marine life.

From the visitor center, you can walk to the **lighthouse,** rising above a high cape on the island's northwest tip. The 108-foot-high (33 m) structure was built with funds donated by the U.S. govern-

ment after one of its ships, the *President Hoover,* sank upon striking rocks nearby in 1937.

Back at Jhongliao Village, head east along the coastal road for about 1.25 miles (2 km) to the fishing village of **Gongguan,** with its pastel houses lining the edge of a small horseshoe-shaped bay dotted with rock formations.

From here it's another 600 yards (550 m) to the former prison—ironically named Oasis Villa by inmates—where thousands of political prisoners were held during the island's long years of martial law.

The prison is now the **Green Island Human Rights Memorial Park.** In the park stands Asia's only monument to human rights, with the names of all the former incarcerated political prisoners. It stands as an impressive monument to the freedoms that have swept Taiwan since the martial law era ended in 1987. The renovated prison's museum highlights the conditions to which the detainees were subjected.

Just beyond the memorial park, the road swoops south and heads down the island's west coast. A few hundred yards after the turn you come to **Guanyin Cave.** Inside is a small temple where a stalagmite donned in a red cape represents Guanyin, the goddess of mercy.

The island's rugged west coast has some lovely white-sand beaches—although low-lying coral precludes swimming at some. At **Haishenping,** a steep path leads to a small pagoda and panoramic views.

At the island's southeastern tip, right on a rocky beach, awaits one of Green Island's most popular attractions: the unusual **Jhaorih (Zhaori) Hot Springs.** The springs are one of only three in the world fed by seawater. Authorities have also built a pavilion, a store, and showers.

About a mile (1.6 km) across from the hot springs, in the southwest corner of the island, is **Dabaisha Beach.** A boardwalk takes you down to the beach sand before continuing out into the sea over coral exposed at low tide. At the end of the boardwalk you can jump into the water and snorkel.

A little more than half a mile (1 km) northwest of Dabaisha on the island's west coast are two sea caves, **Longsia (Longxia)** and **Basian (Baxian).**

The island's main village of **Nanliao,** about half a mile (1 km) northwest of the caves, is where you can hire motorbikes and bicycles and book glass-bottom boat tours. There are also a couple of dive shops here, where you can arrange diving trips if qualified. ∎

Getting there by air
Many flights daily from Taitung Airport.

☎ Mandarin Airlines, (02) 2717-1230 (reservations center in Taipei); (089) 362-669 (reservations hotline in Taitung)

Green Island is known for its rugged coastline and weathered rock formations; General Rock (below) supposedly resembles a human face on the right side, with an imperial-era general's headgear on the left.

Orchid Island

Orchid Island (Lanyu)
⚠ Map p. 131

Getting there by ferry
Many departures daily from Fugang Harbor, 10 minutes north of Taitung City on Provincial Highway 11. See pp. 238–239 for more information.

Elaborately decorated canoes are prized possessions for Orchid Island's native Dahwu families.

ORCHID ISLAND (LANYU) LIES 40 MILES (65 KM) OFF THE southeast coast of the Taiwan mainland. This small, 17-square-mile (44 sq km) isle is dominated by a volcanic landscape of steep mountains soaring high above lush valleys and a precipitous coastline overlooking sweeping bays. It is inhabited by about 2,000 Dahwu aborigines, Taiwan's smallest ethnic group, which is also called the Yami, who despite the odds have managed to cling to many of their traditional beliefs. Although there is some tourism, the island is much less developed than the larger Green Island (see pp. 152–153).

The Dahwu maintain their traditional lifestyle as much as possible, living off the land and sea, fishing in traditional richly decorated canoes, growing yams and taro, foraging for shellfish along the rocky coast, and raising pigs and goats.

Some still live in traditional houses built partially underground, dug out of embankments and on hillsides for protection against the severe typhoons that sweep across the island. Low walls of stone or

wood surround the structures, and the roofs are thatched. Pavilions are built beside the houses to take advantage of more comfortable weather conditions.

Like Green Island, Orchid Island has a paved road running along the coast and encircling the island. The island's six villages are dotted along this 31-mile (50 km) road. Ferries arrive near the main village and administrative center of **Yeyou** on the west coast, while the airport is a little farther south at Yeyou. At Yeyou you can hire scooters or rent taxis.

Heading north from Yeyou about 2 miles (3 km) brings you to a knob-shaped headland and the island's lighthouse, overlooking rock formations whose names—Crocodile and Tank Rocks—pretty much describe their appearance. The road then tops the northwestern tip of the island and, just before heading east, arrives at the **Wukong Caves,** a series of five huge but shallow adjacent caves burrowed into the side of tall sea cliffs. Cave entrances are marked with crucifixes (missionaries made it to Orchid Island and managed to convert a sizable number of the population), while recesses in the cliff face near the entrances house clay statues depicting biblical scenes.

The road then skirts the northern coastline for about 0.6 mile (1 km) before reaching **Langdao,** where you will find the best examples of Dahwu architecture. On a hillside overlooking the Pacific sits a cluster of houses with only the roofs visible. Most of the dwellings have small vegetable gardens and stilted pavilions in their yards.

The island's east coast is studded with a number of unusual rock formations weathered out of the stony coral that makes up the coastline. One of the more interesting is **Twin Lions Rock,** two facing walls sculpted to resemble guardian lions similar to those found in temples, jutting out into the sea at the northeastern tip of the island.

About 1.25 miles (2 km) south on the west coast is **Battleship Rock,** so named because of its ship's-hull shape and outcrops resembling gun turrets. About 110 yards (100 m) farther south, an inviting crystal-clear pool marks the entrance to **Lover's Cave.**

Just beyond Battleship Rock, **Dongcing (Dongqing) Village** is a good place to see fleets of Dahwu fishing canoes. The village sits on a beautiful crescent-shaped bay. ∎

Getting there by air
Numerous flights daily from Taitung Airport.
☎ Mandarin Airlines, (02) 2717-1230 (reservations center in Taipei); (089) 362-669 (reservations hotline in Taitung)

Celebrate!

During the spring the Dahwu, also called the Yami, celebrate the Feiyu Jie (Flying Fish) Festival with the launch of new canoes. The canoes, the pride of a Dahwu family, are a highly regarded possession not least because of the economic well-being they can bring. They are crafted using native timber, with 27 pieces of wood fitted and held together with pegs. Once completed, the canoes are adorned with splashes of color and designs. During the Feiyu Jie Festival (the fish are a local delicacy and are considered sacred), Dahwu men dress in loincloths and wear ceremonial armor made from rattan and silver. The most prized possession is the conical helmet

made from silver, which covers the head, with slits for the eyes. The helmets are made by pounding coins. Previously, metal from shipwrecks was used. ∎

Traditional Dahwu costumes, including a conical helmet banged from silver, are worn during festivals.

More places to visit along the East Coast

CARP HILL PARK (LIYUSHAN)

This Taitung City park sits on a small hill, so named because it is said to resemble a carp. On its eastern slopes is the **Dragon and Phoenix Temple** (Longfeng/Fotang); although not a particularly noteworthy piece of temple architecture, you can climb the pagoda for a panorama of Taitung City and the Pacific. The temple has a small collection of ancient artifacts of the Beinan culture found in the area, dating back some 3,000 to 5,000 years, including stone coffins and tools. A looping pathway then takes you to the top of the hill for more views, including **Green Island** (Lyudao/Ludao; see pp. 152–153). Map p. 131 ✉ Boai Rd., Taitung City

DRIVE FROM SUAO TO HUALIEN

This 122-mile (180 km) coastal ride between the port cities of Suao and Hualien serves up some truly spectacular scenery. The highway, much of it edging precariously along the cliff faces of the Central Mountain Range, dips and rises roller-coaster fashion, climbing to superb views of the Pacific Ocean crashing into sheer cliff faces hundreds of feet below. The route was originally carved in 1875 as a trail south. It was opened to convoy traffic in 1932, and it has been gradually widened to allow vehicles to travel both ways The highway reaches its dramatic best at **Cingshuei (Qingshui) Cliff,** where the winding road edges along 12 miles (20 km) near the bottom of sheer cliffs that plummet more than 3,000 feet (914 m) to the Pacific. Buses from Taipei take this route and offer the best views. A lot of the scenery is missed in the faster, more comfortable trains from Taipei because of the numerous tunnels. Map p. 131

JHIHBEN (ZHIBEN)

The Japanese built Jhihben, one of Taiwan's largest and oldest hot-spring resorts, at the turn of the 20th century. At first glance it's now a rather shabby place of numerous high-rise hotels, but their quality improves as you drive farther up the valley to the newer buildings. Spring water is tapped from the mountain into the hotels for guests and visitors willing to pay. If you feel like a soak, head to the **Hotel Royal Chihpen** (23 Lane 113, Longcuan/Longquan Rd., Wencyuan/Wenquan Village, Beinan Township, Taitung County, tel (089) 510-666), which has pleasant outdoor and indoor hot-spring facilities. Map p. 131

JHIHBEN (ZHIBEN) FOREST RECREATION AREA

This pleasant park, a few minutes' drive from the Hotel Royal Chihpen, has sculpted gardens, a visitor center, and lots of pictures and information about the park's flora and fauna (only in Chinese). It is also the starting point for a number of trails. The **Scenic Trail** is a pleasant 45-minute amble through mostly landscaped areas. It ends at the 1.1-mile (1.8 km) **Green Shower Trail,** which takes you through heavily wooded areas of mahogany, ash, and camphor trees. The more challenging 1.3-mile (2.1 km) **Banyan Shaded Trail** climbs through thick forests of ferns, camphor, and fig trees, and giant banyan trees. The mother of all trails at Jhihben is the **Brave Man's Slope,** which takes you straight up to the top of the park via 729 steps. From here—1,600 feet (500 m) above sea level—there are outstanding views of Jhihben resort, Taitung City, and distant mountains. http://recreate.forest.gov.tw Map p. 131 ✉ 3.6 miles (6 km) west of hot-springs resort area on Longcyuan (Longquan) Rd., Wencyuan (Wenquan) Village, Beinan Township, Taitung County ☎ (089) 513-395 $ $

RUEISUEI (RUISUI) HOT SPRINGS

This top hot-springs spa, built in 1919, has a public bathing area and the rustic Japanese-style **Rueisuei Hot Springs Hotel** (23 Hongye Village, Rueisuei Township, Hualien County, tel (03) 887-2170). The water temperature is a scalding 118° F (48° C), and because of its rich iron content, it has a rather off-putting orange tint. But it is said to be ideal therapy for rheumatism and skin allergies. You can join other bathers in the public pool, or rent individual, family, or group tubs. The spa is 47 miles (75 km) south of Hualien on Highway 9. Map p. 131 ☎ (08) 872-179 ■

Taiwan's oldest city, Tainan reveals an architectural wealth and a religious and colonial past, while Kaohsiung's bustling harbor is at the heart of Taiwan's export-driven economy. Life is more laidback along the tropical south coast.

The South

**Mazu, the protector
of seafarers**

The South

THE SOUTH OF TAIWAN STRETCHES FROM THE CULTURAL CITY OF TAINAN—Taiwan's oldest city and first capital—to the island's glorious tropical tip at Eluanbi in Kenting National Park. The area was once the island's most populated, but since the main economic and political forces moved to the Taipei region, so have many of the people. Kaohsiung, Taiwan's second largest city, still remains the island's most important industrial center, but for the most part, visitors to the south will find a noticeably slower pace.

At the region's northernmost realm, Tainan carries its long history proudly. It is here where the Ming dynasty loyalist Koxinga drove the Dutch occupiers out of Taiwan in 1662; the remnants of a couple of Dutch forts are still in evidence. The city is home to nearly a quarter of Taiwan's nationally listed cultural sites, mainly centuries-old temples, and it maintains them with diligence.

The busy city of Kaohsiung may look like a place to avoid. It carries the legacy of an oceangoing port and industrial city, but it has its share of attractions, especially some fine modern museums. Its massive port facilities, where huge container ships squeeze through a narrow channel into Kaohsiung Harbor, are the lifeblood of Taiwan's export-based economy. The city is also known for its raucous nightlife—it is a port city, after all.

Foguangshan, about 40 minutes northeast of Kaohsiung, is well worth the trip. This Buddhist monastery resembles a small town as much as it does a temple complex. What began as a small mountaintop retreat in the late 1960s has grown into the headquarters of the wealthiest of Taiwan's Buddhist sects, featuring grandiose shrine halls and temples, and museums and art galleries full of priceless artifacts and antiquities.

The most alluring attraction, however, and the one that draws the most people (especially on summer weekends), is Kenting National Park, at the island's southernmost tip. With its white-sand beaches, coral reefs, and turquoise waters, this is the island's tropical playground, popular for its diving, snorkeling, hiking, bicycling, and bird-watching. ■

Surf rumbles onto the shore at Nanwan, one of Kenting's numerous beaches.

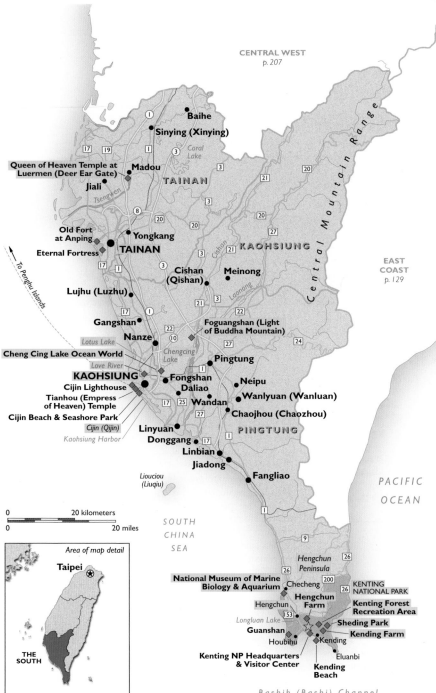

CENTRAL WEST
p. 207

Baihe

Sinying (Xinying)

Coral Lake

Queen of Heaven Temple at
Luermen (Deer Ear Gate)

Madou

Jiali

TAINAN

Tsengwen

Old Fort
at Anping

Yongkang

TAINAN

Eternal Fortress

To Penghu Islands

Lujhu (Luzhu)

**Cishan
(Qishan)**

Meinong

KAOHSIUNG

Cishan

Laonong

EAST
COAST
p. 129

Central Mountain Range

Gangshan

Lotus Lake

Nanze

Cheng Cing Lake Ocean World

Love River

Chengcing Lake

Foguangshan (Light
of Buddha Mountain)

Pingtung

KAOHSIUNG

Cijin Lighthouse

Fongshan

Daliao

Neipu

Tianhou (Empress
of Heaven) Temple

Wandan

Wanlyuan (Wanluan)

Cijin Beach & Seashore Park

Cijin (Qijin)

Chaojhou (Chaozhou)

Kaohsiung Harbor

Linyuan

PINGTUNG

Donggang

Linbian

Jiadong

*Liouciou
(Liuqiu)*

Fangliao

PACIFIC
OCEAN

SOUTH
CHINA
SEA

0   20 kilometers
0   20 miles

Area of map detail

Taipei

THE
SOUTH

*Hengchun
Peninsula*

Bashih (Bashi) Channel

National Museum of Marine
Biology & Aquarium

Checheng

KENTING
NATIONAL PARK

**Hengchun
Farm**

Kenting Forest
Recreation Area

Hengchun

Longluan Lake

Sheding Park

Guanshan

Kending Farm

Houbihu

Kending

Eluanbi

Kenting NP Headquarters
& Visitor Center

**Kending
Beach**

Tainan

Tainan

🅐 Map pp. 159 & 161

Visitor information

✉ Tourism Information Service Center, Tainan Branch, 2F, 90 Jhongshan (Zhongshan) Rd., Tainan

☎ (06) 226-5681

TAINAN WAS TAIWAN'S POLITICAL AND MILITARY CENTER between 1624 and 1885 and its capital between 1683 and 1885. It is the island's oldest city and home to nearly a quarter of its nationally listed cultural sites, mainly ancient temples, shrines, and forts. Many of the temples and shrines are found in the city's lanes and alleyways. You may chance upon them, but taking a guided walking tour is recommended.

One of these structures, the **Eternal Fortress** (*16 Nanwen Rd., Anping District, $*), in the western section of the city, was constructed in 1874 in the later years of the Qing dynasty. It was the first Western-style fortification built in Taiwan by the Chinese. A moat surrounds the fort's high walls, which are accessed through a redbrick arched tunnel from a bridge over the moat. The tunnel runs through to a central drill area. To the left of the entrance, you can climb to the fort's ramparts to two huge Armstrong cannon—copies of the originals—facing Taiwan Strait.

The **Old Fort at Anping** (*28 Guosheng Rd., Anping Distict, $*), also in the city's western precinct, was constructed by the Dutch between 1624 and 1634 using bricks imported from Batavia (today's Java) and mortared with a combination of glutinous rice, sugarcane syrup, and crushed sea shells. It was named Fort Zeelandia. All that is left of the original fort these days is part of one wall. During the Japanese occupation (1895–1945), surviving walls were leveled to allow the building of a three-layer platform on top of which the residence of the director of customs was built. The residence's small rooms are crammed with historical relics and illustrations. At the back of

Old imperial customs building dating from the late Qing dynasty, on the grounds of the Old Fort at Anping

the building is a watchtower built with little regard to the fort's architecture. From the top of the tower await city and ocean views.

The Dutch followed the construction of Fort Zeelandia in 1653 with **Fort Provintia** (*212 Minzu Rd., Sec. 2, Central District, $*). All that is left of the original fort is its foundations. After the deified pirate-warrior hero Koxinga forced the Dutch out of Taiwan in 1662, the fort went through a number of incarnations and name changes. In place of the superstructure in what is now called the **Chihkan (Chikan) Towers** sit two classical imperial-style buildings. In front of one of the walls of the base are nine inscribed Qing dynasty *steles,* each sitting on stone turtles in a moat in which carp swim. A small bridge takes you over the moat, and through a moon gate to the base

of the old fort and access to the towers. A limited collection of period artifacts is found in the main building.

Opposite the towers, a long, red exterior wall—notable for its roof moldings and decorative eaves—leads to the entrance of the **Sacrificial Rites Martial Temple** (*229 Yongfu Rd., Sec. 2, Central District*). Dedicated to Guangong, the god of prosperity and war, the temple is one of the oldest Taoist temples in Taiwan, built during the Yongli period of the Ming dynasty (1647–1683), and it is recognized as one of the island's most authentic.

A facade of stone carved in deep relief graces the entrance to the central temple, where the red-faced, bearded Guangong sits inside a shrine. The shrine is decked with sculptured stone panels depicting a

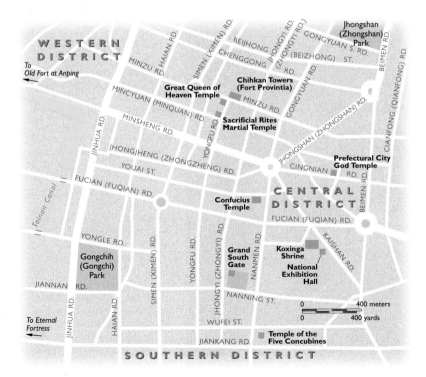

menagerie of animals, along with Taoist immortals and old tablets. There is a large pagoda for burning spirit-money, and a circular ceiling featuring carved, gilded gods.

Nearby, the **Great Queen of Heaven Temple** *(Lane 227, 18 Yongfu Rd., Sec. 2, Central District)* is one of 17 temples in Tainan dedicated to Mazu, goddess of the sea. This one is said to be the oldest in Taiwan, built in 1664 to enshrine an icon of the island's most popular deity. The entrance portico leads past stone pillars to a gilded Mazu, sitting on an altar in the main hall and flanked by two stone statues of mythical generals on pedestals. The murals on the walls memorialize Prince Ning Jing, one of the last members of the Ming dynasty royal family, who donated his residence so the temple could be built.

About a half mile (1 km) southeast of the Great Queen of Heaven Temple, you'll find the city's **Confucius Temple** *(2 Nanmen Rd., Central District)*, the oldest in Taiwan dedicated to the philosopher. Jheng Jing (Zheng Jing), the son of Koxinga, originally built it in 1665, and it has since been renovated nearly 20 times. The temple is a fine example of classical Chinese architecture. Rooftop ornaments and roof-ridge decorations are more subdued than those of the temples of other Chinese religions. The entrance is set in a small park full of banyan trees. From here, the entrance leads to buildings divided by arched gates, corniced walls, and courtyards. Confucius is memorialized in the twin-eave **Central Hall of Great Success** with a spirit tablet, flanked by a gilded wood lattice. The spirit tablets of 12 disciples sit on separate tables. Wooden tablets inscribed with calligraphy written by past emperors and the R.O.C.'s presidents of Taiwan hang from near the ceiling.

The restored **Grand South Gate** *(Lane 34, Nanmen Rd., Central District)*, about half a mile (1 km) south of the Confucius Temple, is one of the few remaining gates that once protected Tainan from the evils of the outside world. Its outer and inner block-stone and concrete walls surround a classical-style Chinese building, which has been turned into a café. You can now enjoy coffee and snacks and look upon a few old cannon—though not as old as the gate itself—still in place.

East of the Grand South Gate, the **Koxinga Shrine** *(152 Kaishan Rd., Central District, $)* is another example of classical Chinese architecture—this time in northern Fujian style—without overzealous embellishment. The shrine, set

Mazu and protector in the Great Queen of Heaven Temple

among cool gardens and pavilions, was built in 1875 by Qing dynasty imperial edict but damaged during World War II. This more substantial structure replaced it in 1962.

The shrine is modeled after a traditional courtyard house consisting of a portico entrance, main hall, and rear hall, all framed by colonnaded corridors built off the outside walls. Behind the entrance portico are statues of Koxinga's trusted generals, Gan Huei and Jhang Wan-di (Zhang Wandi), while the corridors hold spirit tablets of 114 loyal officers who followed Koxinga to Taiwan from the mainland.

A statue of Koxinga sits in the timber-walled main hall. Koxinga's mother is honored in the rear hall. A contemporary, abstract granite-carved statue of the war hero also sits in the lobby of the **National Exhibition Hall,** to the southeast of the main shrine. The hall exhibits antiquities including pottery, paintings, and documents.

In 1683, Prince Ning Jing, anguished over the imminent fall of the Ming dynasty, decided to commit suicide. On hearing the news, his five concubines preempted their lord and lover by hanging themselves. Ning Jing then took his own life. The **Temple of the Five Concubines** (201 Wufei St., Central District) was built to enshrine them. This small temple siting in an untended park is decorated with a retinue of portrait paintings. Behind the temple you'll find the concubines' tomb.

The **Prefectural City God Temple** (133 Cingnian/Qingnian Rd., Central District) is the largest of a number of Tainan's City God temples. Just beyond the imposing carved stone dragon columns at the entrance portico, the facade is set with gilded timber panels carved into mythological figures and patterns. Inside, timber tablets describe etiquette and good manners, and two giant abaci symbolize the number of good and bad deeds in one's lifetime, which will decide one's fate in the afterworld. ■

The deified pirate-warrior Koxinga, who drove the Dutch from the island in 1662, is honored in numerous temples around Taiwan, especially at the Koxinga Shrine in Tainan.

Taipei's Baoan Temple exhibits decorative eave elements typical of Taiwan's Taoist temples.

Temple architecture

Temples in Taiwan tend to be a swirling fusion of different deities, practices, and rituals. Buddhist and Taoist icons reside side by side, often in the same temples, with an iconic representation of the sage sometimes thrown into the mix outside Confucius temples. Buddhist and Taoist elements are often mixed together, and are sometimes joined by a host of lesser folk gods, many of whom are heroes from Chinese myth.

You can pick out a Taoist temple by its sweeping roof with long lines of icons marching along the ridges. At or near the apex will often be a pearl, a dragon, or a pagoda, surrounded by a parade of dragons, phoenixes, monkeys, and other animals, and often, Fu, Lu, and Shou, the three wise old men called the star gods that represent prosperity, posterity, and longevity, respectively. Taoist temples are often dedicated to Mazu, goddess of the sea; Guangong, the god of prosperity and war; and Tudigong, the earth god. You'll also find that Taoist temples are hectic places. Devotees burn incense, throw divining blocks, and set fire to large bundles of faux paper banknotes called spirit- or ghost-money.

Buddhist temples are quieter than their Taoist counterparts, and are geared more toward reflection than worship. Many are located in monastery complexes, and these have a more hushed and reverent tone. By the standards of many other religions, however, they are not exactly quiet. Guanyin, the goddess of mercy and from the Buddhist pantheon, is featured in many of the island's Buddhist temples.

Some general rules apply to temple layouts in Taiwan. Most temples are designed on a rectangular pattern. The standard layout consists of a front courtyard, and then a wall with three doors—a main door and two side doors that flank it—leading to the shrines. A gate or a fence, which keeps malevolent influences from entering and good luck from exiting, often blocks the main door. The main door is sometimes opened to make way for visiting deities or icons, with great blasts of firecrackers to clear away any lurking evil.

If the main door is blocked, visitors enter through one of the side doors. All doors have curbs that must be stepped over; this keeps ghosts and other baleful influences at bay. Door guards flank the doors leading to the deity: A pair of stone lions might sit at the main portals, and various fierce, brightly

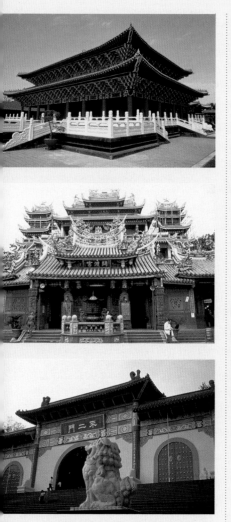

Kaohsiung's Confucius Temple (top left) lacks elaborate decoration, while the multitier roof at Taipei's Gaundu Temple (middle left) sports mythical figures, and stone lions guard Kaohsiung County's Foguangshan monastery (bottom left). The bronze doors of Taipei's Martyrs' Shrine (above) are a rare element.

painted guardians adorn both main and side doors. Dragons are often carved into the main pillars. To the Chinese, dragons signify all things good: strength, goodness, wisdom, and fertility.

Larger temples often have three halls, and the main deity is usually in the second hall, with the other halls used for lesser gods or, in Buddhist temples, as a classroom. The main deity is obvious by its size, the magnificence of its surroundings, and its position in the center of the biggest hall, attended by servants and accompanied by a smaller image of the same god. This miniature is sometimes taken from

the temple for festivals, to go on local patrol, or to bless the homes and workplaces of devotees. Lesser deities dwell at the sides and in the back of the temple, and on either side is a drum tower or bell tower. The bell summons people to worship, and it is also used to drive out bad spirits.

Temples are key features of every city in Taiwan. The Taiwanese are utilitarian when it comes to religion—they visit temples to seek help, and if it does not come from one god, many will decide to go to another one. For the most part, temples are relaxed and sociable places, mixing worship and commerce. ■

Kaohsiung

Kaohsiung
�**A** Map p. 159
Visitor information
✉ Tourist Service Center, Kaohsiung International Airport, Arrivals Lobby, 2 Jhongshan (Zhongshan) 4th Rd., Kaohsiung
☎ (07) 805-7888, hotline: 0800-252-550
✉ Tourism Bureau, Kaohsiung branch, 5F, 235 Jhongjheng (Zhongzheng) 4th Rd., Kaohsiung
☎ (07) 281-1513

Kaohsiung Museum of History
http://w4.kcg.gov.tw/~khchsmus
✉ 272 Jhongjheng (Zhongzheng) 4th Rd.
☎ (07) 531-2560, ext. 312
🕐 Closed Mon.
💲 $
🚌 Bus: 1, 2, 14, 25, 56, 60, 76, 77, 78, 248

Kaohsiung Museum of Fine Arts
✉ 20 Meishuguan Cian (Qian) Rd.
☎ (07) 555-0331
🕐 Closed Mon.
💲 $
🚌 Bus: 73, 205

WITH A POPULATION OF 1.5 MILLION, KAOHSIUNG IS Taiwan's second biggest city. It is the island's largest port and one of the world's largest as well, and it is Taiwan's major industrial center. It is also a city that can easily keep the visitor busy for a day or two with its wealth of museums and historical buildings. Although its nightlife is not as rambunctious as it once was, it remains lively.

The summit of **Shoushan** (Longevity Mountain), which is mostly given over to parkland, overlooks Kaohsiung's sprawling harbor. On its eastern slopes is **Yuanheng Temple,** which was originally built in 1679 and rebuilt in 1926. Its imposing main hall houses three giant gilded Buddha images, part of a collection of many gleaming images of the Enlightened One inside the multistory temple. Toward the peak of the 1,165-foot (355 m) mountain is the city's **Martyrs' Shrine,** an impressive complex in classical Chinese style featuring sturdy red pillars that support sweeping tiled roofs and huge wooden gates and doors. However, it lacks the pomp and ceremony of its namesake in Taipei (see p. 79), and the small karaoke cafés outside of the complex tend to denude it of its solemnity. A number of hiking trails in the park take you through wooded areas to sweeping coastal views.

From the shrine, the road winds down toward the exceedingly narrow northern entrance |to Kaohsiung Harbor and the restored **Former British Consulate** (closed Sat.–Mon. & day after national holidays, $, tel (07) 525-0007), which is placed on a steep hill overlooking the sea and harbor. Built in 1858, the redbrick consulate is one of the oldest examples of colonial architecture in Taiwan. It is now a museum housing historical photographs, maps, models, and relics offering insight into the city's past. Views down to the harbor from the consulate are spectacular.

Liouhe (Liuhe) Tourist Night Market—running along Liouhe 2nd Road between Jhongshan (Zhongshan) 1st Road and Zihli (Zili) 2nd Road a few blocks south of Kaohsiung Railway Station—offers Taiwanese snacks from hundreds of vendors lining both sides of the street, as well as pubs and beer houses. Tables and chairs are laid on footpaths and along the road. It opens at 6 p.m., but it's most lively after 9 p.m. The market closes at 2 a.m.

One of the city's most beautiful buildings—the former offices of Kaohsiung's municipal government during the Japanese occupation—is now the **Kaohsiung Museum of History.** The museum, fronted by a paved plaza and trimmed gardens, incorporates both Chinese and Western architectural elements. The building is sided by turretlike walls and topped with swooping tiled roofs, while the facade—with huge windows on its two levels all but forming a glass curtain—is dominated by a grandiose columned entrance, again topped with a classical Chinese-roof structure. Inside, exhibits of artifacts, antiquities, models, and maps trace city history.

To the north of town, the

Kaohsiung Museum of Fine Arts is located on expansive grounds, including an amphitheater, a sculpture park, and a natural lake. A lot of the museum's space is given over to international exhibitions.

Climb the pagoda just inside the entrance to the resort area at **Chengcing (Chengqing) Lake,** on the city's northeastern outskirts. There you will find views of the lake—a reservoir supplying the city with water—and surrounding well-tended and peaceful parklands. A path winds through wooded areas around the lake. A nine-cornered bridge cuts across the water in the direction of the **Grand Hotel–Cheng Ching Lake** (see p. 255), a big place rendered in classical Chinese-palace architectural style in the image of the same-named

The Love River cuts its way through Kaohsiung, Taiwan's second largest city and one of Asia's major ports.

Chengcing (Chengqing) Lake

✉ 32 Dabei Rd., Niaosong Township

☎ (07) 370-0821

💲 $$

🚌 Bus: 60 from Kaohsiung Railway Station

Cijin (Qijin) Lighthouse guards the north entrance to Kaohsiung's harbor.

and more famous hotel in Taipei (see p. 79).

CIJIN (QIJIN)

Cijin is an island running parallel with the mainland, its north tip at the narrow entrance to Kaohsiung Harbor. The north area—which has been spruced up in recent years—has a collection of sites within easy walking distance of one another. A four-minute ferry ride from a small dock next to the entrance to Binhai fishing wharf lands you on a jetty near the head of **Cijin Seafood Street,** a collection of seafood restaurants and stalls featuring an often-raucous atmosphere.

Seemingly struggling for space among the busy restaurants is the lively and colorful **Tianhou (Empress of Heaven) Temple,** dedicated to Mazu, the protector of mariners and fishermen, and one

of Kaohsiung's oldest structures, dating back to 1691. Highly decorative roofs with ship-prow ridges flush with mythical figurines, and rows of cylindrical tiles flowing down the sweeping roofs, are the temple's most attractive features.

From the temple head north along Tongshan Road to steps leading to the dome-capped **Cijin (Qijin) Lighthouse** (closed Mon.) and whitewashed colonial-style watchman's residence, guarding the north entrance to the harbor. As far as lighthouses go, it's small, only 36 feet high (11 m), but there are enthralling views down to huge container vessels squeezing through the harbor entrance. Just to the west of the lighthouse, and also guarding the harbor entrance, are the remnants of the 125-year-old **Cihou (Qihou) Fortress** (closed Mon.), a faded redbrick fortification carved into a hillock.

On the western side of Cijin, not far beyond Cijin Seafood Street, is the exotically black-sanded **Cijin Beach** and **Cijin Seashore Park,** with a promenade—interspersed with collections of sea-themed artifacts—overlooking parkland and the coast.

NATIONAL SCIENCE AND TECHNOLOGY MUSEUM

Located east of Kaohsiung Railway Station in the northeast part of the city, this museum is one of the largest of its type in the world. Wandering its seven floors, through its numerous galleries and exhibits—many interactive—is a fun way to while away an afternoon. If you bring the kids, plan on spending even more time.

Taking pride of place on the museum's entrance floor is the **Hall of Chinese Achievements,** which replicates an ancient Chinese city demonstrating day-to-day life, along with exhibits showing the amazing number of Chinese inventions that were eventually adopted by Western culture. You are shown how electricity has been utilized over the past couple of centuries at the **Electronic World** exhibit, from its discovery to the development of silicon chips and miniature integrated circuits. The **Food Industry** section has a "computerized" chef sharing culinary tips.

You can experience an earthquake on a simulated earthquake platform at the **Dwelling and Environment** exhibit, while an antivibration table shows how architects of modern buildings take earthquakes and typhoons into account during construction. The **Biology and Technology** exhibit details the brave new world of biotechnology, showing how it combines microbiology, biological chemistry, genetics, and electronic engineering for medical diagnosis and treatment, agricultural development, and environmental protection.

Jungle drums and smoke signals join telephones and Internet paraphernalia to explain the history of communications in the **Communications** exhibit. The **Plastic and Rubber** exhibit demonstrates the almost infinite uses of plastic, while the **Petrochemical Products** exhibit uses a model of a processing tank to illustrate how crude oil is refined and how a variety of products can be manufactured. The **Air Navigation and Aerospace** area has a mock-up of the International Space Station, and an exhibition on the Lockheed F-104 Star Fighter, once considered Taiwan's most sophisticated fighter aircraft.

The museum also has an IMAX theater ($). ∎

National Science and Technology Museum

www.nstm.gov.tw

✉ 720 Jiouru (Jiuru) 1st Rd., Sec. 1

☎ (07) 380-0089

🕐 Closed Mon.

💲 $

🚍 Bus: 57, 60, 73, 201

Beloved Mazu

Of the more than 100 Chinese deities, Mazu is the most popular. The Heavenly Mother and protector of seafarers, she was the daughter of a government official in Fujian Province in the 10th century. She was said to have the ability to warn fishermen and mariners of impending sea disasters. After she died, a temple overlooking the sea was erected in her honor. Temples sprang up all along China's south coast, and a cult following emerged. Every year on the 23rd day of the third lunar month, Taiwan's grandest of all religious events, the Dajia Mazu pilgrimage, kicks off. Over the following week, her image is carried around central Taiwan, accompanied by a riot of costumes, pageantry, music, and noise. A million people turn out to watch her image pass by. ∎

Lotus Lake

Lotus Lake

▲ Map p. 159

✉ Huantan Rd., Zuoying
District, Kaohsiung

THE PAGODAS AND PAVILIONS OF LOTUS LAKE HAVE A wonderful fairy-tale air about them. Perched on the edge of the placid lake, and introduced by colorful and imaginative—and very large— renditions of mythical beasts and gods, these are fun places to explore.

A nine-cornered bridge zigzags to the fantasy-like Dragon and Tiger Pagodas on Kaohsiung's Lotus Lake.

The identical and adjacent **Dragon and Tiger Pagodas** reach out into the lake via a nine-cornered bridge. At the end of the bridge you pass through the gaping mouth of a dragon and into its

throat to view friezes of China's 24 most obedient sons from its mythology. The walls of the pagodas are also embellished with similar paintings, along with scenes of heaven and hell. From the bottom of the Dragon Pagoda, a small bridge connects to the second pagoda, with more friezes on its walls. From here you enter the rear end of a tiger and finally emerge from its mouth and back onto the nine-cornered bridge.

The entrance to the **Summer** and **Autumn Pavilions**—less than 110 yards (100 m) north of the pagodas—exhibits a huge statue of a serene Guanyin, the goddess of mercy, rising above a writhing dragon. Two identical three-story pagodas sit each side of the statue. A long pier begins between the pagodas and runs to **Wuli Pavilion,** some 200 yards (182 m) out on the lake.

Enclosed by walls enameled in brilliant red and fringed with gold tiles, and done in a somewhat rare ——for Taiwan——Song dynasty architectural style, the sprawling **Confucius Temple,** at the northern end of Lotus Lake, is the largest in Taiwan. Its three courtyards and grottoes of potted bonsai plants and trees are divided by corniced walls and moon gates, and like most Confucius temples in Taiwan it eschews the ornate complications of Taoist and Buddhist temples. The original Confucius Temple at this site was built in 1624, but this one was completed in 1976. ■

Foguangshan (Light of Buddha Mountain)

LOCATED NORTHEAST OF KAOHSIUNG, THIS SPRAWLING Buddhist temple complex began in 1967 as a mountaintop retreat under the guidance of its founder, the Venerable Sing Yun (Xing Yun), and has grown into the largest and wealthiest Buddhist monastery in Taiwan and a site of pilgrimage for Sing Yun's followers. It is a remarkable place of funerary niches, shrine and meditation halls, colonnades, pavilions, gardens, ponds, grottoes, libraries, and art galleries, and it has an extraordinary collection of Buddha statuary.

Hundreds of gilded Buddha images stand in line at Foguang-shan, one of the numerous weird and wonderful attractions at this sprawling Buddhist monastery.

You enter the monastery from the parking lot, past a hillside with a seven-level cemetery containing 50,000 grave niches reserved for the deceased followers of Sing Yun (Xing Yun). Above the graves stands a 120-foot-tall (36 m) gilded **statue of the Amitabha Buddha,** flanked by 480 smaller but identical images.

Take the path that leads from beside the Buddha to the **Cultural Exhibition Center,** which exhibits artwork donated by followers. From this exhibit you move into a mirrored corridor with identical marble seated Buddha images from 3 feet (1 m) to 8 feet tall (2.5 m) lining the wall, to another gallery featuring knots of timber twisted and polished into all shapes and sizes. The next gallery features the Venerable Sing Yun's published works, along with his robes and a travel case.

The **Main Shrine** fronts the Cultural Exhibition Center, where three huge gilded Buddha images sit under a 65-foot-high (20 m) patterned ceiling. Natural light from windows running along the top of the walls streams onto 14,000 Buddha images encased in tiny niches covering the shrine's four walls. In the corners you'll spot a huge hanging drum and bell, while on either side of the main altar two 33-foot-high (10 m) cones are inscribed with the names of temple benefactors.

The main shrine opens to a colonnaded plaza, past the Pilgrims Lodge to another plaza and a grotto backing the monastery's main gate. Inside the main gate, the galleries of the **Buddhist Cultural Museum** hold a priceless collection of ancient and contemporary Buddha images.

To the right of the main gate is the wonderfully kitschy **Pure Land Cave.** You enter to a wide path lined with images of Buddha's disciples and life-size *arphans,* then pass through a corridor made to resemble a cave, with Buddha's Eight Precepts inscribed on the walls, until you finally reach enlightenment and nirvana. Low-tech animatronic figures abound, and there's a gift shop. ∎

Foguangshan (Light of Buddha Mountain)
www.fgs.org.tw
- Map p. 159
- Dashu Township, Kaohsiung County. E-mail fgs6205@ fgs.org.tw
- (07) 656-1921, ext. 6203–6205
- Free English language tours; contact temple in advance
- Dining hall open 11:30 a.m.–12 p.m.

Just another sunset at Kenting, Taiwan's tropical playground

Kenting

Encompassing much of the Hengchun Peninsula, southern Taiwan's crescent-shaped coastline of white sandy beaches, coral gardens, and lush tropical uplands is mostly protected within Kenting National Park, one of Taiwan's natural treasures. This beautiful region, boasting the warmest winters in Taiwan, serves up plenty of opportunities befitting a beach resort.

The coastline has been worn ragged by relentless winds and crashing waves. On the park's east coast, windswept sea cliffs overlook broad expanses of the Pacific Ocean, while on its western edges, weird rock formations—including one that resembles a former U.S. President—and huge boulders add drama to the panoramas.

Tablelands of uplifted coral rise quickly inland of this craggy coastline, providing lots of recreational opportunities for hikers, birdwatchers, and nature lovers alike. At Kenting Forest Recreation Area, you can climb through thick rain forest and past pockmarked coralrock boulders that long ago shoved up from the ocean floor to stunning 360-degree views of the park. Gentle hikes through Eluanbi Park, with its historic lighthouse marking the southernmost tip of the Hengchun Peninsula (and Taiwan), is an enjoyable option. Forested pathways meander past ridges, caves, and curious formations of limestone and coral shaped

by wind, waves, and rain. More challenging trails can be found at Sheding and Nanrenshan parks, although you need permission and a guide from the Kenting National Park Headquarters and Visitor Center, as these two areas are ecological-protection areas and off-limits to visitors without a permit. Cycling, sea canoeing, sea kayaking, pleasure cruises, and fishing are other recreational possibilities.

Offshore, the south coast has been gifted with a fringing coral reef teeming with unbelievable amounts of marine life (see pp. 184–187). Diving and snorkeling are understandably two of the most popular pursuits here. Dive schools provide for experienced divers, as well as offer courses for beginners.

Kending Town, right along the water, and Hengchun, farther inland, are where you'll find most of the hotels, restaurants, shops, car rental agencies, and activity centers; the national park visitor center is just west of Kending Town. ■

Kenting National Park

KENTING BECAME TAIWAN'S FIRST NATIONAL PARK IN 1982. Each year more than five million people crowd into its 125 square miles (324 sq km), mostly on weekends—making it Taiwan's most heavily populated and popular national park. Visit during the week to avoid the tour buses, traffic jams, and crowds.

The centrally located **Kenting National Park Headquarters and Visitor Center,** found just to the west of Kending Town, has displays and photographs of the park's geography, topography, corals, and flora and fauna, making it a good place to get familiar with the park's offerings. You can also hire an English-speaking guide to show you around, provided you have your own transportation (call the day before to arrange). The visitor center also has multimedia displays in English and good maps and other information.

West from the visitor center along Provincial Highway 26 is **Nanwan** or **South Bay,** a 660-yard (600 m) arch of yellow sand popular with sunbathers, fishermen, and people using personal watercraft. Unfortunately, the number of Jet Skis roaring close to shore makes swimming a risky proposition.

If you feel like a dip, **Kending Beach** (see p. 178) or **Baisha Beach** (see p. 174) are better bets. The line of guesthouses, souvenir shops, restaurants, and dive and surf shops opposite the bay add a beach-resort character to the place. Here you can book scuba-diving trips to explore the splendid abundance of corals (see pp. 184–187) and other marine life that inhabit the offshore segment of the park. If the urge hits, you can also take a PADI diving course spread over three or four days. It costs around $350.

Follow Provincial Highway 26 west to County Road 153, which takes you to the western

section of the national park and **Longluan Lake.** This combination of reservoir and wetlands has been touted as one of the best locations in Taiwan to view migratory waterfowl as they make their way from Japan, mainland China, and Siberia along the Australasian migratory route (see pp. 176–177). From October to May snipes, plovers, ducks, egrets, cormorants, and wild geese fill its placid waters. At the **Longluan Lake Nature Center,** which sits on a slight bluff overlooking the lake, you can get a close-up view of the bird life through telescopes.

County Road 153 runs into the stubby peninsula in the west of the national park to **Houbihu,** with its small but lively fishing port and marina. Late in the afternoon, bright blue fishing boats with prominent sloping bows return with their catch, some of which is sliced up immediately and dished

Kenting National Park encompasses Taiwan's best beaches and, on the weekends, its largest crowds.

Kenting National Park
www.ktnp.gov.tw

🅜 Maps p. 159 & p. 179

✉ Kenting National Park Headquarters and Visitor Center, 596 Kenting Rd., Hengchun Township, Pingtung County

☎ (08) 886-1321

Seawater sprays over coastal layered rock formations. Rocks, weathered into endless shapes, are a startling feature of Kenting National Park.

up sashimi-style at an outdoor harborside market/eating area. Pleasure craft berthed at the marina are available for cruises and fishing trips, and glass-bottom boats leave the marina regularly to explore the nearby coral beds and marine life.

At the tip of the peninsula on which the lake is located, County Road 153 runs to **Maobitou (Cat's Nose Cape) Park** *(tel (08) 886-7520),* a cape that pokes into the Bashih (Bashi) Channel in a jumble of exposed coral-rock formations. The area earns its moniker from some of these formations, which when seen from a distance—and with the use of some imagination—resemble a crouching feline's nose, with the promontory as the body. Climb the steps to the pavilion at the highest point of Maobitou for superb views of the jagged, coral-rock-fringed coastline, a dominant

feature of the national park.

On the western side of the promontory, a few kilometers from Maobitou Park along County Road 153 at **Baisha** (White Sand Beach), hidden behind a small village also called Baisha, is a 440-yard (400 m) sweep of glittering yellow-white sand locked between rocky knolls and backed by groves of palm, hibiscus trees, and rice paddies. Much of the beach's charm comes from its relative seclusion. It nudges a rustic and peaceful part of the peninsula, complete with hamlets, rice fields, and banana and pineapple plantations. Plans are afoot to develop the area, which will likely suck much of the charm from this delightful spot.

From Baisha, County Road 153 begins a gentle climb north about 3 miles (5 km) to 564-foot-high (172 m) **Guanshan** and more

hurricane 500 years ago.

From Guanshan, the national park is confined within a narrow strip of western coastline ending at the **National Museum of Marine Biology & Aquarium** (see pp. 182–183), about 6.8 miles (11 km) north. The waters off this strip are flush with Technicolor coral and marine life, and if you plan on taking a snorkeling or diving trip, this is surely one of the places you'll end up. Gently sloping reefs, teeming with marine life, are found at the southern area of the strip, while farther north, the underwater scenery becomes more dramatic, with large slabs of reef, broken by deep chasms, forming a wonderland of drop-offs, sea canyons, and tunnels (see pp. 184–187)

KENTING FOREST RECREATION AREA

This 1,075-acre (435 ha) recreation area was established in 1906 during the Japanese occupation as a botanical garden and herbarium. Although a section of the park is still used for this purpose, the main attractions are its primary tropical forests, weird coral-rock formations, caves, and unsurpassed views of the Hengchun Peninsula. Well-marked paths wind through groves of towering palms and eerie forests of banyan trees before climbing past huge pockmarked outcrops of coral and thick tropical forest to the magical **Fairy Cave.** The narrow, 150-yard-long (137 m) cavern has hundreds of stalactites and stalagmites accentuated by lights. Leaving the cave, you climb a path leading to the highest point in the national park (705 ft/520 m). Here, an elevator in a concrete tower whisks you up to an observation deck above the forest canopy to magnificent 360-degree views. ∎

Kenting Forest Recreation Area

http://recreate.forest.gov.tw

✉ 201 Gongyuan Rd., Hengchun Township, Pingtung County

☎ (08) 886-1211

$ $

outstanding views. This time expansive vistas sweep north along the coast past fishing villages, and inland to Longluan Lake, South Bay, and the verdant hills to the east. A pathway runs along the edge of Guanshan, with a number of timber observation decks offering more coastal views, before passing though thick groves of banyan, fig, and hibiscus trees to **Fude (Earth God) Temple,** where devotees shove bundles of red paper into a blazing furnace, made ornate by a towering domed chimney, paintings of writhing dragons, and a three-tiered pagoda-style roof. Doing a precarious balancing act next to the furnace is **Feilaishih (Feilaishi),** or Flown Here Rock, a huge coral-rock boulder named for the shaky premise that it ended up in this spot after being blown here from the Philippines by a

For the birds

Taiwan has one of the highest densities of bird species in the world, thanks to its position along the Australasian migratory route and its extensive network of estuaries, coastal marshlands, and sheltered areas along rugged seacoasts and in its mountainous regions.

About 480 local and migratory bird species have been identified on the island—which represents about one-twentieth of the world's 8,600 species. This compares with 500 species in Japan, 800 in the United States, and 1,200 in China.

Taiwan's birds and other wildlife have often been disregarded in Taiwan's rush for economic growth, but in the 1980s a conservation movement emerged and gained momentum, beginning to thrive in the past decade. Environmentalists have won several significant victories, especially in areas where rare bird species are found. Taiwan has 53 major bird habitats, which cover 18 percent of the island. Eighty-one percent of this area is now protected.

Bird-watching sites are common in Taiwan, as are tours that visit various habitats, most in the mountains, along coastlines, and on outlying islands. The best known areas for waterfowl spotting include the Guandu Nature Park on the northwest outskirts of Taipei, the Ilan

delta, Hsinchu's Keya River estuary, central Taiwan's Dadu River estuary, the Zengwun River estuary near Tainan, and the Gaoping River estuary in southern Taiwan.

The most accessible site is Guandu Nature Park *(55 Guandu Rd., Guandu, Taipei, tel (02) 2858-7417, $, closed Mon., www.gd-park .org.tw)*. This beautiful 148-acre (60 ha) wetland is home to countless birds, both local and migratory. In 2001 the city government bought the site from rice farmers for NT$430 million and allowed it to return to its natural state. Within two years it had reverted to a large open wetland filled with tall grasses, small ponds, and native trees, which in turn has lured back some rare bird species. The sanctuary itself is strictly for the birds—entry is strictly controlled—but three shelters provide good sightlines into the sanctuary.

People who know their birds are impressed with Guandu. Great herons are common, as are gray herons, egrets, bush warblers, green-winged teals, kestrels, and marsh harriers. Rarer species are also represented, including ibises and black-tailed godwits. Guandu, perched at the confluence of the Danshui (Danshui) and Keelung Rivers, is a complex ecosystem of marshland and mangrove forest.

Another famous site is Longluan Lake in Kenting National Park (see p. 173). Chinese sparrow hawks stop at Longluan Lake at the end of September, while the gray-faced buzzard eagle arrives in early October. Many other migrating birds—including snipes, plovers, ducks, and geese—join them. The area also hosts the local bird known as the Taiwan bulbul.

The most famous of Taiwan's 14 species of endemic birds is the Mikado pheasant, which is depicted on the New Taiwan one-thousand-dollar bill. Other noted species include the Formosan blue magpie, Taiwan hill partridge, Swinhoe's pheasant, and Taiwan firecrest.

An endemic Swinhoe's pheasant. Taiwan has a large variety of both native and migratory bird species.

The Zengwen River estuary is home to Taiwan's most notorious bird, the black-faced spoonbill. Of an estimated 300 black-faced spoonbills in the world, 200 have been known to winter at the mouth of this river.

Taiwan is also a favored stopover for the rare and colorful fairy pitta, with a population that stands at only 2,000. The fairy pitta is known in Taiwan as the "eight-colored bird" because of its multihued feathers. It is a summer migratory bird that nests and breeds in the cooler parts of Taiwan during the summer hot months, and heads to tropical areas south of the island for the winter. ∎

The vast variety of bird life on the island includes Taiwan laughing thrush (top left), blue-winged pitta (top right), red-combed chicken (above), and Jacana birds (below).

Kenting's Sail Rock (on the right) is also known as Nixon Rock for its likeness to the late U.S. Preside

A drive along the Hengchun Peninsula

Skirting much of Kenting National Park's coastline, this spectacular drive runs along Bashih (Bashi) Channel on the park's west side, dips south to the Hengchun Peninsula's tip at Eluanbi, Taiwan's southernmost point, then heads north along windswept cliffs overlooking the Pacific on the park's east side. Signposts in English lead the way.

Start at **Kenting National Park Headquarters and Visitor Center ❶** (see p. 173), where you can hire an English-speaking guide (call the day before to arrange) and view displays and photographs of the park's geography, topography, corals, and flora and fauna.

Head southeast from the park headquarters, along Provincial Highway 26 (Kenting Road), through **Kending Town.** On the east edge of town, beyond the prominent, curved-backed **Frog Rock** facing out into the Bashih Channel, you'll spot **Kending Beach (Small Bay) ❷.** This pretty yellow-sand beach sits at the bottom of a small bluff, accessible by wooden steps. The café at the base of the bluff adds some tropical character and is a

good place to relax and check out beach life Taiwan style. Unfortunately, roaring Jet Skis have taken over much of the shoreline, allowing only limited roped-off areas for swimming at both ends of the bay. Snorkeling gear can be rented at the dive shop, located on the same boardwalk as the café, to explore the corals just offshore at the southern end of the beach.

Continue southeast along Provincial Highway 26 for half a mile (1 km) to unimpeded views of the Bashih Channel and the curious **Sail Rock ❸** sitting just offshore. This giant 60-foot-high (19 m) boulder is uplifted coral believed to have long ago tumbled down from the tablelands that back the coastline. From a distance it resembles the taut sails of a fishing junk, but as you get closer, its profile begins to resemble that of the late U.S. President Richard Nixon (1913–1994), earning the boulder its second moniker, Nixon Rock. It even comes with vegetation on top, resembling hair.

Sail Rock marks the beginning of a stretch called the **Tropical Coastal Forest ❹**, which before it was taken to with axes and chainsaws, covered 1,250 acres (500 ha) along an 8-mile (12 km) strip of coastline running to the tip of the peninsula at Eluanbi. The forest originally sprouted from Filipino and Indonesian seedlings carried by the Kuroshiu Current. All that is left (and protected) these days is a one-mile (1.6 km) strip, covering just 5 acres (2 ha). But it flourishes with some 180 species of vascular plants, growing from beds of uplifted coral.

Several miles beyond the southern end of the forest are the sparkling sands of **Shadao ❺**, Kenting's most attractive beach. The beach is formed from tiny seashell, coral, and foraminifera fragments, which, because of their high calcium carbonate content, make the sand

glitter. Add to this the crystal-clear waters lapping the shoreline, and you can understand why the 250-yard (220 m) beach at Shadao is such an inviting place. It is also a protected ecological area, so you can't swim there or walk on the sands. Backing the beach is the small **Seashell Sand Exhibition Hall,** where you can view the sands from its veranda. Inside the center a series of displays explain the phenomenon of the beach.

Continue south half a mile (1 km) past

🅽 See area map p. 159
▶ Kenting National Park
  Headquarters and Visitor Center
🔁 17.5 miles
🕐 3 hours
▶ Jialeshuei (Jialeshui)

NOT TO BE MISSED
- Tropical Coastal Forest
- Shadao
- Eluanbi Park
- Longpan Park

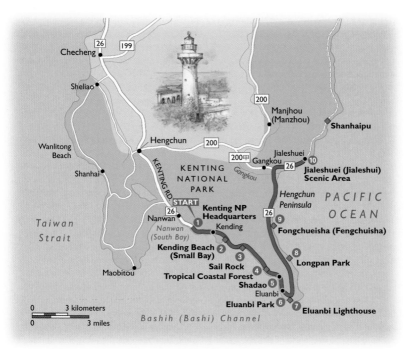

Originally built in 1882 and reconstructed twice since, the lighthouse at Eluanbi is still operational. Eluanbi Park (opposite) mixes parkland and tropical forests.

Shadao to **Eluanbi Park** ⑥ (tel (08) 885-1101), at the tip of the Hengchun Peninsula, where the Bashih Channel meets the Pacific. Much of its 148 acres (59 ha) is given over to cool tropical monsoon forest, with interlaced branches of fig, hibiscus, and banyan trees forming canopies over a maze of winding pathways. Here you'll notice an unusual feature of the park: raised walls of pockmarked coral—some as high as 20 feet (6 m)—topped by shrubs and creeping vines. Sections of the park open to panoramic coastline and ocean views, especially from Tough Guy Rock, Ocean Pavilion, and a boardwalk tracing the coral fringed coast.

The park's most impressive man-made feature is **Eluanbi Lighthouse** ⑦, surrounded by whitewashed stone walls. The 70-foot (21.4 m) structure—originally built in 1882 but its most recent incarnation dating from after World War II, when it was heavily bombed—once served a dual purpose: warning passing ships and as a fort to fend off incursions from local aborigines, making it one of the world's few fortified lighthouses. Next to the gift shop opposite the lighthouse, follow the path down to the ocean and southernmost tip of Taiwan.

From Eluanbi Park, the highway begins to climb north to the grasslands of the peninsula's Pacific coast before opening up to some of the best coastal and ocean views in Taiwan. Make your first stop **Longpan Park** ⑧, about 1.5 miles (2.5 km) north of Eluanbi.

From here, a short walk from the parking lot takes you to clifftop views of the windswept coastline and the Pacific (next stop Hawaii!). Although the coral cliffs are not particularly high—about 200 feet (60 m)—nor steep, the views are expansive and spectacular, with the strong prevailing winds keeping the groves of screw pine and pandanus bushes stunted. The area can offer a surprising sense of isolation, a rarity in densely populated Taiwan. Look over your shoulder at the pleasant green rolling pastureland, another rarity for this crowded island. Trails wind along the cliff edge, with some dropping down to sandy beaches.

Farther on, the road dips inland past grass and pastureland before veering back to the coast to **Fongchueisha (Fengchuisha)** ⑨, 1.5 miles (2.5 km) north of Longpan Park. The area is notable for its phenomenal shifting sands, which sweep down from the tablelands to the coast during summer rains, forming at its widest point a 220-yard-wide (200 m) cascade of patterned sand. Winter winds then blow much of the sand back up to the tablelands. Construction of the coastal highway and planting of vegetation by local authorities have ebbed the annual flow in recent years.

The highway continues to offer splendid ocean panoramas as it follows the contours of the coastline for another 3.4 miles (5.5 km)—occasionally dipping down to sea level and sandy beaches—before passing over a bridge at

the mouth of the Gangkou River and the fishing village of the same name. Here the road reaches a T-junction. Turn right and go another 1.4 miles (2.2 km) to reach **Jialeshuei (Jialeshui) Scenic Area** ⑩ *(tel (08) 880-1083)*, notable for wind-and-wave-sculpted and honeycombed rock formations that run along the coast. From the parking lot, you can follow a path for 1.5 miles (2.5 km) for a closer inspection of some of these weird formations, until you reach **Shanhaipu,** or Mountain-Sea Falls, where

water tumbles down a seaside cliff into the Pacific. Alternatively, you can part with a few dollars and climb aboard one of the fleet of open-decked trucks for a tour.

From Jialeshuei, you can backtrack along the coast or head inland at **Gangkou.** This second route, which twists through the hills, will take you through a pleasant rural area of rice fields and palm groves, small vegetable farms and hamlets, to **Hengchun,** the main town on the peninsula. ■

National Museum of Marine Biology & Aquarium

National Museum of Marine Biology & Aquarium

www.nmmba.gov.tw

⬛ Map p. 159

✉ 2 Houwan Rd., Houwan Village, Checheng Township, Pingtung County

☎ (08) 882-5001

💲 $$

🚌 Kenting Shuttle bus from Kaohsiung International Airport, Pingtung Bus Co.; every 30 min., $$$ one way

THIS WORLD-CLASS MUSEUM AND AQUARIUM, DEVOTED to the education, research, and preservation of Taiwan's marine and freshwater habitats, features visually stunning water tanks, water columns, underwater tunnels, and dioramas filled with live critters to portray Taiwan's various ecosystems. It's educational, and it's also quite a lot of fun.

You are greeted in the front courtyard by an enormous whale, so lifelike it seemingly cavorts in its watery pool.

Upon entering the expansive lobby, you'll spot more life-size models of dolphins, giant squid, whales, and sharks eyeing you from the arched, 69-foot-high (21 m) ceiling.

A tumbling waterfall announces the entrance to one of the museum's three major exhibition areas, the **Waters of Taiwan.**

A procession of tanks traces the voyage that rainwater takes, from high mountain streams, where it first falls, to rivers and reservoirs, into estuaries, and finally ending in the open ocean. The **High Mountain Stream** display gives an above-and-below view of a stream's environment, including a number of rare Formosan landlocked salmon swimming about in the tank. From here you move downriver, to mock-ups illustrating the ecosystems of the middle section of a river, the water's edge, a dam/reservoir environment, and estuaries.

An **Oyster Rack,** with live oysters hanging underwater from ropes tied to racks, demonstrates the traditional form of oyster farming on Taiwan's west coast, while the rocky intertidal coast display explores the ecosystems that exist in areas where the tide ebbs and flows.

Opposite the intertidal coast display, a touch pool lets you feel some less mobile marine life, including sea stars, sea urchins, and sea cucumbers. More of Taiwan's reef ecology is presented in stunning colors at the **Coral Reef Canyon** and **South Bay Reef** displays.

The second major exhibit is the **Coral Kingdom.** You begin at a floor-to-ceiling, curving water tank teeming with live coral and darting technicolor reef fish.

Farther along, in the **South China Sea** exhibition, you enter a clear, 91-yard-long (84 m) underwater tunnel that makes you feel as if you truly are underwater with the rays, reef sharks, snapper, sunfish, dolphin fish, and exceptionally weird-looking bowmouth guitarfish. You finally find yourself in the bowels of a shipwreck, with information on how marine life utilizes sunken ships to create new environments.

After you emerge from the shipwreck, a **coral reef conservation** exhibit draws attention to how coral is damaged by industrial waste and other factors. From here you end up at the **sea mammal tank,** beneath the water, where you can get a fish-eye view of the belugas that reside here.

If you arrive at the aquarium just before 10:30 a.m. or 3 p.m., you can catch the 30-minute perfor-

mance put on by the aquarium's four beluga whales, which take turns doing tricks for enthralled audiences. The performances mainly steer away from the exploitive and are performed more to illustrate how the belugas are taken care of at the aquarium. There is a running commentary (in Chinese) about the mammals: their natural environment; what they eat; their social systems; how they communicate; how they are trained; and so on, with the mammals acting those roles accordingly.

Arrive at the extraordinary **Open Ocean** display in time to see the aquarium's residents get fed (feeding times: 10 a.m., 1 p.m., and 4:30 p.m.). The display looks on to a huge floor-to-ceiling section of one of the tanks. Watch as hundreds of fish—rays, mud sharks, reef sharks, giant trevally, sunfish, and turtles—all but envelop the diver as he or she submerges with bags of feed. The third, and newest, major exhibit is the **Waters of the World** showcase. In the four theme areas—Polar Region, Kelp Forest, Deep Sea, Ancient Oceans—visitors step into these environments through "live" or virtual-reality recreations. The extensive VR exhibits are a great hit; tell friends you've "been there, done that" when a massive sperm whale battles a giant squid. ■

Life-size whale sculptures (opposite) greet visitors to the National Museum of Marine Biology & Aquarium. In the Coral Kingdom exhibit (above), huge tanks are filled with living corals and an amazing array of tropical fish.

A rainbow cloud of parrotfish is just a sampling of Taiwan's extent of tropical marine life.

Underwater rain forests

Taiwan is located near the thermal boundary where coral reefs do not thrive. The powerful, warm Kuroshio Current, however, flows northward from the tropics, splitting in two when it hits Taiwan's southern tip and washing the region with warm water, nutrients, fish, and coral larvae. This situation, combined with the warming factor of seasonal monsoons, creates perfect conditions for corals to thrive. Corals are found in most of Taiwan's waters, but the main area is in the south around Kenting, where a 37-mile-long (60 km) coral reef community, home to some 60 percent of the various species of coral reef to be found in the world, bustles with sea life.

Giant brain corals grow on the rocky bottom closer to shore, joined by staghorn, lettuce, mushroom, and knob coral, while in deeper water undersea meadows of soft coral and grasses wave back and forth in the gentle ocean surge. In all, nearly 300 species of coral live in the offshore waters of the national park. About 250 types of scleractinian coral have been documented in Kenting, together with 39 species of alcyonarian coral.

Like all coral reefs, the Kenting fringing reef is delicate. To thrive, coral needs a precise combination of factors. It is influenced by the temperature of the sea, intensity of sunlight, nutrient content and ocean currents, number of predators, and amount of sediment in the water. In Kenting, the corals have an ideal natural combination.

The corals of Kenting are blessed by Mother Nature but threatened by the forces of economic development. Destructive fishing is one problem. Dynamite fishing is now rare, but fishing boats ply the waters offshore, and their persistent netting and hooking have removed all but the smallest fish from the waters of Kenting. Scuba divers are often astonished by the tiny size of the tropical fish they see and by the lack of edible fish. Nets are commonly found on the coral reefs, both active and abandoned, and present a hazard to divers and fish alike.

But the biggest danger to Kenting's reefs are silt deposits that are flushed into the sea by tropical storms and seasonal rainfall. Large amounts of silt, coupled with sewage from resort hotels and recreational areas, can suffocate coral and other living organisms. Much of the silt is caused by fast-paced development in Kenting National Park. Construction debris is a persistent problem, and piles of dirt and other refuse lie waiting for heavy rainfall to be washed into the sea. Other detrimental factors have been oil spills, devastating typhoons, not to mention the effects of scuba divers who carelessly trample on the reefs—some even carving their names.

There is good news as well. The corals of Kenting are still in reasonably good shape, and authorities in Taiwan are trying to slow the pace and type of development. Kenting National Park was established in 1982; before that, the 81,540-acre (33,000 ha) area was used for agriculture, fishing, whaling, and logging, and it was being subjected to the sort of haphazard sprawl that typifies much of Taiwan. The unplanned growth ended in 1982, although many pre-1982 tenants have been allowed to stay in the park.

National parks in Taiwan, however, are not the same as they are in the United States, where building and even access are strictly regulated, and the emphasis is on conserva-tion. In Taiwan, national park authorities try to balance the conflicting interests of business and preservation, with mixed success. There is plenty of construction in Kenting—mostly hotels and tourist facilities—and the park is a battleground between the forces of development and the forces of preservation. On one side are fishermen, farmers, hotel builders, and Jet Ski operators, and on the other are scuba divers, whale- and bird-watchers, marine biologists, and the national park administration.

The most visible defeat for the national park was the Third Nuclear Power Plant, which looms over South Bay in the heart of Kenting. The Tourism Bureau wanted to build a hotel on the site, but it lost, and hot water flowing from the nuclear plant is responsible for some of the coral bleaching that has taken place in Kenting.

There have also been victories for the forces of conservation. Whaling was stopped in 1986, and cyanide and dynamite fishing have been largely stamped out. Despite this turbulence, Kenting's coral reefs still boast some of the greatest biodiversity in the Pacific. ∎

Sweeps of fringing coral make snorkeling an attractive alternative to scuba diving.

KENTING'S CORAL REEFS

Caves, grottoes, arches, and ridges covered with dense coral and ornamented with shells, sea lilies, sea stars, and roving fish of every variety await beneath the waves.

1. Reef crest
2. Storm-driven pool
3. Smooth starlet coral
4. Brain coral
5. Coral table
6. Reef slope
7. Pillar coral
8. Vase sponge
9. Anemone
10. Stagitom coral
11. Elkhorn coral
12. Elliptical star coral
13. Sea fans
14. Flower coral
15. Plume worm
16. Cattle egret
17–18. Black-faced Spoonbill

19. Chinese Crested Tern
20. Little ringed plover
21. Whale shark
22. Black marlin
23. Sun fish
24. Silver tip shark
25. Reef shark
26. Manta ray
27. Turtle

28. Angel fish shoal
29. Fire fish
30. Angel fish
31. Lion fish
32. Clown anemone fish
33. Butterflyfish
34. Butterflyfish
35. Moray eel
36. Angel fish

37. Oxymon acanthus
38. Clown trigger fish
39. Trigger undulate

More places to visit in the South

CHENG CING (QING) LAKE OCEAN WORLD

In the Cheng Cing Lake resort area on the outskirts of Kaohsiung, this huge underground bunker complex strengthened by a steel door weighing half a ton (500 kg), was built in 1961 to protect a privileged few against nuclear annihilation by Communist China. As the likelihood of such an event happening diminished, the bunker was transformed into an aquarium, which includes tanks of tropical fish, displays of coral, a whale exhibition gallery, and other marine-themed displays.

The once fortified town of Hengchun contains a few historical remnants, including its city gates.

◬ Map p. 159 ✉ 32 Dabi Rd., Niaosong Village, Niaosong Township, Kaohsiung County ☎ (07) 732-5710 $ $ 🚌 Bus: 60 from Kaohsiung Railway Station

HENGCHUN

Hengchun, the main town in the Kenting area, though lying just outside the national park's boundaries, brags that it is the only town in Taiwan where all four gates are still intact. Built in 1879, the gates were once part of walled fortifications that surrounded the town to protect against attacks from disgruntled aborigines and imperialist forces from the West and Japan. The town has long since spread beyond the walls, and the gates have now been all but swallowed up by development. The **West Gate** is in a traffic circle in the center of the town's commercial district. The **North Gate** now breaches the main road into the town, while the **East Gate,** on the outskirts, has a section of the original wall still intact. Follow the road east from here to **Chuhuo** (Fire Coming Out) and a strange geological phenomenon of natural gas seeping from the Earth and feeding flames in a rocky circular pit. Local entrepreneurs sell potatoes wrapped in foil to place on the hot rocks and foil containers (complete with a tin handle) of corn you can hold over the flames to make popcorn. Note that mud often blocks the fissure in the wet season.
◬ Map p. 159

HENGCHUN FARM

This privately run farm, close to Hengchun, is known for its natural, chemical-free farming techniques. Accommodation is available and guests are instructed in organic farming techniques. There is a restaurant, a coffee shop, and a display center with information on organic farming techniques. The farm also sells its own fruits, vegetables, and flowers.
◬ Map p. 159 ✉ 28-5 Shanjiao Rd., Shanjiao District, Hengchun Township, Pingtung County ☎ (08) 889-2633 $ $$

KENDING FARM

The Japanese occupiers established the farm as a research facility in 1904, and it is used for the same purpose today. It is a popular spot for local tourists because of the large expanses of pastureland and herds of cattle, both a rarity in Taiwan. Visitors also get to taste freshly pasteurized cow's and goat's milk at the farm's visitor center. There are superb views to the Bashih (Bashi) Channel from the grasslands, where contented cattle graze freely among the farm's 2,839 acres (1,149 ha). The research station is involved in cattle and sheep breeding and disease prevention among livestock.
◬ Map p. 159 ✉ 1 Muchang Rd., Kending District, Hengchun Township, Pingtung County ☎ (08) 886-1341

An image of the deity Mazu sits amid the gilded grandeur of the Queen of Heaven Temple at Luermen, in Tainan.

The parkland banks of Kaohsiung's Love River are popular with strolling couples.

LOVE RIVER

The banks of the Love River in Kaohsiung have been turned into a fine park and promenade that comes to life in the evening. Open-air cafes and live entertainment now abound. Lovers stroll the promenade hand in hand admiring the lights reflected in the river's waters.
🅜 Map p. 159

QUEEN OF HEAVEN TEMPLE AT LUERMEN (DEER EAR GATE)

This temple, in Tainan's northwest, groans under the weight of hundreds of figurines prancing along the ridges of its tiered roofs. Under the eaves between each tier are gilded pattern carvings, while the stone facade has been etched with more patterns and mythological scenes. In the main shrine writhing dragons protect Mazu, the queen of heaven. Before her is a row of black camphor-wood images turned out in colorful finery.
🅜 Map p. 159 ✉ 236 Lane 1, Siancao (Xiancao) St., Section 3, Annan District, Tainan City ☎ (06) 284-1048

SHEDING NATURE PARK

The park shares much of the characteristics of its neighbor, Kenting Forest Recreation Area. It is notable for trees that have grown out of coral outcrops and been worn by northeasterly winter winds to resemble oversize bonsai plants. The park is kept simple, with just a few pavilions—for bird-watching—and only a few pathways.
🅜 Map p. 159 ✉ Entrance through Kenting Forest Recreation Area; see p. 175

TUCHENG TEMPLE OF THE HOLY MOTHER

What it lacks in antiquity, this temple in the northwestern area of Tainan, built in the 1970s, makes up for in size. Its dominant presence and forced isolation—it is surrounded by a wide moat—add to its grandeur. Finely carved stone dragon pillars stand at the entrance, with two large pagodas sitting on either side. The magnificent main shrine is cavernous and luxuriously decorated.
🅜 Map p. 159 ✉ 160 Lane 245, Chengbei Rd., Annan District, Tainan City ☎ (06) 257-7547 ∎

The rugged, windswept, pristine islands of the Taiwan Strait serve up an entirely different perspective of Taiwan, and they exemplify, through monuments and museums, more than 50 years of strained relations with mainland China.

Strait Islands

Colorful and ornate Kinmen rooftop

Strait Islands

SEPARATING TAIWAN FROM MAINLAND CHINA, STORMY TAIWAN STRAIT harbors three groups of unspoiled and sparsely populated islands a world away from the bustling major island. Midway between Taiwan and the mainland you'll find the largest island group—Penghu—a scattering of 64 small islands spread over 37 miles (60 km) north to south, and 13.6 miles (22 km) east to west. Linked by bridges, the group's three main islands—Penghu, Baisha, and Siyu (Xiyu)—are the most accessible and most visited. The other two archipelagoes, Kinmen and Matsu, each only a mile or so from the Chinese province of Fujian at their nearest points, provide plenty of evidence of Taiwan's tumultuous relationship with its closest neighbor.

Penghu became part of the Chinese empire more than 700 years ago and served for centuries as a way station for immigrants moving to Taiwan from Fujian. This role has left it rich in cultural and historic sites. Taiwan's first Mazu temple, dating back to the 14th century, can be found here, along with the ancient West Fort Sitai (Xitai) on Siyu (Xiyu) and a wealth of restored houses in the southern Fujian architectural style. Penghu also served as a staging post for the imperial thrusts of the Dutch and French.

There is little industrialization on Penghu and, except for the summer tour buses, little traffic. The landscape is mostly flat, covered by brush and grasslands. Combined with basalt-column cliffs rising from the sea, lovely beaches, and fringing coral, these windswept isles serve up a stark beauty. In winter, however, they are subject to fierce winds, and it becomes colder than elsewhere in Taiwan. A visit at this time of year is not recommended.

This harsh climate has made Penghu's 90,000 residents a hardy bunch. They stoically forge their living through peanut, sweet potato, and sorghum farming; and fishing—although tourism is now offering a lucrative alternative.

On Kinmen and Matsu Islands, visitors are supplied with more than enough evidence of the friction between mainland China and Taiwan though museums, memorials, and parks memorializing bloody battles. Getting to the outlying islands generally requires taking advantage of local ferry services or joining chartered boat tours. ∎

Water sports are high on the activity list for visitors to the Penghu islands.

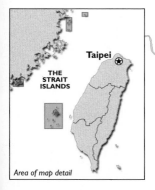

THE
STRAIT
ISLANDS

Taipei

Area of map detail

Liang I.

Dongyin I.

Cinbi (Qinbi) · Beigan I.
Tianhou (Queen of Heaven) Temple · Tangci (Tangqi)
Tanghoudao Beach
Cingshuei (Qingshui) Village · *Nangan I.*

*Matsu
Islands*

Sijyu (Xiju) I.

*Jyuguang
(Juguang) Is.*
Dongiyu
(Dongju) I.

C H I N A

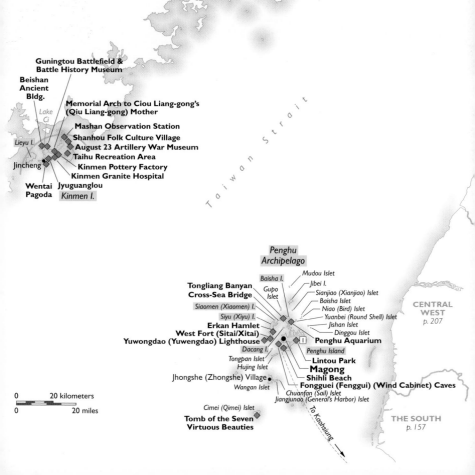

**Guningtou Battlefield &
Battle History Museum**

**Beishan
Ancient
Bldg.**

*Lake
Ci*

**Memorial Arch to Ciou Liang-gong's
(Qiu Liang-gong) Mother**

Mashan Observation Station
Shanhou Folk Culture Village

Lieyu I.

August 23 Artillery War Museum
Taihu Recreation Area
Kinmen Pottery Factory
Kinmen Granite Hospital

Jincheng

**Wentai
Pagoda** **Jyuguanglou**
Kinmen I.

Taiwan Strait

*Penghu
Archipelago*

Mudou Islet

Baisha I.
Jibei I.

**Tongliang Banyan
Cross-Sea Bridge**

*Gupo
Islet*

Sianjiao (Xianjiao) Islet
Baisha Islet
Niao (Bird) Islet
Yuanbei (Round Shell) Islet

Siaomen (Xiaomen) I.

Siyu (Xiyu) I.

Jishan Islet
Dinggou Islet

Erkan Hamlet
West Fort (Sitai/Xitai)
Yuwongdao (Yuwengdao) Lighthouse

Penghu Aquarium

Dacang I.

Penghu Island

Tongpan Islet
Hujing Islet

Lintou Park

Magong
Shihli Beach

Jhongshe (Zhongshe) Village

Wangan Islet

Fongguei (Fenggui) (Wind Cabinet) Caves

Chuanfan (Sail) Islet
Jiangjunao (General's Harbor) Islet

CENTRAL
WEST
p. 207

THE SOUTH
p. 157

0   20 kilometers
0   20 miles

To Koohsiung

Cimei (Qimei) Islet
**Tomb of the Seven
Virtuous Beauties**

Penghu

A stunning ridge of stone columns on Siyu (Xiyu) Island, the most beautiful of Penghu's main island group

MOST VISITORS TO THIS 64-ISLE ARCHIPELAGO WILL probably get to know the main trio first: Penghu, Baisha, and Siyu (Xiyu), thin, curving, convoluted islands linked by bridges and encircling Penghu Bay.

PENGHU ISLAND

The major island in the group, Penghu is home to the major city, **Magong**, a sedate and picturesque place where half of the island group's population resides.

In the city's eastern section, **Tianhou (Empress of Heaven) Temple**—appropriately devoted to the protector of mariners, Mazu—was built in 1593, making it Taiwan's oldest temple. Its interior walls are embellished with finely hewn wooden carvings of patterns and mythical figures, while on the second floor stone tablets recount

the expulsion of the "red-haired barbarians," that is the Dutch, from the islands in 1624. These are thought to be the oldest inscribed tablets in Taiwan. A tablet inscribed with gilded characters from Qing dynasty Emperor Qianlong (R.1736–1796) is also found here.

South of the city along County Route 201, on a string of land near Penghu Bay's south entrance, wind-blown **Shihli (Shili) Beach** stretches more than half a mile (1 km). Its calm, deep-blue waters are nicely offset by the fine grains of coral and seashell that make up the beach.

A little farther west along County Route 201 you'll come to the **Fongguei (Wind Cabinet) Caves.** Wind and waves have eroded the sea cliffs into a craggy collection of formations, and plumes of water burst through blowholes and spit onto the rocks.

On County Route 204 east out of Magong, a forest of casuarinas and lintou trees backs a glorious stretch of white sand and clear water at **Lintou Park,** one of the islands' most popular tourist spots. Gardens of tropical flowers add vivid color to the lovely setting. At the park's western end, a military cemetery has a miniaturized version of Taipei's Chiang Kai-shek Memorial Hall.

BAISHA ISLAND

At the excellent **Penghu Aquarium,** you'll find displays of traditional fishing equipment, aquaculture, life in a fishing village, the evolution of fishing vessels, a futuristic undersea world, mock-ups of a coral reef, and an undersea tunnel for a fish-eye view of local denizens.

The magnificent **Tongliang Banyan,** thought to be more than 200 years old, forms a huge and glorious canopy over the courtyard of **Baoan Temple** in the village of **Tongliang,** on Baisha's western tip. It is likely to be the biggest banyan you will ever lay eyes on, with its aerial roots dropping down from branches and intertwining to form an eerie fairyland forest that covers 7,100 square feet (660 sq m). The tree is revered by the locals who see its ability to survive and thrive in an inhospitable environment as symbolic of their own lives.

From here, the **Cross-Sea Bridge** spans the Houmen (Roaring Gate) Channel, linking the islands of Baisha and Siyu

(Xiyu). At 1.55 miles (2,500 m), it is Taiwan's longest bridge.

SIYU (XIYU) ISLAND

This island, with its convoluted coastline hiding many coves and small bays, is the most beautiful of the three. Midway along County Route 203, off a side road to the

island's east coast, you'll come to the **Erkan Hamlet,** a large clan homestead in classical southern Fujian architectural style. Note the finely crafted reliefs embedded above and below the windows and doors and along the eaves.

Close to the island's southern end, in a lofty position at the south entrance to Penghu Bay, is **West Fort (Sitai/Xitai).** Enclosed between high walls and networked by wide, curved tunnels, the expansive fort was built in 1887 to house up to 5,000 men. You can climb up the ramparts to the gun emplacements for extensive vistas of Taiwan Strait. From the fort, a road heads west through Waian Village to the island's southwest tip and **Yuwongdao (Yuwengdao) Lighthouse,** where more expansive ocean views can be savored. ■

Ferry services and boat charters make island-hopping easy.

Penghu Aquarium
www.ph.tfrin.gov.tw
✉ 58 Citou (Qitou) Village, Baisha Township, Penghu County
☎ (06) 993-3006 or (06) 993-3007
🕐 Closed Mon.
💲 $$

Penghu's other islands

**Penghu's other
islands**
 Map p. 193

**Penghu County
Public Bus & Boat
Administration**
☎ (06) 927-2376

**For more Penghu
islands, see p. 206.**

PENGHU'S SCATTERING OF ISLANDS DISHES UP A FINE
mixture of rugged coastal scenery, attractive beaches, crystalline
waters, and easily accessible coral reefs. Varying in size from a few
square miles to just a couple of hundred square yards, many are unin-
habited. There are scheduled ferry services to some of the islands, or
you can charter a boat from Magong. Tours depart regularly to the
different groups of islands.

SOUTH ISLANDS

Just outside the mouth of the south
entrance to Penghu Bay lies
Tongpan Islet. Its shoreline is
bounded by columnar, stacked,
hexagonal-shaped rock formations
that offer unusual, sometimes
spectacular, scenery. The islands
here were formed by volcanic
activity, and the columns were
formed as lava was quickly cooled
by the seawater and shrank.
Because of its geology, optimistic
local tourism authorities have
tagged the island the "Yellowstone
Park of the Penghus." The
formations can be explored along a
trail that encircles the island.
Surrounding outcrops of coral in
shallow waters make Tongpan
popular with snorkelers. The
island's only village houses the small
but ornate **Fuhai Temple** at the
island's dock.

Just to the southeast of
Tongpan, the larger **Hujing Islet**

shares a similar, but less spectacular, topography of stacked, hexagonal-shaped rock formations. The waters off the island are among the clearest in the Penghu archipelago. Legend holds that the Dutch built a fortification here that sunk during a particularly fierce battle. In recent years, efforts to find the sunken—and apparently poorly built—fort have been unsuccessful.

To the south, **Wangan Islet** has a population of about 4,000, making it the most populated of the outlying islands. But Wangan is large enough to support that many people and still evoke feelings of isolation, especially along its windswept grasslands. On the western edge of the island's highest point, at 170 feet (52 m), **Tiantaishan** is a small crater that legend holds is the footprint of Lyu Dong-bin (Lu Dong-bin), one of the Eight

Immortals. It is not particularly impressive, but it does attract the tourists because of its mythological significance. Uninhibited ocean vistas can be had from here. **Jhongshe (Zhongshe) Village,** on the island's western shoreline, has a well-preserved group of Qing dynasty houses, some still used as residences.

About one mile (1.6 km) east of Tongpan is the much smaller, but more developed, **Jiangjunao (General's Harbor) Islet.** It earned its prosperity from veined-stone mining, which has now ceased. The island is unusual in the Penghu group because of the number of multistory buildings, leading the local tourism authorities to refer to it as "Little Hong Kong." The island celebrated its prosperity by building two richly adorned temples, **Jiangjun** and **Mazu.** A third, much older temple on the island,

A number of historical buildings add to the allure of the Penghu islands.

Drying fish in the sun. Fishing remains a mainstay for many islanders.

Yongan, dates back to the Ming dynasty, when a general used the island as a base while plotting to expel the Dutch from Taiwan. Just to the east of the island is **Chuanfan (Sail) Islet,** named for its sail-like shape. You can walk there at low tide.

Cimei (Qimei) Island, the southernmost of the Penghu archipelago, is named after seven legendary local beauties who threw themselves down a well rather than have their virtue despoiled by a gang of marauding pirates. The simple **Tomb of the Seven Virtuous Beauties** at the island's southern tip honors their sacrifice; the tomb is built over the well. Columns of basalt rock that have been carved by erosion into myriad shapes rim the island's east coast. At **Longcheng** you'll find a weird landscape of wrinkled and folded rock terraces. **Nioumuping (Niumuping)** is a slab of stone weathered into a surprisingly accurate shape of Taiwan, which has earned it the moniker "Little Taiwan." Just off the north coast, an ingenious stone fish trap, built in the shape of two adjoining hearts, draws the crowds; this type of trap can be found throughout the islands.

NORTH ISLANDS

Tiny **Mudou Islet**—only 2,260 square feet (210 sq m)—on the archipelago's northernmost edge, is dominated by a black-and-white-striped, 131-foot-high (40 m) **lighthouse,** built during the Qing dynasty in 1902. At the island's small, white-sand beach, shallow, crystal-clear waters attract shoals of tropical fish.

South of Mudou, sparkling beaches of finely ground coral—among the best in the archipelago—scallop **Jibei Islet**'s western coastline. Coral can be found only a few yards off the island's southern tip.

Two sandy bays on the eastern side, along with coral reefs flush with marine life lying just off the coast, make worm-shaped **Gupo Islet**—to the southeast of Jibei—ideal for beach fun and snorkeling. The island has gained some renown for the seaweed that grows in abundance in its waters and is harvested at the start of winter.

To the south of Jibei and the east of Gupo Islet, **Sianjiao (Xianjiao) Islet** is blessed with wide, white-sand beaches and offshore coral teeming with marine life. Sand makes up much of this little island, giving it a shimmering, mirage-like effect as you approach.

WEST ISLANDS

The west coast of **Baisha Islet** (not to be confused with Baisha Island), to the southeast of Sianjiao Islet, is strung with a series of white-sand beaches that broaden as you move farther south. Columnar rock formations along the southern coastline are particularly spectacular. Sea terns make their nests within these cliffs, luring bird-watchers.

A few hundreds yards south is **Niao (Bird) Islet,** although it has no birds. What it does have are stacked rows of basalt columns

forming high sea cliffs along its eastern shore. Below the cliffs, blowholes spit spray onto the cliff faces. Cliffs along the island's northern coast have been weathered into onion shapes.

Between Niao Islet and the main Penghu island group, columnar rock formations rim **Yuanbei (Round Shell) Islet's** northern coast. On the east coast, the fan-shaped rows of basalt columns resemble pleated skirts. Waters between Yuanbei and Baisha and Niao Islets are rich with coral beds.

South of Niao Islet, **Jishan**

comprises two islets, connected at low tide. Sea cliffs almost totally enclose the smaller island, making it a haven for birds.

To the southeast, **Dinggou Islet's** rock columns have been weathered into an array of angles and differing heights, giving the impression of a gigantic petrified forest. Seabirds flock here in the thousands from March to September, setting up colonies among the craggy landscape. Their overhead wheeling and screeching makes for a memorable experience. ■

Workers repair fishing nets in an increasingly uncommon scene, as employment in the tourism industry gradually draws locals away from traditional occupations.

Kinmen

Kinmen

Map p. 193

**Visitor
information**

www.kmnp.gov.tw

Kinmen National
Park Administration
Center, 460 Boyu
Rd., Sec. 2, Jinning
District

(082) 313-100

Note: Guningtou Battle-
field, Guningtou
Battle Museum,
August 23 Artillery
War Museum, &
Taihu Recreation
Area are all part of
Kinmen NP.

SITTING OFF THE SOUTH COAST OF MAINLAND CHINA'S
Fujian province, the Kinmen archipelago was the site of fierce fighting
between Communist and Nationalist forces soon after the latter with-
drew from the mainland in 1949. The island group, along with Mazu
(see p. 203), was also bombarded by mainland Chinese artillery in 1958.
For many years, the Kinmen islands remained heavily fortified, with up
to 70,000 troops stationed there. They stayed under martial law until
1992, and civilian visits to the island were prohibited up until that time.

Not surprisingly, Kinmen now
relies on its military past to attract
visitors. But the archipelago also has
its share of natural beauty, along
with a wonderful collection of
restored Qing and Ming architecture.

Kinmen is the main island, and
Jincheng is Kinmen's main town,
offering most of the accommodation and other services. Here you'll
also find **Jyuguanglou,** one of a
number of monuments, buildings,
and museums glorifying and
memorializing the feats of Taiwan's
military against mainland China.
This particular one is the earliest,

built in 1952. The imposing structure comprises a two-story granite-
wall "base" topped by a Chinese
palace-style roof. A room on the first
floor is given over to a multimedia
presentation of Kinmen's history.

In Kinmen's Jincheng District, at
the island's southwestern end, the
five-story, hexagonal, stone-built
Wentai Pagoda was originally
built in 1387. The solid granite
tower served as a navigational
marker for ships negotiating the
treacherous waters near Kinmen.

On Kinmen's northwest tip, in
Jinning District, the **Guningtou**

A smiling resident of Kinmen (right), where military personnel outnumber civilians. Dug into solid rock on Mount Taiwu (opposite), Cingtian (Qingtian) Hall was long used for military purposes; it now is sometimes open for public tours.

Battlefield was the scene of a 56-hour bloodbath that began when Communist troops landed on the shore in the early hours of October 24, 1949. The Communists initially made inroads but were eventually pushed back out to sea by the Nationalist forces. According to the victors, the end result was 3,000 Nationalist troops and 12,000 Communist killed. You enter the battlefield through a Chinese-style city gate. A memorial tablet on the waterfront commemorates the battle.

The facade of the nearby **Guningtou Battle Museum** resembles a medieval fortress. Three charging soldiers made of bronze and set on a plinth guard the main entrance, while large bronze reliefs of heroic battle scenes line the outside walls. Inside, you'll find 12 large oil paintings that depict the battle, along with displays of materials, documents, and photographs relating to the fighting and ensuing victory.

Bullet holes from the battle pockmark the **Beishan Ancient Building** on the shores of nearby Lake Cih, which the Communists used as a command post before being overrun by the Nationalists. A tablet in front of the derelict building records in Chinese the events

that took place here. **Lake Cih (Ci)** is now used mainly for fish farming.

Erected in 1812, the **Memorial Arch to Ciou Liang-gong's (Qiu Liang-gong) Mother,** on Jyuguang (Juguang) Road in Jinhu District, to the east of Jinning, celebrates the virtuous mother of Ciou Liang-song (Qiu Liang-gong), a

Wind lions

During the Ming dynasty, Kinmen was denuded of forest by the voracious ship-building appetite of Koxinga, the famed warrior who, among other things, forced the Dutch from Formosa. The island became wind-swept and desolate. In desperation the villagers turned to the wind lion—who they believed could control the savage winter winds—for salvation. Reforestation efforts undertaken under the Nationalists have resulted in significant forest cover, but the wind lion still features prominently. You will find its statues at the edge of every village and guarding important buildings and places, standing upright and often bedecked with a red bib. ∎

governor-general of Zhejiang province in mainland China who was a resident of Kinmen. His mother was virtuous because she lived 28 years in widowhood without remarrying. Carved stone beams, figurines, and inscriptions adorning the tiered stone monument mark that fact.

The **Kinmen Pottery Factory** turns out embellished containers for the local firewater, Kaoliang, which are snapped up by souvenir hunters and collectors. To the west, **Kinmen Granite Hospital** burrows deep into the granite of Kinmen's highest mountain, the 830-foot (253 m) Taiwushan.

Mashan Observation Station sits on a tongue of land on the island's northeastern tip in Jinsha District. From here, mainland China is only 1.3 miles (2.1 km) away. A trench takes you to a bunker equipped with powerful binoculars, so you can check out fishing villages on the mainland shore opposite.

A showcase of Qing architectural style is found at the **Shanhou Folk Culture Village,** featuring neatly packed rows of 28 southern Fujian-style houses dating from the turn of the 20th century, some of which are still lived in. The houses feature orange-tiled roofs shaped like ships' prows. One residence built by a senior imperial official stands out, with intricately carved beams and elaborate wall murals.

Taihu Recreation Area ($) centers around Lake Taihu. Three small islands in the lake are topped with elegant pavilions, and a Ming dynasty-era residence in the park has been fully restored.

Also in the recreation area, the **August 23 Artillery War Museum** commemorates the 587 soldiers lost during a 44-day bombardment by mainland Chinese of Kinmen in 1958, in which 470,000 shells—including 57,500 in the first 24 hours—rained down on the island. The names of those who died are carved on either side of the entrance gates. The museum has a collection of tanks, aircraft, and artillery on its grounds. Inside, 12 display areas take you through the battle with photos, documents, models, relics, and, of course, numerous spent artillery shells. ∎

Military relics on display at the August 23 Artillery War Museum. Military museums on Kinmen recount Taiwan's tumultuous relationship with mainland China.

Matsu

LIKE KINMEN, MATSU NESTLES ALONG THE COAST OF MAIN-land China's Fujian province. It is an isolated place with a large military presence. Few visitors journey to the island group, which in itself is a good reason to visit, as the islands are not without attractions. The group consists of 18 islands, though some are off-limits to visitors.

BEIGAN

Assuming you fly to Matsu, this is where you will arrive. This mountainous island is the group's second largest and has a population of 1,300 civilians. A paved road leads east from the main settlement of **Tangci (Tangqi) Village** to **Tanghoudao Beach,** a spit of sand connecting Beigan's two mountainous island sections. On the island's north coast, the tiny village of **Cinbi (Qinbi)** is made up almost entirely of east Fujian-style stone houses. The ornate **Tianhou (Queen of Heaven) Temple,** dedicated to Mazu, fronts the sands of **Banli Beach** on the island's south coast.

NANGAN

This is Matsu's largest and most populous island, with 3,700 civilians sharing just 4 square miles (10.4 sq km). You'll find a few attractions in and around **Cingshuei (Qingshui) Village.** The **Wenchien History and Folk Culture Museum** covers the area's marine life and traces the history and culture of the islands' people. Next door, you can't miss the **Fushan Illuminated Wall,** a huge sign with red Chinese characters on a white background declaring: "Sleep with one's sword ready." Its purpose was to brace the islands' Kuomintang troops and to warn off the Communist troops always watching from just across the waters.

In nearby **Cingshuei (Qingshui) Park,** a pretty reservoir sits amid gardens. The park is home to the **Matsu Military History Museum,** with lots of displays relating to the stormy relations with mainland China. ■

The isolated Matsu island group has some golden beaches but very few visitors.

Matsu
🄰 Map p. 193
Visitor information
www.matsu-nsa.gov.tw
✉ Matsu National Scenic Area Administration, No. 95-1, Renai Village, Nangan Island
☎ (08) 362-5630

Trouble across the strait

Economically speaking, Taiwan and China couldn't be much closer. Taiwanese investment in China has surged over the past two decades, and the mainland absorbs the lion's share of Taiwan's exports. Politically, the two countries are enemies. China considers Taiwan a breakaway province and repeatedly threatens to take it back by force, while Taiwan prefers to remain independent.

Most Taiwanese prefer the status quo. Polls consistently show that the vast majority of citizens want to remain separate from China. That stance has strengthened in the past decade-plus, as the China-born "mainlander" generation has lost much political influence, and a pro-Taiwan identity has emerged.

The Taiwanese see no reason to rejoin China, which they view as a badly governed country where business is dominated by corrupt officials, personal freedom is limited, and quality of life is low. However, China insists that Taiwan return to the motherland, and threatens to use military might to achieve unification. By constantly threatening to use force, including launching missiles near Taiwan in 1995 and 1996, China has left itself little room for diplomatic maneuver.

Despite having opposite goals, the two sides have talked. In 1992 and 1993, discussions were held under a One China platform, which held that Taiwan and China were one country, but with two governments. That was the high point of the relationship.

The third major player in the ongoing tug-of-war—the United States—does not promote Taiwanese independence. But the Taiwan Relations Act, a 1979 declaration by the U.S. Congress, implies that the U.S. will provide Taiwan with sufficient defensive weaponry, and will help defend it against attack.

As the political stalemate drags on, Taiwan continues to behave like an independent country, electing its own leaders and conducting its own foreign policy. It is not a member of the U.N., but it has nearly 30 diplomatic allies, and every year it requests admission to the world body.

Nor has Taiwan neglected its military. Its Air Force has bought 150 Lockheed F-16 fighter jets and 60 French-built Mirage 2000 fighters, and built 130 locally designed Indigenous Defense Fighter jets. Military service is mandatory, and more than 300,000 soldiers serve full time.

In March 2000, the two countries looked like they were headed for a crisis, as Taiwan first elected an independence-minded president, Chen Shui-bian (1951–). Just as they did in 1996—when they elected Lee Teng-hui (1923–)—Taiwan's voters ignored threats from China and elected the candidate most disliked by Beijing. China reacted cautiously, but repeated its main theme: There is but one China, Taiwan is part of China, it can never be independent. President Chen says he is willing to discuss any topic, including One China, but he firmly believes that the future of Taiwan should be decided by the people of Taiwan.

Meanwhile, on Taipei's streets, China is not discussed much, and daily life remains the same regardless of the political tension. The presence of a vague threat does little to dampen the good good times and general prosperity. ∎

Constant threats leveled by mainland China to someday retake the island has forced Taiwan to build a large, modern, and efficient military (left and right).

More places to visit in the Strait Islands

DACANG ISLAND

This island, located in Penghu Bay and encircled by the three main Penghu islands, is known for its huge tidal movements. You can walk the 2 miles (3 km) to the island from Baisha Island during the lowest tides. It takes about an hour.  Map p. 193 **Visitor information** ✉ See Penghu National Scenic Area Administration, p. 194

JYUGUANG ISLAND

This is the southernmost inhabited island in the Matsu archipelago, actually consisting of two islands, Dongjyu (Dongju) and Sijyu (Xiju). About 600 civilians live on the islands, most in the village of **Dapu,** in the center of **Dongjyu.** At the island's northern tip is the **Dongjyu Lighthouse,** built by the British after the Opium Wars of the mid-19th century and still in use. A stone tablet recounting the adventures of a local Ming dynasty general who drove away marauding pirates some 400 years ago—the Tapu Inscription—sits on a cliff about half a mile (1 km) southwest of Dapu Village. **Sijyu** is a little more lively, but you'll likely be the major attraction, given the island's lack of actual tourist sights. ⬛ Map p. 193 **Visitor information** ✉ See Matsu National Scenic Area Administration, p. 203

LIEYU ISLAND

This island, about 2 miles (3 km) west of Kinmen Island, is also referred to as Little Kinmen. You can catch a ferry from Jincheng on the main island. From the pier at **Sijhai (Xizhai) Village** on Lieyu, you pass through **Victory Gate**—celebrating Nationalist troop heroics against the mainland Communists— and through to the **Bada Memorial,** which honors local soldiers who died in 1933 fighting in the Sino-Japanese War. ⬛ Map p. 193 **Visitor information** ✉ See Kinmen National Park Administration Center, p. 200

SIAOMEN (XIAOMEN) ISLAND

A bridge links small, scenic Siaomen (Xiaomen), sitting at the edge of the Houmen Channel, to Siyu (Xiyu), one of Penghu's main islands. On the island's northwestern coast is **Whale Hole,** a large gap in the cliffs said to resemble a whale when viewed from a distance. Golden sand covers a small plateau to the southeast of Whale Hole, one of Taiwan's few arid landscapes. ⬛ Map p. 193 **Visitor information** ✉ See Penghu National Scenic Area Administration, p. 194 ■

Craggy boulders and steep stone cliffs, here on Liang, typify Matsu Islands scenery.

The urbanized and industrialized areas along the coast are not without their attractions, but the beauty of the central west unfolds in the Central Mountain Range, revealing the most magnificent scenery in Taiwan.

Central West

Pineapples in abundance in the fertile Central West

A Taichung street near Fengle Park is the place to stop for an afternoon snack.

Central West

THE CENTRAL WEST REGION'S WIDE COASTAL CORRIDOR REVEALS JUST how crowded Taiwan is. Almost every square inch of land is utilized in constantly switching landscapes of urban, industrial, and rural life. The outskirts of one city merge into the beginnings of the next. In between paddies of rice and patchworks of pineapple and banana plantations nudge the perimeters of smoke-belching factories and the perimeter fences of suburban homes. On the east side, the scene changes markedly. Here, the low-lying coastal plains abruptly yield to the towering peaks of the Central Mountain Range.

The Central West region radiates from the urban hub of Taichung, Taiwan's third largest city, which is easily accessible from Taipei along the arterial Sun Yat-sen Freeway. Many visitors use the city as a base for trips to the region, drawn not only for its geographical convenience, but also for a nightlife that many believe surpasses that of Taipei.

While the coastal area does have a few attractions, including the historic former river port of Lugang and the riotously ornate Chaotian Temple in Beigang, it is the region's mountains that attract most interest.

A little northeast of Taichung, at Dongshih (Dongshi), begins the north branch of the extraordinary Central Cross Island Highway, an engineering marvel that climbs to over 10,000 feet (3,300 m) on its 172-mile (277 km) serpen-tine journey to the east coast. High up into the mountains at Lishan, the highway branches; one route continues northeast to Ilan County and the other east to Dayuling. At Dayuling is another split, where one branch heads east through to Taroko Gorge (see pp. 134–139), while another swings southwest, reaching its highest point near the snow-dusted slopes (in winter at least) of Hehuanshan, before a steep and winding descent to picturesque Wushe, nestled in a lush valley and surrounded by mist-shrouded mountains. About 16 miles (25 km) southwest is the city of Puli, near the geographic center of Taiwan. (Note that because of instability the Central Cross-Island Highway has been closed indefinitely from just east of Guguan to just west of the Deji Reservoir. All traffic now goes through the Puli-Wushe branch.)

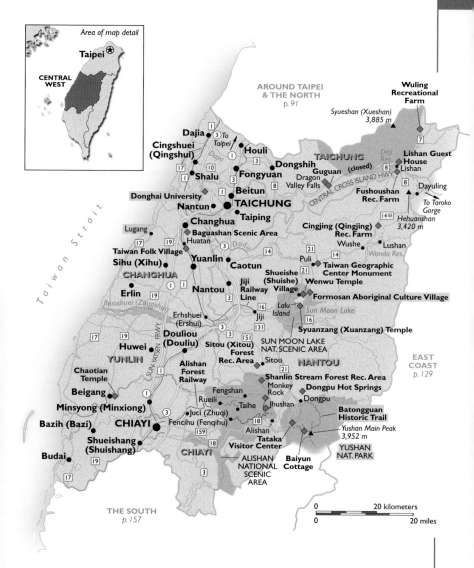

South of Puli, the evocative beauty and serenity of Sun Moon Lake has made it one of Taiwan's most popular resorts, especially among honeymooners.

The narrow-gauge Alishan Forest Railway begins its amazing 44.7-mile (72 km) climb into the mountains of Alishan National Scenic Area from the city of Chiayi. The railway climbs from 100 feet (30 m) above sea level to 7,460 feet (2,274 m) in three and a half hours.

You'll find the head of Taiwan's most popular trail, leading to the peaks of the country's tallest mountain, Yushan (Jade Mountain), about 12 miles (20 km) east of Alishan. Tackling the summit of Yushan Main Peak (the highest peak at 12,966 feet/3,952 m above sea level) and other nearby peaks is for experienced climbers only. Views from the peaks reveal the drama of Taiwan's Central Mountain Range at its best. ■

Taichung

Taichung

⬛ Map p. 209

Visitor information

✉ Taichung Tourism
Information Service
Center, IF, 95
Gancheng St.,
Nantun District

☎ (04) 2254-0809

🕐 Closed Sat.–Sun.

**National
Museum of
Natural Science
& Botanical
Gardens**

www.nmns.edu.tw

✉ Guancian
(Guanqian) Rd.

☎ (04) 2322-6940

🕐 Closed Mon. &
Chinese New Year's
Eve and Day; open
Mon. if national
holiday

💲 $ (free Wed. before
10 a.m.)

**National Taiwan
Museum of Fine
Arts**

www.tmoa.gov.tw

✉ 2 Wucyuan
(Wuquan) West Rd.,
Sec. I

☎ (04) 2372-3552

🕐 Closed Mon.

🚌 Bus: 10, 11, 30,
40, 59

**Taiwan's third
largest city,
Taichung has one
of the island's
liveliest nighttime
entertainment
scenes.**

WITH A POPULATION OF ABOUT ONE MILLION, TAICHUNG
is Taiwan's third largest city. Its economic success comes from its
wealth of small and medium-size enterprises. It also has a reputation
as an educational and cultural center, and its nightlife is renowned
around the island. The city is a good base for travel in the region.

Boutiques, tea shops, outdoor cafés,
restaurants, and art galleries flank
busy **Jingming 1st Street,** a 110-
yard-long (100 m) pedestrians-only
road in the city's hotel and shopping
district—a popular place for locals
and tourists alike to gather.

Fronting the city's Botanical
Gardens, about half a mile (1 km)
east of Jingming 1st Street, the
**National Museum of Natural
Science** has plenty of interactive
exhibits to keep you—and the
kids—amused. At the entrance to
the museum, the **Path of
Evolution** runs 240 yards (220 m)
to the main building, with plants
and trees arranged to represent
Taiwan's different seasons and
climactic conditions. There are also
IMAX shows in the Space Theater.

The adjoining **Botanical
Gardens,** with its enormous
covered area that simulates the
climate and ecology of a tropical
rain forest, is worth a look.

From the Botanical Gardens, a
belt of parkland runs south for a
mile (1.6 km) to the gardens of the
**National Taiwan Museum of
Fine Arts.** In the gardens, along
with numerous sculptures, are 50
stone tablets embellished with
calligraphy representing different
calligraphic schools and styles from
imperial China. The museum,
which was badly damaged during
the September 1999 earthquake but
since rebuilt, concentrates on Chinese
art and antiquities; it also has temporary Western art exhibitions.

Heading east from the National
Museum of Natural Science along

Jiansing (Jianxing) Road, you can't
miss the blue glazed-tile roof of
Baojue Temple *(140 Jiansing/
Jianxing Rd., tel (04) 2233-5179).*
The temple's showpiece is a huge
gilded statue of a portly, laughing
seated Buddha. The 88-foot-high
(26.8 m) image sits on a hollow
pedestal used as a meeting hall, and
the pedestal's facade is inscribed
with Chinese characters meaning

"happiness to all." Smaller pot-bellied Buddha images are scattered around the temple complex.

At the end of Jiansing (Jianxing) Road, a right turn onto Shuangshih (Shuangshi) Road, Section 2, brings you to the city's **Martyrs' Shrine**—a fine example of classical Chinese palace architecture. It commemorates 72 Chinese who were beheaded in 1911 by the Manchu court at the beginning of the republican revolution. Next door, the **Confucius Temple** *(30 Shuangshih/Shuangshi Rd., Sec. 2, tel (04) 2233-2264, closed Mon. & Sept. 15–28 for Teachers' Day prep)* differs from other temples dedicated to China's most famous philosopher because of its Song dynasty palace-style architecture, where the section of temple roof extending over the eaves curves downward rather than flaring heavenward.

The **Folk Hall** in **Taichung Folk Park,** north of Baojue Temple on the city's outskirts, is built in splendid Hokkien architectural style, with its characteristic U-shaped layout and needlepoint roofs. The park's plaza is used for various cultural and folk performances.

For something a little different, head to the privately run, 74-acre (30 ha) **Encore Garden,** 6 miles (10 km) northeast of the city center. The neatly kept patchwork of European- and Japanese-style landscaped gardens is dotted with models of famous European statuary. ■

Taichung Folk Park

- ✉ 73 Lyusyun (Luxun) Rd., Sec. 2
- ☎ (04) 2245-1310
- ⏱ Closed Mon.
- 💲 $
- 🚌 Bus: 14, 34, 105

Encore Garden

- ✉ 41 Boyuan Ln., Minjeng Li
- ☎ (04) 2239-1549
- 💲 $$$
- 🚌 Bus: 2, 60

Changhua

Changhua

◭ Map p. 209

Visitor information

www.chcg.gov.tw

✉ Cultural Affairs Bureau, Changhua Cty. Govt., 416 Jhongshan (Zhongshan) Rd., Sec. 2, Changhua City

☎ (04) 722-2151

CHANGHUA IS A NON-DESCRIPT CITY JUST TO THE SOUTH-west of Taichung, generally visited briefly as a transit point for international tourists traveling to the nearby historic town of Lugang (see pp. 213–214). But locals flock here to see its famous hilltop Buddha image. A few other sights in the town and surrounding countryside nicely round out a visit.

(272 tonnes)—is hollow, allowing you to climb inside and check out the views through the image's ears and eyes. Dioramas inside the statue trace the Buddha's life, teachings, and philosophy. Behind, a three-tiered pavilion and an eight-level pagoda flank a three-story temple.

The city's **Confucius Temple** (*6 Gongmen Rd.*) was built in 1726, making it one of Taiwan's oldest Confucius temples. Although it has been rebuilt eight times, it maintains some of its original Qing dynasty architectural elements. The temple is notable for its carvings in the main shrine and inscribed tablets praising Confucius from the Qing Dynasty ruler, Emperor Qianlong (*R. 1736–1796*), and the late R.O.C. President Chiang Ching-kuo.

About 3 miles (5 km) south of Changhua, along County Route 137 in Huatan, the **Taiwan Folk Village** (*30 Sanfen Rd., Wanya Village, Huatan Township, tel (04) 787-2029, $$$ (NT$ 620), closed Mon., www.tfv.com.tw*) show-cases traditional Taiwanese culture—and more. In the "Historic Taiwan" section, about a hundred build-ings—houses, workshops, small factories—are modeled after typical Taiwanese and ethnic-minority structures. The village also includes areas devoted to "Taiwan Today," with arcade games and waterslides; "Taiwan of Tomorrow," with an aquarium and biology museum; and "Space-Time Performance," featur-ing a boat ride in which visitors experience natural disasters. ■

You can walk inside Changhua's giant hilltop Buddha to view dioramas of Buddhist teachings.

On the eastern outskirts of Chang-hua city, the main attraction at **Baguashan Scenic Area** (*13-7 Guashan Rd., Changhua City, tel (04) 728-9608, www.trimt-nsa.gov .tw*), is the 100-foot-tall (30 m) black concrete statue of the Buddha at **Great Buddha Temple.** The Buddha—which weighs 300 tons

Lugang

DURING THE QING DYNASTY, LUGANG BUSTLED WITH THE arrival of immigrants and trading junks from the mainland Chinese province of Fujian. But the Japanese closed this river port soon after they occupied Taiwan in 1895 to stop the flow. The port's waters thereafter silted over and became useless, and the town receded into a place of little consequence. These days, preservation and restoration of its Qing dynasty architecture—much of it hidden in narrow winding lanes—along with its temples and craftsmen's shops lure visitors.

Lugang

Map p. 209

Visitor information

www.lukang.gov.tw

Lugang Cultural Foundation, 66 Fusing (Fuxing) South Rd.

(04) 778-0096

Most of Lugang's attractions lie on the main avenue of **Jhongshan (Zhongshan) Road,** which cuts through town, or in the lanes that run off it. Off the southern end of Jhongshan Road, on Cingyun (Qingyun) Street, more than 300,000 sacred texts are housed at the **Civil Shrine/Martial Temple/Wenkai Academy,** a combination of shrine, school, and temple built in 1824. Classical buildings with sweeping tiled roofs and minimal ridge ornamentation, along with detailed wall inscriptions, lend a peaceful air to the compound, befitting its history as a center for Taiwan's 19th-century Taiwan's scholars and literati.

North from the academy along Jhongshan Road—just past the junction with Changlu Road—a left on Sanmin Road leads to the **Longshan Temple,** devoted to Guanyin, goddess of mercy. Longshan, or Dragon Mountain, was first built early in the 17th century and moved to its present location in 1786. It is regarded as one of Taiwan's most architecturally significant and best-preserved Qing dynasty temples, famed for the circular carved ceiling in its main hall that towers above the enshrined image of the goddess, and classical Chinese murals by famed artist Guo Sin-lin (Xin-lin). Its courtyards and halls exude a more tranquil ambience than other Taoist temples, enough to earn it the

moniker "Taiwan's Forbidden City."

Looking distinctly out of place in a town that sells itself as a Chinese cultural center is a European-style villa housing the **Lugang Folk Arts Museum** *(152 Jhongshan/Zhongshan Rd., tel (04)*

777-2019, $ (NT$ 130). The building, designed for a wealthy local landholder by a Japanese architect in 1919, is imposing with its bold, cream-colored facade, arched windows, and flanking cupola-topped cylindrical towers. Inside, displays include old furniture, fittings, jewelry, photos, handicrafts, books, clothing, and plenty of interesting Chinese curios.

Farther north along Jhongshan Road, a left turn on Minzu Road takes you to the brick-paved **Nine Turns Lane (Jinsheng Lane).**

The imposing facade of the Lugang Folk Arts Museum draws as much interest as the displays housed inside.

Lugang's Putou Street

The narrow lane, often called Breast-Rubbing Lane because people have to turn sideways to pass, was built to prevent the entry of bandits and protect against strong northeasterly winds that hit the town starting each September.

Traditional handicraft shops—some dating back more than a hundred years—line Jhongshan Road. A number of them craft religious images, decorations, and paraphernalia (given the number of temples in the town, that's not surprising), while others turn out wooden furniture, tinware, fans, lanterns, embroidery, and pottery. Worth a visit is the **Wu Dun-hou Lantern Shop** *(312 Jhongshan Rd., tel (04) 777-6680)*, where Taiwan's greatest master of this delicate craft creates exquisitely painted lanterns. A few doors up (No. 439), the smell of sandalwood pervades the 200-year-old **Shih (Shi) Jin-yu Incense Shop** *(tel (04) 777-9099)*, which uses a secret blend of ingredients to produce handmade incense famous throughout Taiwan.

Running parallel to Jhongshan Road, **Old Market Street** comprises three narrow lanes—Putou, Yaolin, and Dayu—edged with renovated Qing dynasty-style shophouses selling crafts, toys, clothing, and other nostalgic paraphernalia.

The image of Mazu, enshrined in the town's **Tianhou (Empress of Heaven) Temple** farther north at 430 Jhongshan Road, is thought to have been brought to Lugang in 1684 after Qing dynasty forces took the island from Ming dynasty loyalists. This legend has made this ornate temple extremely popular with pilgrims. ■

Nantou County

LYING AT THE GEOGRAPHICAL HEART OF TAIWAN, NANTOU County is mainly mountainous. A number of forest recreation areas that can be explored by car or on foot exemplify its natural beauty.

One of these—the best known—is **Sitou (Xitou) Forest Recreation Area,** where National Taiwan University cultivates more than one million tree and bamboo shoots every year on its terraced nurseries; they are distributed throughout Taiwan for reforestation projects. The recreation area also comprises vast groves of bamboo (40 percent of Taiwan's bamboo comes from here), cypress, cedar, and pine. Numerous trails lead through the forest. The most popular hike follows a creek south from the main gate for about a mile (1.6 km) to a 150-foot (46 m) cypress tree, reckoned to be 2,800 years old. Its size and age have earned it the privileged title of "sacred tree." Bamboo is put to practical use at the bamboo bridge spanning **University Pond,** found along a hilly trail about three-quarters of a mile west of the main gate (1.2

km). Shops at Sitou's tourist village, just outside the main gate, sell souvenirs made mainly from bamboo.

About 12.5 miles (20 km) south and higher into the mountains, **Shanlin Stream Forest Recreation Area** *(contact Nantou Cty. Govt. Tourism Bureau)* presents a more rugged face. From just inside the tollgate, a trail leads off along a boulder-strewn creek and through thick forests of cedar and pine for about half a mile (800 m) to tumbling **Green Dragon Waterfall.**

East of Shanlin Stream, **Dongpu Hot Springs** *(Dongpu Rd., Dongpu, tel (049) 270-1616)* is a high-mountain resort that combines hot-springs soaking with some scenic—and rigorous—hikes. After hiking all day, soothe your muscles at any of a number of the hotels that have spring water tapped into their premises. ∎

Nantou County
- Map p. 209

Visitor information
- ✉ Nantou County Government Tourism Bureau, 66 Jhongsing (Zhongxing) Rd., Nantou City
- ☎ (049) 222-2106, ext. 226 & 308

Sitou (Xitou) Forest Recreation Area
- ✉ Visitor center, 10 Forest Ln., Neihu, Lugu Village, Nantou County
- ☎ (049) 261-2111

Vast bamboo forests in Sitou (Xitou) Forest Recreation Area explain the abundant use of it as a building material.

The glorious Deji
Reservoir is
just one of the
many superlative
vistas along the
Central Cross
Island Highway.

Central Cross Island Highway

THE CENTRAL CROSS ISLAND HIGHWAY STRETCHES FOR 172
miles (277 km) from Dongshih (Dongshi), northeast of Taichung, to
Taroko Gorge on the island's east coast, with branches going north
to Ilan and southwest to Puli. The scenery along the route offers continuous beauty unsurpassed in all the rest of Taiwan. You get it all:
subtropical forests, waterfalls tumbling from cliff faces, roaring rivers,
placid lakes, mountain hot springs, cloud-filled valleys, alpine forests,
and mountain peaks that—if you're lucky—are dusted with snow.

Ten thousand workers—many
decommissioned Nationalist soldiers originally from the mainland
and with little or no means of support—toiled on the construction of
this spectacular engineering project
for four years, until its completion
in 1960. The route follows early
aboriginal trails, widened by the
Japanese, through tortuous ravines,
under cliff faces, and along steep
and friable mountainsides.

From **Dongshih (Dongshi),**
a town severely damaged in the
September 21, 1999, earthquake
(see sidebar p. 218), the highway

just to the north of the village.

Less than half a mile south of Lishan village, an arched gate marks the entrance to **Fushoushan Recreational Farm** (*29 Fushou Rd., Lishan Village, Heping Township, Taichung County, tel (04) 2598-9205, $*). The farm grows a variety of temperate-climate fruits on its terraced hills, which you can gaze upon from a lookout. Ponds and pavilions dot the farm, while walking trails head farther into the mountains. The farm is especially beautiful between March and May, when peach and apple trees blossom and azaleas and mountain dandelions carpet the hillsides.

From Lishan, you have a choice: Go northeast on the Ilan branch to Syueshan (Xueshan) and Wuling Recreational Farm; or southwest toward the junction at Dayuling.

ILAN BRANCH

If you choose the northern route, in **Wuling** you can arrange mountaineering expeditions to **Syueshan (Xueshan),** or Snow Mountain, Taiwan's second highest peak at 12,746 feet (3885 m). The difficult ascent begins at Wuling and takes between 10 and 12 hours. Views on the way up, as you would expect, are magnificent. The climbing seasons are between October and December and March and April. At other times, snow, rain, wind, or the chance of landslides make the ascent too risky.

The popular mountain resort of **Wuling Recreational Farm** (*3 Wuling Rd., Pingdeng Village, Heping Township, Taichung County, tel (04) 2590-1259, $$*) was established in 1963 to provide work for decommissioned military servicemen. Pear, peach, and apple orchards and tea plantations, spreading over 1,730 acres (700 ha) of terraced hillsides, flourish in the crisp alpine air.

passes emerald rice paddies and orchards for 12 miles (20 km) to **Guguan (Valley Pass),** a hot-springs resort that also received its share of quake damage. From the resort, a mile-long (1.6 km) trail leads through a lush valley to the 250-foot (76 m) **Dragon Valley Falls.**

From Guguan, the highway climbs steeply, winding to the mountain resort of **Lishan,** a spectacular two-hour drive from Guguan (see note). Lodges and restaurants cling to precipitous mountainsides flush with apple, pear, and peach orchards. Trails take you to views of towering peaks, broad valleys, and the huge emerald green **Deji Reservoir** far below,

Note: The Central Cross-Island Highway has been closed indefinitely from just east of Guguan to just west of the Deji Reservoir. All traffic now goes through the Puli-Wushe branch.

Hehuanshan Visitor Center

✉ 170 Renai Rd.,
Renai Township,
Nantou County

☎ (049) 280-222

Among the casualties of the devastating 9-21 Earthquake was this temple in Jiji, Nantou County.

Earthquake!

Taiwan gets its share of earthquakes. The most devastating recent one occurred at 1:47 a.m. on September 21, 1999, measuring 7.3 on the Richter scale. The quake, with its epicenter along the Chelongpu fault line near the resort area of Sun Moon Lake, was so violent that it toppled buildings in Taipei, 93 miles (150 km) away. A total of 2,405 people were killed, 10,718 injured. Around 30,000 buildings were destroyed and 25,000 damaged. The number of homeless was estimated at 100,000. The worst of the devastation was in the Central West region, with just about every city, town, and village suffering damage. ∎

Trails lead to magnificent views of surrounding mountains.

SOUTH TO DAYULING & BEYOND

If you go south from Lishan, you'll come to Dayuling in 19 miles (30 km), and another choice: You can go east to the unforgettable **Taroko Gorge** (see pp. 134–139). Or, you can take the highway southwest, rising steeply along wide expanses of grassland and arrow bamboo, with stands of pine, with views to distant rocky summits, to **Hehuanshan**—the Mountain of Harmonious Happiness—rising 11,220 feet (3,420 m) above sea level. Gentle slopes and a relatively regular winter snowfall once made Hehuanshan the only place in Taiwan suitable for skiing, but warmer climactic conditions over the past few decades have affected ski conditions, and the ski lift has been dismantled. Even so, as soon as the media report that one of the infrequent snows is expected, droves of people show up for the unusual Taiwan experience.

Even without snow, Hehuanshan serves up plenty of nature-appreciation opportunities. From highway stopping points near the summit, you can take a number of short hikes that offer riveting views of the lofty area. The **Hehuanshan East Peak Trail** leads up past the site of the old ski lift to the summit of the mountain's eastern peak, offering fantastic views of the Central Mountain Range. The round-trip takes two hours.

Heading southwest beyond Hehuanshan, the highway begins a steep, winding descent, past the grassy plains of Kunyang and the maple forests of Yuanfeng, before reaching **Cingjing (Qingjing) Recreational Farm** (*Young Lion Mountain Hostel, Jenai Township, Nantou County, tel (049) 280-2748*),

one of the numerous (and popular) farms that offer urban Taiwanese the chance to watch cattle and sheep graze in green fields.

Misty mountains all but enclose the aboriginal settlement of **Wushe** (*visitor center, 2 Renhe Rd., Renai Township, Nantou County, (049) 280-2205*), 2 miles (3 km) south of Cingjing. In 1930 a bloody uprising by local aborigines was put down by Japanese troops, leaving 1,000 aborigines and 200 Japanese officials dead. A plaque in the village's temple recalls the event. The village has a few stores selling artifacts and handicrafts. Nearby, a trail winds down to the emerald **Wanda Reservoir.**

The hot-springs resort of **Lushan,** 5 miles (9 km) east of Wushe, sits on both sides of a rock-strewn river gorge. A long, slightly swaying suspension footbridge high above the river joins the two sections, giving you a choice of

hot-springs inns on either side.

Following the highway's southern section for another 16 miles (26 km) southwest brings you to sprawling **Puli.** The city suffered greatly from the 1999 earthquake, as the many vacant blocks (now cleared of rubble from ruined buildings) attest. The town is famous for its beautiful women, pleasant weather, and its rice wine, which is said to get much of its taste from the quality of the area's water. The **Puli Winery** (*219 Jhongshan/Zhongshan Rd., Sec. 3, tel (049) 290-1649, www.plwinery.com .tw*) was founded in 1917, when it began producing its famous Shaohsing rice wine. It has a small museum and display center, and offers samples. The **Taiwan Geographic Center Monument,** half a mile (1 km) northeast of town, by the Central Cross Island Highway, marks the dead center of Taiwan. ■

The scenery at Cingjing (Qingjing) Recreational Farm, seemingly more Alpine than Asian

Sun Moon Lake

Sun Moon Lake

🅰 Map p. 209

Visitor information

www.sunmoonlake.gov.tw

✉ Sun Moon Lake National Scenic Administration, 136 Jhongsing (Zhongxing) Rd., Sun Moon Lake, Yuchih (Yuchi) Township, Nantou County

☎ (049) 285-5668

SUN MOON LAKE IS ONE OF TAIWAN'S MOST POPULAR resorts, especially favored by honeymooners. It is at its best at dawn and dusk, when the low-set sun washes its waters in gentle hues of orange and red and mist swathes the surrounding hills in a scene redolent of a classic Chinese painting. On bright, cloudless days, the bluish green lake waters sparkle with stunning intensity. The man-made attractions of temples and pagodas that dot Sun Moon Lake's shoreline add to the area's beauty.

The lake gets its name from two lakes, Sun and Moon, which existed side by side before a hydroelectric dam project undertaken by the Japanese flooded them into one. The construction of the dam had an upside. Sun Moon became Taiwan's largest lake, spreading over 3.5 square miles (9 sq km) and creating a beautiful, evocative place.

The dam project, however, also had it downside. The Thao, a local

Sun Moon Lake's mood changes moment to moment, according to the whims of the light and swirling mists.

results can be savored in lakeside restaurants. The tribe also has been given a say in the development of **Sun Moon Lake National Scenic Area,** established in response to the 1999 earthquake to help reattract tourism and help locals recover more quickly from the devastation (see sidebar p. 218). The scenic area comprises the lake and surrounding hills.

On its north shore, **Sun Moon (Shueishe/Shuishe) Village** is the lake's main settlement, with a number of hotels, restaurants, and souvenir shops. It is also one of a number of places you can rent rowboats, canoes, and paddleboats, or take an organized lake cruise. Here is also the main pier for boat cruises *(Shuishe Pier, tel (049) 285-5054)*, now framed by a lovely boardwalk that reaches around the lake. The shore-hugging boardwalk will eventually circle the lake.

DRIVING AROUND THE LAKE

A winding road rings the lake, serving up some lovely lake and mountain views along its route and allowing you to reach most attractions without too many navigational problems.

East from Sun Moon Village, past the scenic area's north tollgate, is **Wenwu Temple,** built grandly into the hillside in three ascending levels. At the lower levels, shrines honor warrior deities Guangong and Song dynasty hero Yueh Fei (Yue Fei). A hall dedicated to Confucius sits on the upper level, the lofty positioning symbolizing the power of knowledge over the path to war. At the foot of the stone steps leading to the temple, balancing on concrete globes, are the two largest stone lion temple guardians in Asia. Both are painted bright red and look suitably fearsome. The lack of clambering ceramic statuary

aboriginal tribe that lived and still lives by the lakeshore, were forced off the slopes of the high hill sitting between the two lakes to allow flooding of the basin. The top of the hill—today's **Lalu Island**—is still exposed, but the tribe's burial grounds on the lower reaches were flooded, as was their main village. The Thao consider the isle a spiritual place—the maples you see on it are sacred—and local authorities are no longer allowed to cruise boats or land tourists on the island. The government is working toward reconciliation with the Thao. The isle is now in the tribe's control, and they use the surrounding waters for aquaculture—their

Nationalist leader Chiang Kai-shek built Cihen (Cien) Pagoda, or Pagoda of Filial Virtue, in honor of his mother.

along the ridges enhances the graceful lines of the temple's classical multitiered roofs, which sweep over the colorful patterned eaves and are supported by carved dragon columns. Meticulously trimmed bonsai and animal topiary decorate the temple's courtyards, while ornate colonnades and stairways connect its side halls and pavilions. From the hill behind the Confucius shrine you can gaze down over serene Sun Moon Lake.

Above the northeastern shore of the lake, nearby **Peacock Garden** was built in 1968 at the behest of President Chiang Kai-shek, who reasoned it would help bring tourists to the lake. It's unlikely you'll ever see more peacocks gathered in one spot.

The road meanders south to **Dehuashe,** on the lake's southeastern edge. What was a few years ago a half-hearted attempt to portray an authentic aboriginal village is now in the control of the Thao, who have reclaimed the area as ancestral land and developed it into a community whose housing and lifestyles reflect traditional styles. The settlement, which because of

its concentration of aboriginal denizens is also appropriately called Sun Moon Village, has a handicraft center and holds cultural performances for tourists.

Syuanzang (Xuanzang) Temple perches high on a bluff off the lake's ring road along the lake's southern shore. It was built in 1965 to house and display some of Taiwan's holiest Buddha relics. Illuminated in a gold, jewel-encrusted, miniature pagoda on the altar in the main shrine are seven *shelizih (shelizi)* nuggets—found among the cremated ashes of highly revered monks that Tang dynasty monk Syuanzang (Xuanzang) brought back from his pilgrimage to India.

Like many temples in Taiwan, Syuanzang Temple combines Buddhism and Taoism, evidenced by the shrine to Guanyin, the goddess of mercy, on the second floor. Another small pagoda on the third floor holds what is believed to be a small piece of the skull of Syuanzang.

Near Syuanzang Temple, a 550-yard (500 m) steep climb leads to **Cihen (Cien) Pagoda** (Pagoda of Filial Virtue). Climb to the top level of the 157-foot (48 m) structure for superb lake views. This is one of the more peaceful places you'll find in the area, on weekdays at least. Decorative elements lace the ridges of its nine-tiered roofs, while its white balustrades contrast neatly with the tower's ocher walls. Chiang Kai-shek, who had the pagoda erected in honor of his mother, inscribed the tablet over the front archway entrance.

At the tip of the same promontory on which Syuanzang Temple sits is the similar-sounding minor **Syuanguang (Xuanguang) Temple.** From a pier in front, you can hire rowboats or motorboats for the short trip around Lalu Island. ∎

Formosan Aboriginal Culture Village

SPRAWLING OVER 153 ACRES (62 HA) ABOUT A MILE AND A half (2.5 km) east of Sun Moon Lake, the Formosan Aboriginal Culture Village presents a cultural microcosm of Taiwan's 11 government-recognized aboriginal groups. The park also has tacked on an incongruous European-style chateau and garden and an enormous amusement park. Although these features tend to belittle any attempt to seriously showcase Taiwan's indigenous minorities, the park does allow visitors to gain some understanding of their history and culture.

Formosan Aboriginal Culture Village
www.nine.com.tw
 Map p. 209
✉ 45 Jintian Ln., Dalin Village, Yuchih (Yuchi) Township, Nantou County
☎ (049) 289-5361
💲 $$$ (NT$ 650)

Structures and lifestyles of Taiwanese aboriginal groups are displayed at the Formosan Aboriginal Culture Village.

The **Aboriginal Village Park** organizes the Tao, Ami, Atayal, Saisiat, Tsou and Thao (together in one area), Bunun, Puyuma, Rukai, and Paiwan ethnic minority groups each within its own "traditional village." You can catch a cable car from the entrance to the park's highest point, then wander along pathways leading down the hillside to explore the "villages." Despite the park's exploitative tinge, much effort has gone into the reproduction of the dwellings and attendant arts and crafts of the minority groups, with authentic materials used in their construction. The aboriginal village employs aborigines from each of the 13 tribes to work in the "villages," acting as guides, creating local handicrafts, selling inexpensive traditional snacks, and putting on song and dance performances. Signs throughout the park let you know of the times of performances.

The **European Palace Garden** is an expanse of lawn, flowerbeds, statuary, and fountains fronting a faux-baroque chateau. A restaurant inside the chateau serves Chinese and Western dishes. **Future World** offers several movie theaters, including the enormous-screen Showscan Theater. Between the European-style gardens and the Aboriginal Village Park, **Amusement Isle** serves up some adrenalin-surging rides. At its entrance, **Cultural Square,** festooned with aboriginal totems and sculptures, features aboriginal music and dance performances and demonstrations of traditional craftmaking. ■

Taiwan's aborigines today

The fortunes of Taiwan's 455,000 indigenous peoples (or aborigines, as they are called on the island) have followed a similar path to those of the native peoples of the United States, Canada, and Australia, where recognition and appreciation of their culture exists, but, in the main, they're still marginalized from mainstream society.

Beginning in 1945, during Nationalist rule, little thought was given to the welfare and cultures of the aboriginal groups. Many had been assimilated, adopting Chinese names, while a dwindling number still held to their traditional lifestyles high in the mountains and in more remote areas in the east and offshore. The physical resemblance of some of the aborigines to the Chinese led to a "don't ask, don't tell" policy, in which people of native heritage kept their origins to themselves.

In the 1990s, the fortunes of Taiwan's aborigines began to improve. In keeping with a global trend, the groups became more assertive in their demands, and the government responded. In 1992 it launched a six-year plan to promote aboriginal culture and provide subsidized medical care, legal advice, and business loans. At the same time, it began to improve roads that link isolated aboriginal villages with nearby cities, and native land in mountainous regions was zoned as reservation land and cannot be sold to non-natives.

The government programs fuelled a renewed interest in all things aboriginal. The first native theme bars opened in Taipei in the early 1990s, and the trend picked up as aboriginal restaurants became popular and native food items appeared on Chinese restaurant menus. Aboriginal music and dance became trendy, and annual tribal festivals are now well attended. Woodcarving demonstrations are common in public parks in Taipei, native-motif clothing is fashionable, and authentic souvenirs—some of them very expensive—decorate homes and outdoor public spaces around the island.

Even the standard Chinese appellation has changed, from *shandiren,* or mountain people, to *yuanzhumin,* or original people. Some aborigines are beginning to forsake their Han Chinese names and return to traditional tribal names.

The overall educational and income levels of Taiwan's native peoples, however, lag behind those of the Chinese-descent majority, and many suffer from chronic social problems like alcoholism, unemployment, and prostitution. Another concern is the fading away of native languages and traditions. Facial tattooing is long gone, and shamanism has largely given way to more conventional religion, especially Christianity. Aboriginal languages are still spoken, but native speakers are declining in number, and young people are speaking Mandarin and Taiwanese. Tribal chiefs and other leaders are still respected, but elected officials hold the real power and have undermined their traditional authority.

A movement is afoot in Taiwan to return some tribal lands to the aborigines and to give them autonomy in those lands. Such a move, combined with the recent assertiveness of the aboriginal tribes and the surge of interest in aboriginal culture, would help ensure that tribal traditions are maintained. ∎

Top left: Aboriginal groups celebrate the Harvest Festival. Bottom left: Elders maintain traditions and culture. Below: Rukai aborigines perform a tribal dance. Cultural performances are common among Taiwan's aborigines and draw increasing crowds of tourists.

Beigang's
Chaotian Temple
www.matsu.org.tw
🅰 Map p. 209
✉ 178 Jhongshan
(Zhongshan) Rd.,
Beigang, Yunlin
County
☎ (05) 783-2055

Pilgrims flock to Chaotian Temple, one of the island's most important and colorful temples honoring the deity Mazu, the protector of seafarers.

Beigang's Chaotian Temple

BEIGANG IS FAMED FOR ITS OUTSTANDING CHAOTIAN Temple, dedicated to popular deity Mazu, the goddess of the sea. Of the 400 or so Mazu temples scattered around Taiwan, Chaotian— originally constructed in 1694—is one of the most important. It stands out as an extravagant example of temple architecture, exceeding the riotous flamboyance found in most of Taiwan's temples.

More than a million pilgrims visit Chaotian Temple (Palace Facing Heaven) every year, so it is usually crowded. During the week-long festival running up to Mazu's birthday, which falls on the 23rd day of the third moon of the lunar year (April or May), it erupts into a cacophony of noise and color.

Chaotian's most striking element is its multitiered roofs, with their ridges, eaves, and curving beams piled high with glazed ceramic figurines and images that depict a vast array of mythological characters and scenes.

A curving beam rising heavenward tops the main shrine hall. In the center sits a pagoda flanked by two balancing dragons. A colorful muddle of ceramic deities, beasts, and mythological scenes supports the beam. Below, rising from both sides of the ridge of the top tier, dragons and other figures balance on more curving beams. The central tier is completed with large ceramic figures of the star gods of longevity, prosperity, and posterity.

The intricate and masterly stone dragon pillars inside the main building were carved in 1775. A lot of the other decorative work inside also dates from the Qing dynasty. In the temple's courtyard, devotees burn paper offerings at a three-level pagoda, while the temple's benefactors—of which there are many—are honored in tall Buddha image cones flanking the temple's altars, with each cone featuring hundreds of small images of the Buddha lit up by a small light. ∎

Alishan

Alishan
🗺 Map p. 209

ALISHAN IS ONE OF TAIWAN'S MOST FAMOUS TOURIST attractions. People come here mainly to see the sunrise at Jhushan (Zhushan), when thick clouds throw a fleecy white carpet of clouds into the valleys, leaving only jagged mountain peaks pointing heavenward. Alishan can be reached by road, but a far better journey is on the scenic Alishan Forest Railway, which departs from Chiayi.

The Alishan Forest Railway winds its way up into the mountains from Chiayi to Alishan.

ALISHAN FOREST RAILWAY

The delightful Alishan Forest Railway is one of the world's great short train rides, not least because of the superlative scenery and the magnitude of the feat of engineering involved in its construction. From the town of **Chiayi** (see p. 232), locomotives haul postcard-pretty red-and-cream carriages from 100 feet (30 m) above sea level on a narrow-gauge railway for 45 miles (72 km), reaching 7,461 feet (2,274 m) above sea level at Alishan Forest Recreation Area, home of one of the world's highest-altitude railway stations. Along the way, the railroad crosses 77 bridges and passes through 50 tunnels. In 1899 the Japanese, intent on exploiting these inaccessible and heavily forested mountains for logging, began building the railway. It was not until 1912 that the line reached Alishan.

The railway begins its three-and-a-half-hour climb in a mundane fashion, rumbling past fields of banana and pineapple plantations on the outskirts of Chiayi for 8.5 miles (14.2 km), before beginning its dramatic climb into the mountains. It corkscrews around lofty **Dulishan** before pushing farther up the mountain along precariously steep inclines. The train negotiates the final, and steepest, section of the climb through a series of switchbacks before pulling into Alishan.

Along the way, passengers are treated to scenes of precipitous pointed peaks shrouded in mist and

dropping thousands of feet to distant valleys. Bamboo forests dominate the lower reaches of the track before giving way to dense cedar and pine forests clambering up steep mountainsides.

The main destination for most people is the **Alishan Forest Recreation Area,** Alishan's main hub. From here, toylike steam locos pull carriages even farther into the mountains to nearby Jhushan and Alishan's famous sea of clouds (see p. 228); the Mianyue Line branches off along the way, moving 5.7 miles (9.2 km) from Alishan Station north past sweeping valley scenery below to the end of the line at **Monkey Rock,** 8,041 feet (2,451 m) above sea level.

ALISHAN FOREST RECREATION AREA

This forest recreation area has plenty of hotels, restaurants, and

Alishan Forest Railway

✉ Taipei Main Railway Station ((02) 2311-1024); Chiayi Beimen Railway Station ((05) 276-8094); Alishan Station ((05) 267-9833)

🕐 Leave Chiayi at 9 a.m. & 1:30 p.m. daily; Alishan at 1:18 p.m. & 1:40 p.m. daily. Trip takes 3.5 hours.

💲 $$$

Alishan National Scenic Area

www.ali.org.tw

⚠ Map p. 209

✉ 3-16 Chukou Village, Fanlu Township, Chiayi County

☎ (05) 259-3900

💲 $ (certain sections, including Alishan Forest Recreation Area)

Harbinger of a new day, the sun peeks over the mountains at Jhushan (Zhushan) in Alishan.

other amenities. Peaceful and serene during the week, Alishan metamorphoses into a noisy, jam-packed mess of traffic, tour buses, and people on weekends.

Roads and a number of trails wind around the recreation area, taking you to all the requisite sights, although trying to find a decent map of the trails can be the most challenging part of the experience.

The easy-to-negotiate, 2.5-mile (4 km) **Alishan Loop Trail** begins from behind Alishan House—spectacular in springtime with its many blossoms. Among its many sights are the thousand-year-old **Three Generations Tree**—a massive cypress crowned by a 10-foot-high (3 m) second tree; and **Tree Spirit Pagoda,** which commemorates a stand of noble and ancient trees ignobly cleared in 1936. It also passes by two temples, the simple Buddhist **Cihyun (Ciyun) Temple;** and the ornate Taoist **Shoujhen (Shouzhen) Temple,** reconstructed in 1969. The peaceful **Sister Ponds** are said to be the manifestation of two aboriginal girls who drowned themselves rather than submit to the demands of a brutish local chief. This part of the trail, called the **Wood Forest Corridor,** slices through one of Taiwan's densest stands of ancient red cypress.

JHUSHAN

An early morning, 30-minute train journey from Alishan's quaint railway station takes you farther up the mountain to Jhushan, famed for its beautiful sunrise views of sawtoothed peaks poking out of a sea of fluffy clouds. The clouds move in huge billowing waves, which sometimes swallow the island-like mountain peaks. Because of fickle weather, this unforgettable sight cannot always be guaranteed. Dress warmly; it's always fairly cold

before dawn on the mountaintop.

It's best to start the trip up the mountain about 45 minutes before sunrise. Your hotel will tell you when the sun will rise and wake you in time to catch the train or minibus.

Jhushan can also be reached on a one-hour walk along a paved path and stone steps. The route is easy to pick out in the dark, especially if you visit on a weekend when hundreds of other tourists lead the way.

At the large deck at the summit, a board points out the positions of **Yushan** (see pp. 230–231) and other mountains, as well as sunrise points in different seasons; you can buy local breakfast foods while you wait for the sun to appear. When it does, peeking diamondlike above a ridgeline, the crowd gasps, hundreds of cameras click, and the rush for a space on the train for the ride back down begins.

OTHER AREAS IN ALISHAN

The scenery around the small village of **Fengshan,** northwest of the forest recreation area, is a magnificent collection of primeval forests, steep rocky precipices, and tumbling waterfalls set in one of the most pristine environments in all of Taiwan. Hiking is the main attraction here, with a number of forest trails leading off to superlative vistas of the mountains, including the 7,008-foot-high (2,136 m) **Siaotashan (Xiaotashan),** which spends most of the year shrouded in mist.

At **Laiji,** south of Fengshan on County Route 149, you can peer over a sheer mountain precipice shaped like the sharpened bow of a huge ship that drops more than 200 feet (60 m).

The **Rueitai (Ruitai) Old Mountain Trail** wends its way east–west through a magnificent bamboo forest for about 2 miles (3 km) between the towns of Rueili (Ruili) and Taihe, west of Laiji. Alishan's bamboo forests are exceptionally tall, rising as high as 30 feet (10 m) in some areas, producing a still, eerie effect. You can get to Rueili from the Alishan Forest Railway's Jiaoliping Station by shuttle bus.

About halfway between Chiayi and Alishan along the Alishan Forest Railway is **Fencihu (Fenqihu),** a heavily forested and scenic area. The place is avoided by most tourists, who head straight to the Alishan Forest Recreation Area, so it is decidedly less crowded. A number of trails lead from the small settlement into the surrounding forests. One winds its way toward the peak of **Dadongshan,** where sunrise-watching crowds also gather. ■

Yushan National Park

Yushan National Park

www.ysnp.gov.tw

⚠ Map p. 209

Shueili (Shuili) Visitor Center

✉ 300 Jhongshan (Zhongshan) Rd., Sec. 1, Shueili (Shuili) Township, Nantou County

☎ (049) 277-3121, ext. 242

$ $

Tataka Visitor Center

✉ 118, Taiping Rd., Tongfu Village, Sinyi (Xinyi) Township, Nantou County

☎ (049) 270-2200

🕐 Closed second and fourth Tues. every month

Note: Class A climbing permits ($) are required to climb Yushan. You can obtain them at the Shueili Visitor Center; forms can also be downloaded from the park website and mailed in.

RISING 12,966 FEET (3,952 M) ABOVE SEA LEVEL, YUSHAN—Jade Mountain—is Taiwan's highest mountain. Paths leading to its peaks are well maintained, but exposed ridges and steep inclines make them challenging. If you're experienced, fit, and equipped, this is the place to discover the intimidating beauty of Taiwan's mountains.

Yushan National Park's 407 square miles (1,055 sq km) are found within the Central Mountain Range, including 11 connecting peaks that form a cruciform shape, with Yushan Main Peak at the apex. Broadleaf forests dominate the park's lower altitudes, giving way to coniferous and bamboo forests at mid-altitudes and, finally, at the highest elevations, to arrow bamboo, conifers, and rocky outcrops. On the mountainsides, endangered species, including the Asiatic black bear and sambar deer, are staging a comeback, though sightings are rare. You are more likely to see Taiwan macaques and goatlike serows.

Among the park's six hiking routes, the most popular is the **Yushan Peaks System,** which allows you to reach up to six of Yushan's 11 peaks, including the Main Yushan Peak. The starting point of the main trail is reached from **Tataka Visitor Center,** 8,563 feet (2,610 m) above sea level. From the visitor center, it's a 1.7-mile (2.7 km) walk along the Tatajia Saddle to the trailhead for the Yushan main-trail. Another 4.1-mile (6.6 km) climb brings you to **Baiyun (White Cloud) Cottage,** which is used as a base for tackling the peaks of the Yushan Peaks System. It is the usual first day goal and the only place on the mountain that has accommodations; it sits 11,550 feet (3,520 m) above sea level.

If you want to catch the sunrise at **Yushan Main Peak,** you'll need to awake at about 3 a.m. for the one-and-a-half to two-hour walk to the summit. Along the last bit, you climb on bare rock face, where fences and chains have been erected to help negotiate the tricky footing, as well as protect climbers against blasts of wind along the exposed rocky area known as **Wind Tunnel.** At the top await the magnificent panoramas of the

Central Mountain Range to the east, Alishan's peaks to the west, and drop-offs to lowlands thousands of feet below.

The trail to the 12,175-foot (3,711 m) **Yushan South Peak**—a series of rocky peaks cut with deep valleys either side—branches off from the Main Peak path a short distance above Baiyun Cottage. The views are just as spectacular as those at the Main Peak, but fewer climbers give the South Peak a more isolated feel. It takes longer (about three and a half hours) to reach the South Peak, but the climb is less arduous.

The 11,575-foot (3528 m)

Yushan West Peak, a 2.5-mile (4 km) hike from Baiyun Cottage, is the easiest of Yushan's peaks to climb. The trailhead is found directly behind the cottage.

To get to the summit of 12,575-foot (3833 m) **Yushan North Peak** from Baiyun Cottage, take the trail toward the Main Peak until it reaches the last ridge before the peak. Instead of turning right to the Main Peak, turn left and head down the steep ridge. The round-trip takes about three hours. An alternate descent route is the **Baton-gguan Historic Trail** (see p. 232), which links Yushan North Peak to the hot-springs resort of Dongpu. ■

Yushan, Taiwan's tallest mountain, has numerous peaks rising over 10,000 feet (3,000 m). Climbing any of these peaks requires a high fitness level and experience.

More places to visit in the Central West

Left: A digoxin, one of lower Yushan's many springtime wildflowers. Right: Stone lions guard the entrances to most temples in Taiwan. This one, at a Taichung temple, also serves as a hat stand.

a perpendicular rock face. From here, a steep section of the trail leads to Dongpu. The trip from Baiyun Cottage to Dongpu takes about 10 hours, so you need to start early.
 Map p. 209 **Visitor information** ✉ See Yushan National Park, pp. 230–232

CHIAYI

This small city between Tainan in the south and Taichung is the departure point for the wonderful **Alishan Forest Railway** (see p. 227). If you plan on traveling up the mountain by train, you'll likely find yourself staying here for at least one night. The city is pleasant enough, but does not have a lot to offer visitors. The city has a number of temples. On Mincyuan (Minquan) Road, in the center of town, **Beiyu Temple** (North Hell Temple) is worth a look for the image of its god of hell, housed on the seventh floor of the temple's main tower. The temple was originally built in 1697 to house the image, which was brought by immigrants from mainland China. It was completely renovated in the 1970s. As you would expect in a temple enshrining such a fearful god, there is a lot of appeasement going on by way of food offerings and paper burning. On Wenhua Road, near the railway station in the city's center, **Chiayi Night Market** is a good place to try the Taiwanese snack foods, especially Chiayi specialties.  Map p. 209 **Visitor information** ✉ Chiayi City Govt. Tourism Bureau, 199 Jhongshan (Zhongshan) Rd., Chiayi City ☎ (05) 225-4321, http:// travel.chiayi.gov.tw.

DONGHAI UNIVERSITY

The university—a 20-minute drive northeast of downtown Taichung—has one of Taiwan's most attractive campuses. Spread over 343 acres (139 ha) of largely wooded area, many of the campus's buildings have been created in the Tang dynasty style, which incorporates a more graceful and subtle form from the more

BATONGGUAN HISTORIC TRAIL

The 95-mile (152 km) trail was completed in 1875 to link the east and west coasts. Much of it is now overgrown, but one section, linking Yushan North Peak in **Yushan National Park** (see pp. 230–231) to the hot-springs resort of **Dongpu**, is maintained for hikers. The route offers an alternative descent route back down from Yushan Main Peak. Instead of returning to the base camp at Baiyun Cottage, you can continue down the trail to Yushan North Peak. Follow this trail until it leads steeply off to the right down a gravel slope; the routes to the North Peak and to the Batongguan trail are marked at the fork. A chain fence helps you from slipping. The actual trailhead is found 3.7 miles (6 km) beyond. This leads down to spectacular views of Yushan. The trail continues to fall gradually with meadows giving way to forested areas. Just before Dongpu, at Father and Son Cliff, the trail has been carved out of

ornate Ming period architecture. The unadorned tiled roofs of the buildings sweep over wide colonnaded eaves, evoking a suitably cloistered air. Clashing with this calm is the university's postmodernist **Christian Chapel,** made to look like two hands in prayer pointed skyward; it was designed by notable Chinese-American architect I. M. Pei. ⓂMap p. 209 ✉ 181 Taichunggang Rd., Sec. 3, Taichung ☎ (04) 2359-0121

JIJI RAILWAY LINE

Until the 1980s, this narrow-gauge railway between Changhua and Nantou Counties hauled logs out of the forest to a lumber mill in the picturesque village of Jiji. Today, it is Taiwan's most popular scenic railway. The trip, which takes just under an hour, starts from the restored colonial-style railway station at Jiji and winds through forests and past spectacular mountain backdrops for 19 miles (30 km). ⓂMap p. 209 **Visitor information** ✉ Jiji Visitor Center, 61 Mingniou (Mingniu) Rd., Jiji, Nantou County ☎ (049) 276-2546

TAICHUNG METROPOLITAN PARK

Expansive Taichung Metro Park sits on a plateau at Dadushan, on the northwest edge of the city. The park's centerpiece is a large semicircular man-made pond set amid willow trees, while its grounds are scattered with assorted artifice. It is a favorite spot for stargazers and lovers taking in romantic views of Taichung city's twinkling lights and the city's harbor on the coast. A walkway leads from the pond to a plaza and a convex chart set into the ground that maps the heavens. After dark, the map is lit up and can be used to plot the current position of stars and constellations, with reference by dates printed on its outer rim. A path winds through a protected area of thick acacia groves on the park's periphery, which in the evening comes alive with sounds of chirping cicadas and blinking fireflies. You can rent bicycles at the main gate. ⓂMap p. 209 ✉ 30-3 Sipin South Lane, Situn District, Taichung ☎ (04) 2461-2483 Ⓢ $ ■

Lights blaze at Taichung Metropolitan Park, a favorite spot for stargazing and moonlight walks.

Travelwise

**Straw figures outside a
Jhudong (Zhudong) shop,
Hsinchu County**

TRAVELWISE INFORMATION.

PLANNING YOUR TRIP

WHEN TO GO

Taiwan is enjoyable any time of the year, although the weather is at its most delightful across the island from mid-September until November. During these months, the skies are sunny, humidity low, and there is little rainfall.

Travel is difficult over the Chinese New Year holidays (January or February). During this period, public transportation is packed; taxis hike their rates; hotels are heavily booked and their rates may double; and shops, offices, and government departments close.

During Ghost Month—late August or early September—many superstitious Taiwanese are reluctant to travel, so crowds at sites are smaller.

Locals tend to visit major tourist sites on weekends. Try to organize your itinerary so that you explore cities on the weekends and favored country-side locations during the week.

CLIMATE

Taiwan straddles the Tropic of Cancer, with two distinct seasons—chilly and damp, and hot and humid. Between December and March, when the winds come from the northeast, the north and east coastal regions are cool with heavy cloud cover and frequent drizzle. Temperatures start to rise in April as the winds shift to the south-southwest. By May across the island, the temperatures consistently rise above 86°F (30°C), and days begin to feel sticky and uncomfortable. However, the average daily temperature is a comfortable 72°F (22°C), with lows ranging from 54° to 63°F (12° to 17°C).

Rains start in May, with the heaviest downpours in June, July, and August. These are typically short, heavy afternoon thun-derstorms, but the skies are clear and sunny between showers. Rainfall drops off and temperatures become milder by mid-September. This is the harbinger of the island's "winter."

In the mountains, summer rainfall is heaviest, but temperatures are mild and afternoon fog common. Winters are drier and colder at higher elevations, but snowfall is not common.

The southwestern section of the island is more subtropical, with two distinct seasons. Characterized by mild to warm sunny days, the cool season runs from November to March. Average temperatures during the hot months hover around 86°F (30°C)—marginally cooler than Taipei. During the hot season, afternoon thunderstorms usually last a couple of hours.

Taiwan is subject to frequent buffeting by typhoons, usually between July and October. Due to the island's closeness to the Asian landmass, temperature swings vary during the winter. Chilling monsoon winds sweep down from Central Asia and can send the mercury plummeting 20°F in just a few hours.

WHAT TO BRING

From May to October, pack light summer clothes, along with a waterproof jacket for the almost daily showers. Smart, casual slacks and a light dress jacket for men and smart dress for women would be suitable for dining in the better restaurants. Also bring a warm pullover or jacket if you plan to visit mountain areas even during the hot summer. For the cooler months pack warmer clothing.

If you plan to hike, bike, or motorcycle, high-quality wet-weather gear is a must. But there is no need to buy it before you come—this type of gear, and camping equipment, is inexpensive in Taiwan.

Don't forget sunglasses and a wide-brimmed hat for protection.

Also remember the umbrella. Footwear should include dress shoes for the best restaurants, sneakers, and sandals. A sturdy pair of hiking boots is also recommended if you plan on taking to the mountain trails.

How you dress can determine how you are treated. Clothes should always be clean and neat. Women should dress modestly. Although long shorts are acceptable street wear, you might feel more comfortable in a skirt or light slacks. For men, clean shorts, T-shirts, and sandals are acceptable city wear. Flip-flops are not proper street wear, nor are vests without a shirt.

Carry toilet paper with you, as most public rest rooms do not supply it. Although sanitary napkins are widely available, tampons are not.

INSURANCE

Arrange for travel insurance to cover penalties for missed flights, medical costs for illness and injury, and lost or stolen property. If you plan some active pursuits like cycling, surfing, paragliding, etc., you may require additional coverage.

If renting a car, check the coverage included in the rental price. You should be able to purchase additional insurance from the car rental company.

Theft or loss of property covered by insurance should be reported to the Foreign Affairs Police (see Emergency Numbers, p. 243). You will need a police report to file a claim.

ENTRY FORMALITIES

VISAS

Citizens of the United States, Canada, Australia, New Zealand, Britain, Japan, and a number of European and other countries (30 in total) can stay in Taiwan for 14 days without a visa. On arrival, those visitors can obtain a 30-day visa by filling out a form, supplying two passport photos, and handing over

NT$1,500. (U.S. citizens are exempt from this charge.)

Visitors must have outbound tickets and valid visas (if required) for their next destination. Their passports need to be valid for at least six months. Neither the 14-day non-visa nor 30-day visa can be extended. If a longer stay is required, an application must be made at representative offices overseas. These types of visas allow you to stay 60 days, and they can be extended twice for a maximum stay of 180 days.

If you overstay your visit, you could be subject to a grilling by police and immigration, and a fine. If you have overstayed, it is best to report to the immigration department first. Trying to explain yourself at the airport could result in a missed flight.

For visa extensions or overstays, contact the Bureau of Consular Affairs, Ministry of Foreign Affairs, 3rd Floor, 2-2 Cinan (Qinan) Rd., Sec. 1, Taipei, tel 2343-2888.

You can get visas for Taiwan from these overseas representative offices:

United States
Taipei Economic & Cultural Office–Washington, D.C.
  4201 Wisconsin Ave., N.W.
  Washington, DC 20016-2137
  tel 202/895-1800
  fax 202/363-0999
  e-mail tecrotcd@erols.com
Taipei Economic & Cultural Office–Los Angeles
  3731 Wilshire Blvd., Ste. 700
  Los Angeles, CA 90010
  tel 213/389-1215
  fax 213/389-1676
  e-mail info@tecola.org
Taipei Economic & Cultural Office–New York
  1, East 42nd St.
  New York, NY 10017
  tel 212/317-7300
  fax 212/754-1549
  e-mail teco@tecony.org
Australia
Taipei Economic & Cultural Office
  Suite 1902, Level 19 MLC
  Center, King Street
  Sydney, NSW

  tel (2) 9223-3233
  fax (2) 9223-0086
  e-mail syteco@bigpond.com
Canada
Taipei Economic & Cultural Office
  151 Yonge St., Ste. 501
  Toronto, ON M5C 2W7
  tel 416/369-9030
  fax 416/369-9189
  e-mail yyz@mofa.gov.tw
United Kingdom
Taipei Representative Office
  50 Grosvenor Gardens
  London SW1W OEB
  tel (20) 7881-2650
  fax (20) 7730-3139
  e-mail tro@taiwan-tro.uk.net

CUSTOMS

Those 20 or over may import one liter of alcoholic beverages, 25 cigars, 200 cigarettes, or one pound of tobacco products duty free. Things prohibited and in some cases punishable by heavy fines and imprisonment include counterfeit currency or forging equipment; gambling apparatus or foreign lottery tickets; pornographic materials; publications propagating communism; weapons (including real or toy gun-shaped devices and assault knives); illicit and narcotic drugs; pirated or copyright-infringed goods; and endangered animals or animal parts.

When leaving Taiwan, an outbound declaration form is required if taking out: gold; antiques; over $10,000 in U.S. currency, or over NT$60,000 currency notes; and commercial samples or dutiable items such as personal computers or professional photo equipment that will be brought back into the country for sale. For information, contact the Directorate General of Customs, Ministry of Finance, 13 Dacheng St., Taipei, tel (02) 2550-5500, http://eweb .customs.gov.tw.

DRUGS & NARCOTICS

Taiwan bans all restricted substances or drugs that are

non-prescription or non-medicinal in nature. Like most places in Asia, Taiwan does not take kindly to the use of illicit drugs. Trafficable amounts of cocaine, opium, heroin, methamphetamines, and other narcotic drugs can bring the death penalty. Even small amounts of marijuana for personal use can result in a prison term. Clearly label medicines for personal use and have a doctor's prescription. If you are required to carry a large amount of pharmaceuticals, have a letter from your doctor to that effect.

HOW TO GET TO TAIWAN

AIRLINES

Taiwan is served by Taiwan Taoyuan International Airport in Taipei, and Kaohsiung International Airport in the south, which serves mainly Asian destinations.

Around 40 international airlines fly to Taiwan's Taiwan Taoyuan International Airport, including American, Continental, and Northwest from the U.S. Taiwan's flag carrier China Airlines and more respected EVA Air also have daily flights from North America, Europe, Oceania, and most of Asia. Other major carriers include British Airways, KLM, and Cathay Pacific.

The flight time from New York is 18 hours; from London and Sydney 13 and 9 hours.
International airline offices in Taipei
  Air Canada, tel 2507-5500
  American, tel 2563-1200
  British Airways, tel 2512-6888
  Cathay Pacific, tel 2715-2333
  China Airlines, tel 2715-1212
  Continental, tel 2719-5947
  Delta Airlines, tel 2551-3656
  Eva Airways, tel 2501-1999
  Northwest, tel 2772-2188
  Qantas, tel 2559-0508

TAIPEI'S AIRPORT
Taiwan Taoyuan International Airport is connected to downtown Taipei by expressway—

about 28 miles (45 km) away. There are two terminals at the airport, the aging Terminal I and the newer Terminal II.

The Taiwan Tourism Bureau (tel (03) 398-2790) has a desk in the arrivals hall of both terminals. The helpful staff will provide maps, book you into a hotel at a discount rate (just about every hotel in Taipei is on their list), and arrange a limo for you. Nearby these desks are a number of hotel representative desks, where you can also book a room and arrange limo transport; the limo cost is NT$1300 to NT$1500—equivalent to taxi fare. Limo charges can be added to your hotel bill, and no driver tip is necessary.

Alternatively, you can follow the signs in the terminals to the taxi stands, where waiting taxis (in various conditions) will transport you downtown or its environs. A 50 percent surcharge is added to the fare—at least NT$1100–1200. There is no surcharge for taxis to the airport, but drivers will be reluctant to take you there for less than NT$1000. Four bus companies provide frequent service from the airport terminals, stopping at designated spots in Taipei, including major hotels. One-way fares range from NT$110 to NT$140.

Car rentals are also available at both terminals.

There are currency exchange booths at the airport, as well as ATMs where you can withdraw cash from credit card accounts or from banking networks such as Cirrus and Maestro.

GETTING AROUND

TRAVELING IN TAIWAN

BY AUTOMOBILE

You need a valid driver's license, an international driver's license, and steely nerves to drive in Taiwan. It certainly takes getting used to. Traffic laws are both enforced and flaunted. Most

roads are heavily traveled, and impatient drivers seemingly have no qualms making death-defying passing maneuvers. Trucks, buses, and military vehicles demand, and usually get, right of way.

If you are not familiar with road conditions, it may be best to hire a driver along with the car. Most hotels can arrange this. A good idea is to use public transport between cities, and hire a car and driver for in and around the cities.

Many road signs are not in English, and English-language road maps are hard to find. Cars in Taiwan are driven on the right, and all occupants are required to wear seat belts. Police sometimes stop cars, and drivers are fined for traffic infringements not always well defined.

If you are intent on renting a car, you can do so at major airports and at downtown locations. Some car rental companies allow customers to return cars to other locations, although a surcharge may apply. Full insurance coverage may not be included in the cost. Make sure you ask, and opt, for a plan that is comprehensive.

BY DOMESTIC AIRLINE

Taiwan's domestic airline network is extensive, with four airlines providing regular flights to numerous cities on the island, as well as to Penghu, Matsu, Kinmen, Green, and Orchid Islands. Fares are inexpensive—a flight from Taipei to Kaohsiung costs about NT$2,200. You can usually buy tickets at the airport before the flight, but it is better to book ahead. You will be required to show your passport before boarding any flight.

Domestic airlines
Far Eastern Air Transport, tel 2715-1921
Mandarin Airlines, tel 2514-2077
TransAsia Airways, tel 2718-6062
UNI Airways, tel 2715-6969

BY FERRY

A regular network of ferries links Taiwan proper to its outlying islands. Travel agents can book trips. Because of frequent inclement weather, service is unpredictable; always confirm ahead by phone.

Strait Islands
Keelung to Matsu takes 8 hours.
Nangan
tel (083) 626-655 (Dongyin)
or (083) 677-555 (Matsu)
Sinhua (Xinhua) Navigation
tel 2424-6868 (Keelung)
Kaohsiung to Kinmen takes 10 hours.
Hefu Marine
tel (07) 551-3112
Jinhan Marine
tel (07) 332-9588
Kaohsiung to Magong (Penghu islands) takes 4.5 hours.
Taiwan Navigation
tel (07) 561-5313

East coast Islands
The ferry from Taitung to Green Island takes 35 to 50 minutes; from Taitung to Orchid Island takes 2 to 3 hours; and from Green Island to Orchid Island takes 1.5 to 2.5 hours.
Victory
tel (08) 928-1047
Jiou-Xin Ferry
tel (08) 932-0413
Long-Hon Marine
tel (08) 928-0226
Xinfa Marine
tel (08) 928-1477

BY INTER-CITY BUS

Frequent and inexpensive luxury coaches travel almost everywhere in Taiwan. You can purchase your tickets through a travel agent, your hotel, or at the bus station. During the holidays, expect to be caught up in crowded conditions.

Inter-city bus companies
Guoguang Bus Corp., tel (0800) 010-138
Free Go Express, tel (02) 2586-3065 (Taipei)
Toward You Air Bus Co., (0800) 088-626
United Highway Bus, tel (02) 2995-7799 (Taipei)

BY TRAIN

Taiwan's rail network is comprehensive, inexpensive, and efficient, albeit a little complicated. It can be crowded on long weekends and holidays, so it is best to avoid trains at these times.

Four main lines—western, eastern, northern, and southern—form the core of the network. Making a reservation through a travel agent assures you of a guaranteed seat. Five types of services exist. The air-conditioned services are Zihciang (Ziqiang), the rapid express; Jyuguang (Juguang), the first-class express; and Fusing (Fuxing), a limited express. The other two, Pingkuai and Putong, are slow, non-air-conditioned, and have no reserve seating. They are not recommended.

The information counter at Taipei Main Railway Station (tel 081-231-919 toll-free) is very helpful in arranging round-trip tickets. Information desks at larger stations generally have someone who speaks English and will be helpful in arranging tickets, but you may need to insist if you want to reserve a seat.

Reservations for express trains can be made up to 14 days in advance. It is best to pick up the ticket at least one day before; you will need to show your passport for identification. You can also book online at www.railway.gov.tw.

Some classes provide complimentary snacks, while meals are available in a casual dining car.

A 215-mile (345 km) high-speed railway (HSR) from Taipei to Kaohsiung came online in Jan. 2007 with stations at Taoyuan, Hsinchu, Miaoli, Taichung, Changhua, Yunlin, Chiayi, and Tainan. It slices travel time from 4.5 hours to just 90 minutes (www.thsrc.com.tw).

TRAVELING IN TAIPEI

BY CITY BUS

Buses run from 6 a.m. to 11:30 p.m. and cost NT$15 for each leg of the route. Drop the money in a coin box next to the driver when getting on the bus if you see a "SHANG" sign. Pay again if the same character shows in red when you get off. Each of the many city routes has both a number and starting-ending points written in Chinese, now often in English, which means it can get a little confusing. "The Bus Guide" to Taipei, available at hotels and major bookstores, may bring a little clarity. You can get to most destinations in the city by combining the MRT and inexpensive taxis, diminishing the need to catch a bus.

BY MRT

Taipei's mass rapid transit (MRT) system is one of the best and most extensive in Asia. Its five interconnecting lines can take you to, or close to, most of the city's attractions. The system's signs, maps, and information are in English. Tickets vary from NT$20 to NT$65 depending on distance, or you can purchase a one-day pass for NT$150. You can also purchase stored-value tickets. Charts at the ticket machines show how much money you need to get to your destination, and exits are clearly marked. Maps in English are also posted in stations showing major points in the immediate area. The MRT runs from 6 a.m. to midnight.

Metro Taipei Service Hot Line, tel (0800) 033-068 or (02) 2181-2345 (8:30 a.m–5:30 p.m.)

BY TAXI

Taipei and other major cities have an abundance of taxis that can be hailed virtually anywhere. Fares around the cities are cheap, with most intra-city trips costing around NT$100 to NT$130. Longer trips in the city or to suburbs may cost NT$300. Charges in Taipei are NT$70 for the first 0.9 mile (1.5 km) and NT$5 for each additional 0.2 mile (300 m). An additional NT$5 is charged for every two minutes of waiting, and a 20 percent

Place-names

A frustration for visitors to Taiwan is the different transliterations of Chinese place-names into English. Various city and county administrations can't seem to agree on a standard method, tussling over the use of Wade-Giles, and the tongyong and hanyu pinyin systems. The transliterative creative flair and individualism of makers of tourist maps, street directories, and road signs around the island—who often circumvent the nation's official tongyong system—make matters even more bemusing. For example, a major road may be spelled variously Pate, Pateh, and Bade. And that's an easy one. Some transliterations are so varied as to defy a logical connection. This guide uses the tongyong method, followed by hanyu in parentheses if the spelling is different.

surcharge is added to fares between 11 p.m. and 6 a.m. An extra NT$10 is charged if you phone for a cab or for luggage placed in the trunk. For out-of-town or long-distance trips, meters are not used, so negotiate a fare beforehand.

Most drivers do not speak English, so have the hotel staff write your destination in Chinese. Hotels have name cards available with their name and address written in English and Chinese. Always carry one. Taipei has a young English-language learning program for drivers, and graduates can carry a special identifying marker in their window; but don't expect much. For complaints you can call the Taipei Foreign Affairs Police at 2556-6007.

PRACTICAL ADVICE

PRACTICAL ADVICE

COMMUNICATIONS

POST OFFICES

Taiwan has fast and efficient postal service. Mail takes five to seven days to reach the U.S. The post office's express mail service speeds the delivery time by about two days, and is less expensive than international courier services. Most articles are delivered within Taiwan in 24 to 48 hours. Post offices are open from 8 a.m. to 6 p.m. Monday through Friday. Some of the bigger post offices are also open from 8 a.m. to 4 p.m. on Saturday.

Taipei's Central Post Office (tel (0800) 099-246) is at the North Gate intersection close to Taipei Main Railway Station. Workers in the international section speak English and packaging can be purchased.

Most hotels will mail items. Otherwise, drop stamped articles into red mailboxes; the left-hand slot is for airmail, right for prompt delivery. With green mailboxes, the right-hand slot is for mail within the city, the left-hand for elsewhere

TELEPHONES

The international dialing code for Taiwan is 886. To call Taipei from overseas, add the prefix "2" to the local number. To call Taipei from within Taiwan, the prefix is "02." From Taiwan dial 002 for international direct dialing access.

For directory assistance in English, dial 106. The international operator can be reached at 100 from private phones only, and dialing 108 will get the reverse-charges operator.

Both local and international calls can be made from pay phones. Local calls are NT$1 per minute. To keep talking, keep adding coins. The digital display keeps count of how much time you have left. For international calls, buy phone cards, International Direct Dial cards or

IDDs from any of the 7-Eleven convenience stores around the island, and find a pay phone that is marked as IDD capable. Some hotels have phones that take major credit cards.

If you bring a mobile phone, buy a replacement SIM card that will give you a local number and a certain number of minutes. The cards can be purchased from mobile phone retailers. Before the number can be used, you must register and provide a few details and passport number. This is done by dialing the number provided on the SIM card packaging. A card with a hundred minutes of calling time will cost about NT$600. This can be added to by buying a phone card from convenience stores with a number code. You dial the number code on your mobile phone and the extra time is allocated.

Alternately, buy a mobile phone when you arrive. Fierce competition in the telecom market has made them available at knockdown prices. The penetration rate of mobile phones in Taiwan is over 90 percent, so you shouldn't have a problem phoning someone.

INTERNET

There are many Internet cafés in the cities—usually inhabited by teenagers playing video games—where you can send e-mails or surf the Web. They charge by the minute but are cheap—sometimes well under NT$1 per minute. Competition also means sites open and close regularly.

Hotels have Internet access from computers in their business centers, and charge about NT$200 per hour or more.

CONVERSIONS

Taiwan uses the metric system for weights and measures. An ancient Chinese system is also used in certain circumstances; it's not necessary to know, but be aware it exists.

1 kilometer = 0.6 mile
60 kph = 30 mph

1 kilo = 2.2 pounds
1 liter = 1.75 pints
Temperatures are in centigrade
0°C = 32°F
Chinese system weights
1 liang (tael) = 1.2056 ounces
1 jin (catty) = 16 liang = 1.32 pounds

ELECTRICITY

Taiwan uses the same standards for electricity as the United States: 110V, 60 Hz AC. Flat two-pin plugs are used for connection. If your devices do not match these, you will need to bring a power adapter and plugs. Hotels also have adapter plugs.

HOLIDAYS

The Taiwanese keep in touch with their traditions and culture with numerous festivals throughout the year. Most have their origins in Taoism, Buddhism, or Chinese folk religion, so the dates vary based on the lunar calendar. In many cases they are raucous and riotously colorful affairs rich in costume, action, and religious symbolism. With the exception of the sedate Chinese New Year festival, it is worth planning your visit to coincide with one of the island's major festivals.
January 1 Founding Day of the Republic of China
January/February Chinese New Year (Lunar New Year's Eve and first, second, and third day of first lunar month)
February 28 Peace Memorial Day
April 5 Tomb Sweeping Day
May/June Dragon Boat Festival (fifth day of fifth lunar month)
September/October Mid-Autumn Festival (fifteenth day of eighth lunar month)
October 10 Double Tenth National Day

LIQUOR LAWS

You must be 20 to buy and consume alcohol in Taiwan. Bars and pubs open between 5 p.m. and

7 p.m. and stay open until around 3 a.m., some stay open until 5 a.m. Eating and drinking are commonly combined into a single pursuit at restaurants. Beers and spirits are sold in convenience stores.

MEDIA

MAGAZINES
Regional and international magazines such as the *Far Eastern Economic Review, Time, Newsweek,* and *The Economist* are sold at large bookstores and in hotels.

Other national English or bilingual magazines in Taiwan include the news and current events magazine *Taipei Review; Taiwan Panorama* covers social and political issues. *This Month in Taiwan* is a travel and listings magazine, as is *Travel in Taiwan.*

NEWSPAPERS
Taiwan enjoys a high degree of press freedom and a vibrant and competitive newspaper industry. There are numerous Chinese-language papers, along with the English-language dailies: *China Post, Taiwan News,* and *Taipei Times.* These papers carry local, regional, and international news. The English publications are available at most newsstands and hotels.

The regional *Asian Wall Street Journal* and the *International Herald Tribune* are printed in Taipei and available on news-stands and in hotels. *USA Today* is also widely available.

RADIO
ICRT (International Community Radio Taipei) is Taiwan's only English-language radio station. Its FM channel broadcasts separate programming, including popular Western music, talk shows, and community service segments. It's at FM100.7MHz (100.1 in Hsinchu and the south) and AM576MHz.

TELEVISION
About 80 percent of Taiwan homes have cable television with more than 90 channels available. Most hotels have cable television

featuring a number of English-language international satellite and cable channels including: National Geographic, Australia Asia Pacific Television, BBC World, Star, Cinemax, CNBC, CNN, Discovery, and ESPN.

MONEY MATTERS

The New Taiwan dollar (NT$) is the unit of currency. While it varies slightly from day to day, the exchange rate generally hovers around NT$33 to the U.S. dollar. You will find 1, 5, 10, 20, and 50 dollar coins, and 100, 200, 500, and 1,000 dollar bills. A 2,000-dollar note is in circulation, but is rarely encountered in everyday use.

Major foreign currencies can be exchanged for NT$ at larger banks (smaller banks do not deal in foreign exchange), international hotels, and the island's international airports in Taipei and Kaohsiung. Most banks charge a fee for cashing traveler's checks.

Traveler's checks can only be cashed at banks and hotels. To exchange money at a hotel, you may need to be a guest—almost always the case for cashing traveler's checks—and hotels tend to exchange at lower rates.

Receipts are given when exchanging currency. Keep them! They must be presented in order to redeem unused NT$ before departure. Wait until you are at the airport to change back your money; the foreign exchanges there are more familiar with the process and have more currencies. (It can be difficult to exchange NT$ outside of Taiwan.) Note, there are no foreign exchange booths once you pass through immigration and customs at the airport.

Many ATMs accept international credit cards such as Visa, MasterCard, Diners Club, and American Express, allowing you to withdraw local currency and eliminating the need to carry large amounts of cash or traveler's checks. A growing number of worldwide ATM

networks are found at banks and convenience stores.

You can open a bank account by showing your passport. Banks are open Monday to Friday from 9 a.m. to 3:30 p.m.

Major credit cards are widely accepted.

OPENING TIMES

Business hours are generally 9:00 a.m. to 5:00 p.m.; government hours are 8:30 to 5:30, Monday through Friday. Government offices close for lunch from 12:30 to 1:30.

Department stores are open seven days a week, usually opening between 10:00–11:00 a.m., and closing 9:00–9:30 p.m. Most other retail outlets open earlier (9:00–10:00 a.m.) and close later, around 10 p.m. The 7-Elevens and other convenience stores are open 24 hours a day, seven days a week.

RELIGION

The main religions in Taiwan are Taoism and Buddhism, with many temples incorporating elements of both faiths. There is a significant Christian minority on the island. Churches can be found in most cities and major towns. Protestants make up about 80 percent of the Christian population—mainly Presbyterian—and the remainder are Catholic. The island's Muslims numbers around 60,000.

TAIWAN TOURISM

For information on Taiwan, visit the website of the Tourism Bureau R.O.C at www.taiwan.net.tw or contact the Tourism Bureau at:
    Ministry of Transportation
    and Communications,
    Republic of China
    9F, 290 Jhongsiao E. Rd., Sec.4,
    Taipei, Taiwan 106,
    Republic of China
    tel (02)2349-1635
    fax (02)2771-7036
    e-mail tbroc@tbroc.gov.tw
You may also contact the tourist offices abroad (see p. 242).

Taiwan's central government Tourism Bureau operates tourist service centers at both Taiwan Taoyuan International Airport Terminal I (tel (03) 383-4631), Terminal II (tel (03) 398-3341), and Kaohsiung International Airport (tel (07) 805-7888). The staff hands out maps, brochures, and other helpful information (see pp. 239–240).

Similar materials can be obtained in downtown Taipei. The Tourism Bureau also has travel information service centers in other major cities around the island.

Taipei
240 Dunhua N. Rd.
tel 2717-3737 or (0800) 011-765 (8 a.m.–7 p.m.)
e-mail tisc@tbroc.gov.tw
Kaohsiung
5F-1, 235 Jhongjheng (Zhong-zheng) 4th Rd.
tel (07) 281-1513 or (0800) 711-765 (Mon.-Fri.)
Taichung
4F, 216 Mincyuan (Minquan) Rd.
tel (04) 2227-0421 or (0800) 422-022 (Mon.-Fri.)
Tainan
10F, 243 Mincyuan (Minquan) Rd. Sec. I
tel (06) 2226-5681 or (0800) 611-011 (Mon.-Fri.)
National park and forest recreation area visitor centers provide maps and brochures of varying quality and quantity—not always in English. The Tourism Bureau manages all national scenic areas and provides English materials.

TIME DIFFERENCES

The time difference from Greenwich Mean Time (GMT) is + 8 hours. From New York it is +13 (one hour less during daylight savings time). From Sydney, the difference is -2 hours in winter and -3 hours in summer.

TIPPING

Taiwan does not have a tipping culture, so there is no need to encourage it. Most hotels add a 10 percent service charge to their restaurants and room service. Bellhops are tipped NT$20 per piece of luggage. Some upscale restaurants also have a service charge. Leaving a few coins in a check tray is becoming a more common practice in bars and cafés that don't have a service charge. Taxi drivers don't expect to be tipped.

TOURS

The Taiwan Tourism Bureau (officially known as the Republic of China Tourism Bureau) has a wealth of suggestions for tours and related contacts (see p. 241).

TRAVELERS WITH DISABILITIES

Modern buildings have wheelchair access ramps, but the law does not require them in older buildings. Most top hotels have facilities for people with disabilities, but it is a good idea to ask in advance.

Taipei's MRT system has elevator access for those in wheelchairs. But the crowds during rush hours can make for an uncomfortable travel experience. Other public transport, save the High Speed Rail system, does not provide for disabled passengers.

On the streets, high curbs and uneven surfaces make things difficult, although ramps onto sidewalks in the big cities are becoming common. Street overpasses and underpasses present insurmountable problems for people with walking disabilities. Although most intersections in cities and towns are now equipped with time-countdown "walk" signals, drivers unfortunately often ignore them.

Most government museums and art galleries have facilities for the disabled.

TOURIST OFFICES ABROAD

United States
Taipei Economic & Cultural Office–Los Angeles
3731 Wilshire Blvd., Ste. 780
Los Angeles, CA 90010
tel 213/389-1158
fax 213/389-1094
e-mail latva@pacbell.net
Taipei Economic & Cultural Office–New York
Travel Section
1 East 42nd St., 9F
New York, NY 10017
tel 212/867-1632 or 212/867-1634
fax 212/867-1635
e-mail nyo@tbroc.gov.tw
Australia
Taipei Economic & Cultural Office
Travel Section
Ste. 1904, Level 19, MLC Center, King Street
Sydney, NSW 2000
tel (2) 9232-6942
fax (2) 9233-7752
e-mail info@taiwantourism.org
Canada
Taipei Economic & Cultural Office
Tourism Representative
Travel Section
Ste. 1960, 45 O'Connor St.
Ottawa, ON K1P 1A4
tel 613/231-5025
fax 613/231-7414
United Kingdom
Taipei Representative Office
Tourism Representative
Travel Section
50 Grosvenor Gardens
London SW1W 0EB
tel (20) 7881-2650
fax (20) 7730-3139

EMERGENCIES IN TAIWAN

REPRESENTATIVE OFFICES

Taiwan has formal diplomatic relations with fewer than 30 countries; other countries are represented by trade and commerce offices in Taipei and a few other cities. These places are not embassies, but they do provide similar functions such as issuing visas and replacing lost or stolen passports.

United States
American Institute in Taiwan
7 Lane 134

Sinyi (Xinyi) Rd., Sec. 3
tel 2162-2000
Australia
Australian Commerce Office
26F, International Trade Bldg.
333 Keelung (Jilong) Rd., Sec. 1
tel 8725-4100
Canada
Canadian Trade Office
13F, 365 Fusing (Fuxing)
North Rd.
tel 2544-3000
United Kingdom
British Trade & Cultural Office
9F, 99 Renai Rd., Sec. 2
tel 2192-7000

EMERGENCY PHONE NUMBERS

Fire, ambulance, tel 119
Police, tel 110
Taipei Foreign Affairs Police,
tel 2556-6007
Taichung Foreign Affairs Police,
tel (04) 2327-3875
Kaohsiung Foreign Affairs Police,
tel (07) 221-5796
English-language directory
assistance, tel 106

LOST OR STOLEN CREDIT CARDS OR TRAVELER'S CHECKS

Visa, tel 080-651019
American Express, tel 2719-0606

MEDICAL SERVICES

Hospital treatment in Taiwan is
of a high standard and compared
to Western countries inexpensive. Hotels can call a doctor on
short notice, and hospitals have
outpatient facilities. Emergency
services are available 24 hours at
most hospitals, including:

Taipei
Taiwan Adventist Hospital
424 Bade Rd., Sec. 2
tel 2771-8151
Mackay Memorial Hospital
92 Jhongshan (Zhongshan)
North Rd., Sec. 2
tel 2543-3535
Veterans General Hospital
201 Shihpai (Shipai) Rd.,
Sec. 2
tel 2871-2121

Chang Gung Memorial Hospital
199 Dunhua North Rd.
tel 2713-5211
Kaohsiung
Kaohsiung Chang Gung
Memorial Hospital
123 Dabei Rd.
Niaosong Township
tel (07) 731-7123
Chung Ho Memorial Hospital
100 Shihcyuan (Shiquan)
1st Rd.
tel (07) 312-1101
Taichung
China Medical University
Hospital
2 Yude Rd., Taichung
tel (04) 2205-2121

HEALTH

No special precautions or inocu-
lations are necessary to visit
Taiwan, and there are very few
risks to your health. There have
been some occurrences of the
mosquito-borne virus Japanese B
encephalitis, and dengue fever,
passed by mosquitoes.

Hepatitis A is prevalent in rural
areas where sanitation is poor.
Make sure eating and drinking
utensils are clean in these areas.
Unused, paper-wrapped chopsticks are the best idea. You can
buy a number of sets, for personal use, as a precaution.

Tap water in major cities and
towns is drinkable, but health
authorities advise it should be
boiled first. It may be best to
stick to bottled water.

Hepatitis B and C, present in
Taiwan, can be contracted from
blood transfusion or sexual contact. Although HIV prevalence is
relatively low in Taiwan, it is still
a threat, along with other sexu-
ally transmitted diseases.

Taiwan, along with Hong Kong,
Singapore, Canada, and mainland
China, was hit by Severe Acute
Respiratory Syndrome (SARS)
in the first half of 2003. The
mystery surrounding the virus
created a media event, causing a
huge drop-off in foreign tourists
throughout Asia. By mid-2003
the virus was under control and
very few, if any, new cases have
been reported in Taiwan.

Taiwan's subtropical climate can
cause problems for the unprepared. If hiking or cycling during
hot, humid weather, drink plenty
of bottled water to prevent de-
hydration. Wear a wide-brimmed
hat and apply liberal amounts of
sunscreen (SPF 15 and above),
even under cloudy conditions.

Weather conditions change
rapidly in mountain areas. You
may start your hike with clear
skies and warm temperatures,
but these conditions can
quickly deteriorate. Carry
wet-weather gear and warm
clothes with you.

A prescription is not always
required for drugs in Taiwan.
However, if you are taking any
medications, it is best to bring
a prescription from your doctor
in case you need a refill or
the drugs are lost. If you are
carrying large quantities of
prescription drugs for your
own use, have a letter from
your doctor saying so in case
you are questioned by customs
on arrival.

Many Taiwanese place faith in
both traditional Chinese medicine practitioners and Western
medical practices. Traditional
medicine is geared to prevention
rather than cure. Taiwan is an
ideal place to get checked over
by a such a practitioner.

SAFETY

Heavy bars guarding the windows and doors of most
Taiwanese homes might give
the impression of a dangerous
place, but Taiwan is in fact an
exceptionally safe place to visit.
There is usually no problem
walking in cities and towns day
or night—even for women.
Violent crime against visitors is
virtually nonexistent, and there
is no animosity shown toward
foreign visitors.

Common sense rules need to
be applied to prevent theft. As
anywhere, don't leave luggage or
bags with valuables unattended
in public places. Pickpockets or
snatch thieves do exist, but are
not a big problem.

HOTELS & RESTAURANTS

There are many hotels in Taiwan—especially Taipei—that are of international standard and reasonably priced compared to Western countries. Service is generally efficient and friendly, although you may encounter a few language problems, even in the best hotels. The variety and quality of food in Taiwan makes it one of the best places in the world to sample the different styles of Chinese cuisine. From the cheap noodle shops to classy establishments in five-star hotels, the food is consistently good. Taipei in particular also has many quality restaurants serving international cuisines.

HOTELS

The best establishments are generally found in the center of the cities as this is where business people stay. Here, amenities are slanted toward corporate travelers, with business centers, secretarial services, executive floors, and in-room fax and Internet connections. The better hotels tend to offer health clubs, swimming pools (some both indoor and outdoor), spacious guest rooms, and quality restaurants.

Outside Taipei and the cities of Kaohsiung and Taichung, choices become more limited. Many of the island's midsize cities have what are called "regular tourist hotels." Don't expect special services from these places.

The more popular tourist areas, such as Kenting, Sun Moon Lake, and the North Coast, have resort hotels with the emphasis on recreation. But again, the choice of luxury hotels in these areas is limited.

Rooms in the best hotels in Taipei start at around $175 in U.S. currency. These generally belong to chains such as Hyatt, Sheraton, Inter-Continental. and Shangri-La. There are also a number of fine hotel chains under local management including the Landis, Howard, and Sherwood, with guest room prices starting at around US$125. Equivalent hotels in other major cities tend to be a little less expensive. A room at "regular tourist" hotels with their basic amenities will cost between US$50 and $100.

A buffet breakfast—often excellent—is normally included in the room rate at most hotels, but ask before booking if you are not sure. Guest rooms nearly always have a kettle along with packages of coffee, tea, whitener, and sugar.

The prices of the hotels listed here are the published rack rates—a 10 percent service charge is often added. Most establishments offer discounts of 30 percent or more if you book ahead, and possibly more if you book online. The plethora of Internet hotel booking services often offer larger discounts, and include service charges and taxes in the quoted rates.

It is best to book hotel airport transfers before you arrive (or check the Taiwan Tourism Bureau desks at the airport). Taipei's Taiwan Taoyuan International Airport is a fair distance from downtown (see p. 238). The cost of a hotel limo, which can be added to your hotel bill, is about the same as the taxi fare (NT$1200–1500).

RESTAURANTS

Taiwan offers innumerable choices for Chinese cuisine (see pp. 24–29). People from all over mainland China have settled in Taiwan, bringing their culinary traditions with them. The result is a varied and consistent quality of dishes. Add to this the obsession for food among the Chinese, and you will find you never have to walk far to find a good restaurant. Increasingly, culinary talents from elsewhere around the world are also finding Taipei a good place to set up, both in major hotels and on a private basis.

If you are new to Chinese food, dining rooms at the better hotels are a good place to begin. Here, staff are more familiar with Western tastes. Menus in Chinese restaurants can be extensive and present a challenge to ordering. Frequently creative use of English can also present a challenge. A Taiwanese friend or acquaintance can help you navigate.

Taipei has many quality international restaurants, with many found in the top hotels. Buffet meals in these hotels are a good value and often have choices of Western, Chinese, Japanese, and other Asian dishes.

Restaurant prices are reasonable. However, if you plan on drinking imported wines, the cost rises substantially. Meals at small local Chinese eateries often costs only a few dollars.

Hygiene standards in Taiwan, generally, are very high. There should be no problem eating food from market stalls.

ORGANIZATION & ABBREVIATIONS

The hotels and restaurants have been arranged alphabetically by price range and within each region. Credit cards are abbreviated AE American Express, DC Diner's Club, MC MasterCard, and V Visa.

PRICES

HOTELS
An indication of the cost, in U.S. dollars, of a double room based on the hotel's standard rate is given by $ signs.

$$$$$	$235+
$$$$	$175–$235
$$$	$120–$175
$$	$60–$120
$	Under $60

RESTAURANTS
An indication of the cost of a three-course dinner without drinks is given by $ signs.

$$$$$	Over $50
$$$$	$25–$50
$$$	$12–$25
$$	$5–$12
$	Under $5

TAIPEI

SOMETHING SPECIAL

⊞ FAR EASTERN PLAZA HOTEL

Western and Chinese tastes blend in this Shangri-La-managed hotel. Spacious rooms feature rosewood furnishings set against light-colored walls. If you feel like indulging, stay in one of the spa suites with sauna, steam room, and Jacuzzi. Spectacular views abound from the rooftop pool. The Marco Polo's (see p. 247) wine list is among the best in Taipei. **$$$$$**

201 DUNHUA SOUTH RD., SEC. 2
TEL 2378-8888
FAX 2377-7777
www.feph.com.tw
ⓘ 420 🅿 ⬆ 🅐 🅢 ⬈
🅖 🅒 All major cards
🚇 Technology Building

⊞ GRAND HYATT TAIPEI
$$$$$

2 SONGSHOU RD.
TEL 2720-1234
FAX 2720-1111
www.taipei.hyatt.com
The rooms are finished in warm pastels with marble bathrooms, while the stunning glass-topped atrium enhances the lobby. The outdoor pool has an underwater sound system—a surprise when you dive in. Haute cuisine and an extensive wine list enhance its Pearl Liang restaurant (see p. 247), while authentic Italian food makes the Ziga Zaga (see p. 250) a joy.
ⓘ 870 🅿 ⬆ 🅐 🅢 ⬈
🅖 🅒 All major cards
🚇 Taipei City Hall

⊞ IMPERIAL HOTEL
$$$$$/$$$$

600 LINSEN NORTH RD.
TEL 2596-5111
FAX 2592-7506
www.imperialhotel.com.tw
Designed to attract the corporate traveler with a well-equipped 24-hour business center. Spacious rooms are decorated in warm tones, rich wood furnishings, and artworks. The 66 business suites have large desks and high-tech accoutrements. The Front Page bar is a favorite haunt for Taipei's expatriates during early evening happy hour and as a jumping-off point for The Zone bar area immediately behind the hotel.
ⓘ 288 🅿 ⬆ 🅐 🅢 ⬈
🅖 🅒 All major cards

⊞ THE WESTIN TAIPEI
$$$$$/$$$$

133 NANJING EAST RD., SEC. 3
TEL 8770-6565
FAX 8770-6555
www.westin.com.tw
One of Taipei's newest hotels built for the business traveler. Rooms are fitted with large desks and Internet access. Decor is a muted blend of Western and Asian. The eight food and beverage outlets provide for all tastes; Danieli's (see p. 247) is considered one of the city's elite Italian restaurants.
ⓘ 288 🅿 ⬆ 🅐 🅢 ⬈
🅖 🅒 All major cards
🚇 Nanjing East Road

⊞ CAESAR PARK
$$$$

38 JHONGSIAO (ZHONGXIAO) WEST RD., SEC. 1
TEL 2311-5151
FAX 2331-9944
www.caesarpark.com.tw
Formerly the Taipei Hilton and now managed by a homegrown hotel group with an excellent reputation, the Caesar Park still maintains first-class standards. Many Hilton staff have stayed on, so you know what to expect.
ⓘ 395 🅿 ⬆ 🅐 🅢 ⬈
🅖 🅒 All major cards
🚇 Taipei Main Station

⊞ GRAND FORMOSA REGENT
$$$$

41 JHONGSHAN (ZHONGSHAN) RD., SEC. 2
TEL 2523-8000
FAX 2523-2828
www.regenthotels.com
This hotel boasts the largest guest rooms in Taipei. Floor-to-ceiling windows and marble bathrooms with soaking tubs are a delight. Some suites open to a Japanese garden. Views of the city from the rooftop pool keep you distracted between dips. There are 10 food and beverage outlets.
ⓘ 539 🅿 ⬆ 🅐 🅢 ⬈
🅖 🅒 All major cards
🚇 Zhongshan

⊞ THE GRAND HOTEL
$$$$/$$$

1 JHONGSHAN (ZHONGSHAN) NORTH RD., SEC. 4
TEL 2886-8888
FAX 2885-2885
www.grand-hotel.org
The red-columned facade, sweeping classical Chinese tile roof, and location atop a hill give this hotel a dominating presence. Recently renovated rooms are appealingly finished with traditional furniture. The decor changes with each floor representing a specific dynastic period. Balconies have views of Taipei city or the mountains.
ⓘ 490 🅿 ⬆ 🅐 🅢 ⬈
🅖 🅒 All major cards
🚇 Jiantan

⊞ HOWARD PLAZA HOTEL
$$$$

160 RENAI RD., SEC. 3
TEL 2700-2323
FAX 2700-0729
www.howard-hotels.com
Chinese rosewood furniture and original artwork lift the large rooms and restaurants a notch. Brunch and afternoon tea in the leafy atrium restaurant are favored pastimes for Taipei residents. Upscale boutiques ring the atrium on four levels.
ⓘ 606 🅿 ⬆ 🅐 🅢 ⬈
🅖 🅒 All major cards
🚇 Zhongxiao-Fuxing

SOMETHING SPECIAL

🏨 THE LANDIS TAIPEI HOTEL

This small classy hotel is an appealing alternative to the larger five-star hotels. Lobby and guest room decor is art deco. The hotel has 100 suites, with starting rates not much higher than the standard rooms. The hotel's Paris 1930 French restaurant (see p. 247) ranks as one of the best, with a superb wine list.

$$$$$

41 MINCUAN (MINQUAN)
EAST RD., SEC. 2
TEL 2597-1234
FAX 2596-9223
www.landistpe.com.tw

ⓘ 209 🅿 ⇄ 🔄 🚫 🏊
🍽 🃏 All major cards

🏨 EVERGREEN LAUREL HOTEL TAIPEI

$$$$

63 SONGJIANG RD.
TEL 2501-9988
FAX 2501-9966
www.evergreen-hotels.com

A boutique hotel room and open-area trappings. Known for outstanding service and dedicated personnel. In a busy area, soundproofing handles external noise. Original Italian furniture brings a continental ambiance. Each room has wireless LAN, free broadband Internet, roomy walk-in closets, facilities for physically handicapped. Eight smoke-free floors.

ⓘ 100 🅿 ⇄ 🔄 🍽
🃏 All major cards

🏨 REBAR CROWNE PLAZA

$$$$

32 NANJING EAST RD., SEC. 5
TEL 2763-5656
FAX 2767-9347
www.crowneplaza-taipei.com

The nearby World Trade Center and financial district make this hotel popular with business travelers. Sleek

furniture adds a stylish appeal. Standards and service are what you expect from the Six Continents chain.

ⓘ 225 🅿 ⇄ 🔄 🚫 🍽
🃏 All major cards

🏨 HOTEL ROYAL TAIPEI

$$$$

37-1 JHONGSHAN (ZHONG-SHAN) NORTH RD., SEC. 2
TEL 2542-3266
FAX 2543-4897
www.royal-taipei.com.tw

The Royal Taipei rooms employ beige colors with floral bedspreads and seat cushions for a comforting boutique style. A lovely greenhouse full of blazing tropical flowers sits next to the rooftop swimming pool.

ⓘ 202 🅿 ⇄ 🔄 🚫 🏊
🍽 ♿ 🃏 All major cards
🚇 Zhongshan

🏨 SHERATON TAIPEI HOTEL

$$$$

12 JHONGSIAO (ZHONGXIAO) EAST RD., SEC. I
TEL 080-231-666/7
FAX 2394-4240
www.starwood.com

This Taipei landmark has a grandiose feel with rich tones and wood furniture in the spacious guest rooms and suites. The fitness center has a whirlpool, hot tub, and golf simulator. Its nine cafés and restaurants serve quality cuisine, among them the fine French dining in the Antoine Room (see below). There is a ladies-only floor.

ⓘ 688 🅿 ⇄ 🔄 🚫 🏊
🍽 🃏 All major cards
🚇 Shandao Temple

🏨 THE SHERWOOD

$$$$$

111 MINSHENG EAST RD., SEC. 3
TEL 2718-1188
FAX 2713-0707
www.sherwood.com.tw

The rooms here don't scrimp on quality furnishings. The decor contains a a mix of classical and modern Euro-

pean styles, embellished with original artwork. The indoor, glass-roofed atrium swimming pool is a special treat.

ⓘ 350 🅿 ⇄ 🔄 🚫
🏊 🍽 🃏 All major cards
🚇 Zhongshan Junior High School

🏨 HOTEL RIVERVIEW

$$$

77 HUANHE SOUTH RD., SEC. I
TEL 2311-3131
FAX 2361-3737
www.riverview.com.tw

Its location in the colorful old Wanhua section of the city near the Danshuei (Danshui) River makes the Riverview a little out of the way and a distance from useful mass transportation. But the lower room rates make up for this. Rooms are large and river views are a bonus, especially from the glass-roofed restaurant.

ⓘ 201 🅿 ⇄ 🔄 🚫
🍽 🃏 All major cards

🏨 SAN WANT HOTEL

$$$

172 JHONGSIAO RD., SEC. 4
TEL 2772-2121
FAX 2721-0302
www.sanwant.com

It's a bit confusing when you first enter the hotel and don't see a check-in counter —it's on the fourth floor. Rooms are comfortable but noticeably small. Excellent location, however, with a MRT station at the doorstep.

ⓘ 268 🅿 ⇄ 🔄 🚫 🍽
🃏 All major cards
🚇 Zhongxiao-Dunhua

🍴 ANTOINE ROOM

$$$$$

SHERATON TAIPEI HOTEL
12 JHONGSIAO (ZHONGXIAO) EAST RD., SEC. I
TEL 2321-5511

This French restaurant has been around for two dec-ades. Top-notch ingredients and thoughtful presentation give it much appeal. You can't go to the Antoine Room without trying the luxurious

seafood salad—fresh seafood mixed with Japanese seaweed, sticky rice, and vinegar and soy sauce dressing. This place possesses one of the best wine cellars in the city.
🛏 90 💳 All major cards

🍽 BEL AIR
$$$$$
GRAND HYATT TAIPEI
2 SONGSHOU RD.
TEL 2720-1200, EXT. 3198
The high-quality Californian cuisine infused with Asian elements emphasize the Bel Air's attention to healthy dining. Classical decor combines muted colors, soft lighting, and natural skylight for an intimate effect.
🛏 76 💳 All major cards

🍽 BEN TEPPANYAKI
$$$$$
2 LANE, 102 ANHE RD., SEC. I
TEL 2703-2296
Experienced teppanyaki chefs prepare choice cuts of Masusaka, Kobe, and Omi beef to perfection, but you pay for the privilege. While most diners come to try the Japanese beef, a set meal of quality U.S. beef is also prepared with skill.
🛏 160 💳 All major cards

🍽 CHEZ JIMMY
$$$$$
27 LANE 50, TIANMU EAST RD., TIANMU
TEL 2874-7185
Waiters in natty French-style uniforms are attentive in this popular restaurant. Diners rave about the award-winning steamed egg in the shell topped with Hollandaise sauce and Iranian caviar. It's an unusual but workable marriage of light and heavy tastes. The unfussy spring chicken flavored with garlic is a popular main course.
🛏 90 💳 All major cards

🍽 DANIELI'S
$$$$$
THE WESTIN TAIPEI
2F, 133 NANJING EAST RD.,

SEC. 3
TEL 8770-6565, EXT. 3255
If the descriptive term "casual elegance" means anything in the reviewer's lexicon, it would apply here. Although nothing is casual about the prices, mere money doesn't dissuade diners from waiting for tables, however. Cost aside, this Italian restaurant does serve up excellent fare. Notable are the antipasto selections. The seafood *guazzetto*, a spicy concoction of broth brimming with clams, shrimp, and scallops, with garlic and chili pepper, zings with flavor.
🛏 80 💳 All major cards

🍽 MARCO POLO
$$$$$
FAR EASTERN PLAZA HOTEL
201 DUNHUA SOUTH RD., SEC. 2
TEL 2378-8888, EXT. 5950
The panoramic views from this 38th floor are engaging at night. The multicultural and mouthwatering Sicilian Maine lobster Catalana style and the assorted fish and shellfish casserole bathed in luscious tomato sauce are standouts. Make sure your credit card is paid up if you are paying.
🛏 144 💳 All major cards

🍽 MOMOYAMA RESTAURANT
$$$$$
SHERATON TAIPEI HOTEL
2F, 12 JHONGSIAO EAST RD., SEC. I
TEL 2321-1818
The nearest you'll get to true Japanese dining in Taiwan. Kaiseki cuisine recipes and preparation techniques are followed precisely. The selection of sashimi arriving at your table exemplifies the emphasis on freshness. The *yamagata* beef sirloin steak—sirloin strips grilled on a volcanic rock brought from Japan—all but melts in your mouth. The sushi bar offers less formal dining.
🛏 140 💳 All major cards

🍽 PARIS 1930
Start with the signature tomato garlic cream soup flambéed with gin and/or the roast goose liver with corn seed beer pancake and cider Carmel Normandy sauce at this renowed French restaurant. Its whole pressed duck requires complicated preparation, so you need to order ahead. The service is flawless, and the list of French wines is extensive.
$$$$$
LANDIS HOTEL
41 MINCYUAN (MINQUAN) EAST RD., SEC. 2
TEL 2597-1234
🛏 80 💳 All major cards

🍽 PEARL LIANG
$$$$$
GRAND HYATT TAIPEI
2 SONGSHOU RD.
TEL 2720-1200, EXT. 3198
Chinese seafood and dim sum are served in elegant and sophisticated surroundings. The wine cellar is one of the most extensive in a Taipei Chinese restaurant, and waiters can advise on what to try with the innovative dishes.
🛏 178 💳 All major cards

🍽 RUTH'S CHRIS STEAK HOUSE
$$$$$
2F, 135 MINSHENG EAST RD., SEC. 3
TEL 2545-8888
Undisputedly the best steak house in Taiwan. Lots of polished wood, brass, glass, and mirrors, while partitioned tables give a sense of space. All cuts of U.S. prime beef are available—New York strip, rib-eye, T-bone, porterhouse. Service is friendly, efficient, and fast.
🛏 170 💳 All major cards

🍽 SHINTORI
$$$$$
68 ANHE RD., SEC. 2
TEL 2702-5588
Salmon roe, soft-shell crabs,

🚭 Nonsmoking 🛗 Elevator ❄ Air-conditioning 🏊 Indoor/🏊 Outdoor swimming pool 🏋 Gym 💳 Credit cards

HOTELS & RESTAURANTS

salmon, and tuna are imported from Japan to maintain the authenticity of the Kaiseki cuisine. Dishes are presented with such meticulous detail that you feel a bit guilty about eating the work of art in front of you. The superb quality of the food and the minimalist Zen-type decor match the presentation.
🛏 185 💳 All major cards

🍴 SUNTORY RESTAURANT
$$$$$
FAR EASTERN PLAZA HOTEL
7F, 201 DUNHUA SOUTH RD., SEC. 2
TEL 2378-8888
Full-length windows overlooking a peaceful garden enhance the spatial design elements of the restaurant. Quality, service, and artful presentation—Kaiseki, sushi, teppanyaki—is first-class.
🍴 114 💳 All major cards

🍴 LAN TING
$$$$$
GRAND FORMOSA REGENT
41 JHONGSHAN (ZHONG-SHAN) NORTH RD., SEC. 2
TEL 2523-8000
This fine dining establishment specializes in Shanghainese seafood delicacies. The elegant restaurant has set lunch and dinner menus.
🍴 65 💳 All major cards

🍴 TUTTO BELLO
$$$$$
15 LANE 25, SHUANG-CHENG ST.
TEL 2592-3355
An imaginative menu, with attention to detail and impeccable service has kept this restaurant at the top of Taipei's Italian establishments. The menu is mainly northern Italian, although other regional influences are incorporated. The rolled spinach pasta with fresh and smoked salmon, mushrooms, and herbed-cream sauce is as near to pasta perfection as you can get.
🍴 55 💳 All major cards

🍴 CAFÉ
$$$$
GRAND HYATT TAIPEI
2 SONGSHOU RD
TEL 2720-1200, EXT. 3198
The more than 160 dishes on the buffet tables offer an enormous choice. Fresh salads are in abundance and the sashimi is deliciously fresh. Like any good buffet, the variety of desserts is expansive. Part of the joy in the brightly sunlit area is watching the 50 chefs preparing your treats in the open kitchen.
🍴 314 💳 All major cards

🍴 CAPONE'S ITALIAN AMERICAN DINNER-HOUSE
$$$$
312 JHONGSIAO (ZHONG-XIAO) EAST RD., SEC. 4
TEL 2773-3782
The intriguing name alone is enough to tempt a visit. Checkered tablecloths, a long bar, and photographs on the walls evoke the gangster theme. The "Italian American" in the place's name indicates American and Italian food. It's a good place for a late-night supper, staying open to 2 a.m. on weekdays and 3 a.m. on weekends. Live bands provide entertainment.
🍴 156 💳 All major cards

🍴 CHEZ MOI
$$$$
28 LANE 240, GUANGFU SOUTH RD.
TEL 2772 7265
The garden entrance adds charm to this intimate and stylish French restaurant. Baked escargot and Burgundy-style appetizers are prepared with butter, cheese, garlic, and herbs, while the country-style pumpkin soup is rich and flavorsome. Steaks are enjoyed, as are the delectable lamb chops, duck's leg, and pig's knuckle, with a selection of French red wines. The set menus offer excellent value.
🍴 55 💳 All major cards

🍴 CHIKURINTEI
$$$$
2F, SPRING CITY RESORT HOTEL, 18 YOUYA RD., BEITOU DISTRICT
TEL 2897-5555, EXT. 225
Featuring grand views of hills and twisting valley from one of Beitou's youngest and most popular hot-spring hotels, the fare here is Japanese. Among the kitchen team's finest are Taraba crab hotpot (crabs flown in from Okhotsk Sea) and sweet persimmons with sesame-flavored miso (when fruit in season in Japan).
🍴 90 💳 All major cards

🍴 DAN RYAN'S CHICAGO GRILL
$$$$
8 DUNHUA NORTH RD.
TEL 2778-8800
This pub/restaurant. emulating a Chicago speakeasy of the 1930s and '40s, serves whopping portions (for Asia) of familiar American dishes. New England clam chowder, Caesar salad, nachos, and buffalo wings appear on the menu for starters. Steaks and the accompanying sauces are

favored main courses. All can be washed down with an American beer.
150 All major cards

FENG ZHUAN TAIPEI
$$$$
B1, 225 DUNHUA SOUTH RD., SEC. 1
TEL 2751-2277
The Oriental decor evokes a tranquil ambience that enhances the innovative approach to preparation and presentation. French and Chinese dishes—primarily seafood—are cooked to bring out the natural flavors using little oil and few spices. Treats include pan-fried lamb chops, abalone in oyster sauce, and fresh shrimp dumplings. Set lunch and dinner meals will soften the effect on your wallet.
80 All major cards

IRODORI
$$$$
GRAND HYATT TAIPEI
2 SONGSHOU RD.
TEL 2720-1200, EXT. 3198
The extensive and high-quality Japanese food spread out on the buffet tables is an irresistible draw, so go before the lunch crowds arrive at noon. Spend your time sampling the extensive array of sushi, sashimi, tempura, teppanyaki, and other styles of Japanese cuisine.
160 All major cards

L'AMICO RISTORANTE ITALIANO
$$$$
10 LANE 55, MINSHENG EAST RD., SEC. 4
TEL 2719-3688
Classic European decor, intimate size, and hideaway location on a narrow lane evokes a romantic ambience. The variety of pasta dishes will appeal, while layers of eggplant and courgette with mozzarella is a tasty antipasto choice. Tender veal dishes smothered in an assortment of sauces are tempting.
56 All major cards

LE JARDIN
$$$$
170 JHONGJHENG (ZHONGZHENG) RD., SEC. 2, TIANMU
TEL 2877-1178
Le Jardin specializes in southern French and Provençal cuisine. Try the pan-fried duck liver with balsamic vinegar and eggplant puree for a starter. You'll find the thick fish soup with garlic saffron sauce hearty. The rack of lamb in rosemary sauce and the pan-fried beef filet with creamy anchovy sauce are as rich as they sound.
80 All major cards

PASTA WEST EAST
$$$$
7 ANHE RD., SEC. 1
TEL 2721-0029
As its name suggests, this place concedes some Italian authenticity to Asian tastes, resulting in a creative menu. The pasta *alle vongole* (spaghetti with a creamy sauce, fresh clams, and chopped basil) is a popular example. Try the homemade breads.
60 All major cards

PORTOFINO
$$$$
2F, 323 DUNHUA SOUTH RD., SEC. 1
TEL 2755-5580
Heavenly fresh bread accompanied by piquant dip—created with capers, black olives, and fresh tomatoes—keeps the hunger at bay while you enjoy the views and await the appetizers' arrival. The al dente pasta that smacks of freshness and flavor is enlivened with sauces that pay attention to detail.
90 All major cards

SALSA BISTRO
$$$$
9 LANE 141, ANHE RD., SEC. 1
TEL 2700-3060
South American decor decorates this small bistro. Try the marinated fresh fish in lemon juice as a refreshing appetizer before tucking into the baked corn and meat pastry entrée. A wide selection of Chilean wines are available, and the owners will help you make a choice.
35 All major cards

SHANGHAI SHANGHAI
$$$$
TAIPEI METRO MALL, B1, 203 DUNHUA SOUTH RD., SEC. 2
TEL 8732-1536
Here in the cheery atmosphere that finds favor with Western expatriates and tourists, you can indulge in a menu prepared with flair. The Shanghainese steamed buns and dumplings are caringly handmade and filled with delicious meats and gravies, seafood, and vegetables. Stir-fry dishes are enhanced with first-rate ingredients and imaginative preparation.
110 All major cards

SHANGHAI STORY
$$$$
2F, 25 SINYI (XINYI) RD., SEC. 4
TEL 2702-1566
Shanghai of the 1920s and '30s is the backdrop in which to enjoy Shanghai soup buns and authentic Jiangsu and Zhejiang cuisine. The chefs excel in their creation of the must-try scallop and shrimp streamed dumplings. Other dishes, like shrimp with vegetables, shredded beef with bamboo, and chicken marinated in Shaohsing rice wine excel because of their unpretentious preparation and dedication to authenticity.
70 All major cards

🍴 SOMMELIER
$$$$
553 MINGSHUEI
(MINGSHUI) RD.
TEL 2532-4707
Both imaginative and familiar
Continental cuisine is available
in this town-house-style
establishment. Seafood
Delight is aptly named for the
shrimp, scallops, squid, and
other seafood sautéed in
butter and enhanced with
spices and Pernod. The
popular sautéed shrimp and
wild mushrooms in garlic
sauce has a more Asian background. The wine list is varied
and reasonable.
🪑 60 🃏 All major cards

🍴 SOWIESO
$$$$
88 SIHWEI (SIWEI) RD.
TEL 2705-5282
While labeled Italian, this
place is known to wander off
the culinary trail. The baked
escargot in garlic butter,
served with mashed pota-
toes, is one example. More
on track is the penne with
crab meat and lobster sauce,
one of the more popular
pasta dishes. The Sowieso
also tends to waver when it
comes to decor.
🪑 50 🕐 Closed Sun. 🃏 All
major cards

🍴 TIEN HSIANG LO
$$$$
LANDIS TAIPEI HOTEL
41 MINCYUAN (MINQUAN)
EAST RD., SEC. 2
TEL 2597-1234
A top-notch restaurant that
serves Hangzhou cuisine—
known for it subtle taste and
presentation. Some dishes
might be a bit too exotic for
Western tastes, but there are
plenty that will appeal. The
chicken and wonton soup is
a favorite. For something
different, try the shrimp fried
with tea leaves.
🪑 90 🃏 All major cards

🍴 TOSCANA ITALIAN RESTAURANT
$$$$
THE SHERWOOD
111 MINSHENG EAST RD., SEC. 3
TEL 2718-1188, EXT. 3001
Floor-to-ceiling windows separate the indoor and alfresco
sections. The kitchen specializes in authentic Italian
cuisine with some variations.
The porcini mushroom soup
is delicious, while the vegetable broth is indeed hearty.
The satisfying. poached Maine
lobster on a bed of couscous
salad can be enjoyed as an
appetizer or main course.
🪑 120 🃏 All major cards

SOMETHING SPECIAL

🍴 TAINAN DANZAI NOODLES
At the north end of famed
Huaxi St. Tourist Night
Market, the signature dish here is
a traditional noodle specialty
long ago invented in southern
Tainan City, "danzih mian/tan
tsu mian" or "passing-the-lean-
months noodles," carried on
shoulder poles to make cash
when fishermen couldn't put to
sea in winter. Here are probably
Taiwan's most expensive noodles,
improbably served amidst
overdone Wedgwood china,
chandeliers, and Corinthian
columns. The restaurant's
seafood is also praised.
$$$$/$$$
31 HUASI (HUAXI) ST.
TEL 2308-1123
🪑 140 🃏 All major cards

🍴 TRADER VIC'S RESTAURANT
$$$$
7F, 135 MINSHENG E. RD., SEC. 3
TEL 2545-9999
Here, the rattan furnishings
evoke a South Seas theme,
and what would a South Seas
restaurant be without bongo
bongo soup? Despite the silly
name and it being served in a
large seashell, this thick,
creamy oyster soup is worth

a try. So, too, are the tender
and sweet pork spareribs and
the marinated, crispy chicken
cooked to a juicy smoke-
flavored meat. Finishing the
delicious mud pie dessert is a
chore, but worth the effort.
🪑 150 🃏 All major cards

🍴 ZIGA ZAGA
$$$$
GRAND HYATT TAIPEI
2 SONGSHOU RD.
TEL 2720-1200, EXT. 3198
The selections at this
excellent buffet vary daily.
The dishes include a large
range of salads, pastas,
seafood, and meat dishes.
The desserts are irresistible.
Dinner is à la carte, and
diners like to stay after their
meal to listen and dance to
the bands and DJs.
🪑 120 🃏 All major cards

🍴 BAMBOO VILLAGE
$$$
81 NANJING EAST RD., SEC. 2
TEL 2551-1838
If you desire delicious dim
sum in the early morning
hours, then head here. It stays
open until 4 a.m. (having
opened at 5:30 p.m.), and it
remains crowded. Besides dim
sum, this Cantonese restaurant also places emphasis on
seafood. Pick your favorite
fish from the tank, and the
chefs will cook it for you.
🪑 110 🃏 All major cards

🍴 PENG YUAN
$$$
2F, 380 LINSEN N. RD.
TEL 2551-9157
The original in the locally
renowned "Peng's Garden"
chain. Expansive, relatively
unadorned, and always busy,
the Hunanese food's the
thing here. The best selection
is Hunan ham cooked with
honey—rich and smoky.
Another popular item is
frog's legs in hot sauce. You'll
need a Chinese speaker in
your group.
🪑 110 🃏 All major cards

◫ HSIN YEH RESTAURANT
$$$
34-1 SHUANGCHENG ST.
TEL 2596-3255
The main branch of a popular chain that serves Taiwanese cuisine to a bustling clientele of locals and tourists. The seafood—squid, grilled eel, fried shrimp rolls, and grilled clams—is excellent and a good value.
⊞ 120 ⊗ All major cards

SOMETHING SPECIAL

◫ HO NG YUN CANTONESE RESTAURANT
An innovative and extremely long menu keeps this 24-hour-a-day establishment busy. Chefs have created wonderful dim sum, including asparagus and codfish dumplings, and a skillful mix of scallops and beans. The satay mushroom beef stew blends Hongsi (Hongxi) mushrooms with tender beef for outstanding results. The yam and snow-clam soup is the equivalent of clam chowder. For dessert the chrysanthemum cake with matrimony vine—a traditional Chinese herb—is not only delicious, but its health-giving properties are said to soothe both body and mind.
$$$
2F, 275 NANJING EAST RD., SEC. 3
TEL 2713-3877
⊞ 120 ⊗ All major cards

◫ JAKE'S COUNTRY KITCHEN
$$$
705 JHONGSHAN (ZHONGSHAN) NORTH RD., SEC. 6, TIANMU
TEL 2871-5289
This restaurant serves up an array of Mexican favorites—enchiladas, quesadillas, and tacos. It is popular with expatriates and Western visitors. The food portions are generous, and prices reasonable.
⊞ 80 ⊗ All major cards

◫ MING GARDEN
$$$
AMBASSADOR HOTEL
63 JHONGSHAN (ZHONG-SHAN) NORTH RD., SEC. 2
TEL 2100-2100, EXT. 2183
The buffet has a "Chinese cuisines area" where you can sample an extensive mix. Western dishes are laid on in equal abundance. At the afternoon tea buffet, the food tends to be a little lighter but abundant.
⊞ 120 ⊗ All major cards

◫ MOROCCAN RESTAURANT
$$$
1 LANE 165, DUNHUA NORTH RD.
TEL 2719-4469
One of the best of Taipei's limited number of Mid-East/African restaurants. Its Harira soup combines diced lamb, paprika, saffron, tomatoes, beans, and lime juice in an exotic and tasty dish. Lamb and chicken dominate the entrées. Lamb is stewed with olives, almonds, vegetables, and beans, and served on a bed of couscous.
⊞ 76 ⊗ All major cards

◫ PIAO LIU MU (DRIFT-WOOD) ABORIGINAL RESTAURANT
$$$
4 ALLEY 9, LANE 316, ROOSEVELT RD., SEC. 3
TEL 2365-7413
Some of the island's best aboriginal artists painted the pub murals that depict scenes from legend. The excellent grilled wild boar is served with a special sauce and wild vegetables. Aboriginal performers take to the stage on weekends at 9 p.m.
⊞ 50 ⊕ Closed Mon. ⊗ All major cards

◫ TANDOOR INDIAN RESTAURANT
$$$
10 LANE 73, HEJIANG ST.
TEL 2509-9853
Tandoor's excellent menu includes mixed grill of chicken, lamb kebab, fish, and prawns sizzling on a bed of onions. The ovens turn out an assortment of unleavened breads to complement the range of rich curries.
⊞ 80 ⊗ All major cards

◫ TAPAS BAR
$$$
50 HEPING WEST RD.
TEL 2362-8777
Western expatriates crowd the small yet cozy place where waiters circulate explaining the dishes. The daily salad is a hearty combination of crisp lettuce, baby radishes, tomatoes, red and green bell peppers, onions, squid, green olives, and boiled egg, all tossed in vinaigrette sauce. If you are in a group, call ahead and order paella. French food is also available.
⊞ 30 ⊕ Closed Mon.

◫ VUVU ROCK ABORIGINAL RESTAURANT
$$$
3 JHIHSHAN (ZHISHAN) RD., SEC. 2
TEL 2880-3043
One of the new aboriginal restaurants to pop up in recent years. Stucco walls, sculptures, and murals are a little overdone, but the diners don't seem to mind, tucking into some unusual dishes. The betel-nut flower with either beef or pork is popular, along with the mixed stir-fry that includes wild boar and flying fish. The pork and papaya stew lends an appealing sweetness to the meat. Sweet red rice wine can be ordered by the pitcher, and enjoyed while watching live performances by aboriginal artists.
⊞ 105 ⊗ All major cards

◫ NIU JIA ZHUANG BEEF RESTAURANT
$$
136 SINYI (XINYI) RD., SEC. 4
TEL 2754-1658

A variety of basil leaves, spring onions, garlic, soy sauce, ginger root, and other flavors are added to stir-fry beef dishes. Some dishes feature various innards that may test your fortitude. The "cow penis chicken stew" must be ordered in advance, presumably so the restaurant can find a cow that has the desired appendage.
🔳 85

🍴 TIEN XIANG HUI WEI
$$
2F, 16 NANJING EAST RD., SEC. 1
TEL 2511-7275
The litany of spices added to the hot pots makes this chain a favorite for the tasty food and its professed healthy properties. The herbs are mixed with other special ingredients to create warming and flavorful hot pots. The homemade fish balls and seafood dish make fine companions The melon platter, with winter melon, squash, and sweet potato, is a tasty and healthy way to round out the meal.
🔳 200 🚫 All major cards

🍴 JHEN SIANG (ZHEN XIANG) BEEF NOODLES
$
196 SONGREN RD.
This small, unassuming eatery serves up noodles with distinction. That accounts for the crowds of diners. So pleased are the diners that they even lend a hand clearing their dishes. Chunks of tender beef swim in a rich broth. Dry beef noodles (without the broth) are also available. For less than $1.50 (NT$50) you can buy what regulars profess to be the best beef noodles in Taipei.
🔳 30

🍴 OLD JHANG'S (ZHANG'S) BEEF NOODLES
$
19 LANE 31, JINSHAN SOUTH RD., SEC. 2

TEL 2396-0927
Beef noodles were introduced by mainland north Chinese soldiers in the late 1940s and are now one of Taiwan's most popular dishes. If you are after the most tender beef of all, then this is the place. Every local knows Jhang's, so going there with a Taiwanese acquaintance will elicit smiles. Dishes come in a choice of light broth or a thick, slightly spicy broth.
🔳 60

AROUND TAIPEI & THE NORTH

BEITOU

🏨 SPRING RESORT HOTEL
$$$$
18 YOUYA RD.
TEL 2897-5555
FAX 2897-3333
www.springresort.com.tw
The nearby MRT Xin Beitou station makes staying here a viable alternative to Taipei hotels—30 minutes away— especially during the week when room rates halve and the staff is more attentive. Hotel decor mixes art deco with Chinese and Japanese. Deep in-room soaking pools are filled with hot water piped in from the springs.
ℹ️ 90 🅿️ 🔄 🔳 🚫 🏊
📺 🚫 All major cards
🚇 Xin Beitou

🏨 WHISPERING PINES INN
$$
21 YOUYA RD.
TEL (02) 2891-2063
This inn is one of only a few traditional Japanese-style hotels remaining in the area. Large tatami rooms and slate-floor hot spring bathing rooms are set amid tranquil Japanese gardens. The inn is popular among Taipei's actors and entertainers.
ℹ️ 20 🔳 🚫 🚫 All major cards

JHONGLI (ZHONGLI)

🏨 KUVA CHATEAU
$$$
398 MINCYUAN (MINQUAN) RD., TAOYUAN COUNTY
TEL (03) 281-1818
FAX (03) 281-1616
www.kuva-chateau.com.tw
Located 15 minutes from Taiwan Taoyuan airport, and 25 minutes from Taipei, this newer facility is the only deluxe hotel in the area. It is aimed at the corporate traveler, with Internet access in the rooms. There is a nonsmoking floor and airport shuttle.
ℹ️ 116 🅿️ 🔄 🔳 🚫 🏊
📺 🚫 All major cards

KEELUNG

🏨 EVERGREEN LAUREL HOTEL
$$$
62-1 JHONGJHENG (ZHONGZHENG) RD.
TEL 2427-9988
FAX 2422-8642
www.evergreen-hotels.com
On the edge of Keelung Harbor, some rooms offer unlimited harbor and ocean views. Decor and amenities in

the ample-size guest rooms justify its four-star status. An indoor pool, steam room, and sauna are found in the health center. Near most of Keelung's attractions.

🛈 140 🅿 🔁 ❄ 🚭 🏊 🏋 🏧 All major cards

NORTH COAST

🏨 HOWARD BEACH RESORT
$$$
1-1 FEICUEI (FECUI) RD., WANLI TOWNSHIP, TAIPEI COUNTY
TEL 2492-6565
FAX 2492-6588
www.howard-hotels.com.tw
Multistory hotel right on the beach with innumerable recreational facilities, including indoor and outdoor pools, a spa, and all sorts of beachside accoutrements for rent. All the spacious rooms have ocean views.

🛈 241 🅿 🔁 ❄ 🚭 🏊 🏋 🏧 All major cards

TAOYUAN

🏨 WESTIN RESORT TA SHEE
$$$$
166 RESIN (REXIN) ROAD, DASI (DAXI) TOWNSHIP, TAOYUAN COUNTY
TEL (03) 387-6688
FAX (03) 387-5288
www.tasheeresort.com.tw
In the hills 40 minutes south of Taipei, 20 minutes east of the international airport. The key attraction is the adjoining Ta Shee Golf & Country Club; hotel guests have special access. There is also an excellent sports & fitness facility, with outdoor tennis, a business center, and conference facilities.

🛈 208 🅿 🔁 ❄ 🚭 🏊 🏋 🏧 All major cards

🏨 EVERGREEN TRANSIT HOTEL
$$
4F, TERMINAL 2, TAIWAN TAOYUAN INTERNATIONAL

AIRPORT, TAOYUAN COUNTY
TEL (03) 383-4510
FAX (03) 383-4610
www.evergreenhotels.com
The Evergreen Transit Hotel was officially opened in 2003. There is a limited but state-of-the-art range of recreational facilities in the small facility.

🛈 21 🅿 🚭 🏋 🏧 All major cards

YANGMINGSHAN

🏨 LANDIS RESORT YANGMINGSHAN
$$$$
237 GEJHIH (GEZHI) RD.
TEL 2861-6661
FAX 2861-3885
www.landisresort.com.tw
This boutique hot-springs resort is located in Yangmingshan National Park. Modern Japanese decor in the lobby, restaurants, and guest rooms lends serenity and intimacy. Water from the nearby hot springs is piped into the deep soaking pools in guest room baths.

🛈 47 🅿 🔁 ❄ 🚭 🏊 🏋 🏧 All major cards

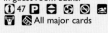
EAST COAST

HUALIEN

🍴 GARDEN TERRACE
$$$$
CHINATRUST HOTEL, 2 YONGSING (YONGXING) RD.
TEL (03) 822-1171
The Garden Terrace, a popular European-style buffet, sports an oasis feel. The head chef states that in the evening the most popular dish is the honey chicken leg, but his personal favorite's the lamb chop with house-specialty (and very secret) sauce.

🍽 125 ❄ 🚭 🏧 All major cards

🍴 LOTUS PAVILION
$$$$
CHINATRUST HOTEL
2 YONGSING (YONGXING) RD.
TEL (03) 822-1171

The Lotus Pavilion specializes in Cantonese fare; the most popular dish is the Fugui prawn ball, but the head chef's recommendation is the Shansu salmon roll. The large facility is almost always bustling. Try to get a seat near the windows overlooking the palm-tree-fringed pool.

🍽 140 🚭 🏋 🏧 All major cards

HUALIEN COUNTY

🏨 HUALIEN FARGLORY HOTEL
$$$$$/$$$$
18 SHANLING, YANLIAO VILLAGE, SHOUFENG TOWNSHIP
TEL (03) 812-3999
FAX (03) 812-3988
www.bellevista.com.tw
The plush Victorian Farglory takes care of every need you might desire. Hotel guests enjoy special rates at the Hualian Ocean themepark. Shuttle pickups from the airport and train station.

🛈 391 🅿 🔁 ❄ 🚭 🏊 🏋 🏧 All major cards

🏨 PROMISED LAND RESORT
$$$$$/$$$$
1 LISIANG (LIXIANG) RD., SHOUFENG TOWNSHIP
TEL (03) 865-6789
FAX (03) 865-6555
www.plcresort.com.tw
Located in the East Rift Valley, this young resort is about 25 minutes south of downtown Hualien. Luxury cottages surround a lagoon where you can take boat rides. There is nothing better than lounging outdoors by the poolside bar while looking up at hills and the nighttime star extravaganza in the unpolluted rural skies.

🛈 260 🅿 🔁 ❄ 🚭 🏊 🏋 🏧 All major cards

🏨 SHIN KONG CHAO FENG RANCH AND RESORT
$$$/$$

20 YONGFU ST., LINRONG WARD, FENGLIN TOWN
TEL (03) 877-2666
FAX (03) 877-1433
www.skcf.com.tw
In the middle of the broad north end of the East Rift Valley, a perfect place to spend the nights gazing at the stars from the verandas of the Dutch-style cabins. This resort is perfect for families with its bird park, animal area, and water-fun arena—a treat for children of all ages.
🛏 122 🅿 🔄 📶 🚭 🏊
🍴 All major cards

TAITUNG

🏨 FORMOSAN NARUWAN HOTEL & RESORT
$$$
66 LIANHANG RD., TAITUNG
TEL (089) 239-666
FAX (089) 239-777
www.naruwan-hotel.com.tw
The aboriginal-theme decor and spacious well-appointed rooms embellished with dark wood-panel inlays work well in this young hotel, which offers aboriginal song and dance performances almost daily. A pleasant lobby lounge bar looks out over a sparkling swimming pool. Wonderfully relaxing outdoor spa. A shuttle bus runs to the absorbing National Museum of Prehistory nearby.
🛏 276 🅿 🔄 📶 🚭 🏊
🍴 All major cards

🏨 HOTEL ROYAL CHIHPEN
$$$
23 LANE 113, LONGCYUAN (LONGQUAN) RD., WENCYUAN (WENQUAN) VILLAGE, BEINAN TOWNSHIP
TEL (089) 510-666
FAX (089) 510-678
www.hotel-royal-chihpen.com.tw
One of a few so-called upscale hotels in the popular Jhihben (Zhiben) hot-springs resort town. Facilities are aimed at the soaking crowd, with various indoor, outdoor,

and in-room hot-springs options. And that is why you would stay here.
🛏 183 🅿 🔄 📶 🚭 🏊 🍴 🍷 🍴 All major cards

🍴 ESOD VEGETARIAN RESTAURANT
$$
320 JHONGSING (ZHONGXING) RD., SEC. 1, TAITUNG CITY
TEL (089) 232-106
In the heart of the city, vegan fare is served here, the décor simple and straightforward. The menu is wide-ranging, concentrated on rice, noodle, and pasta dishes. The ramen is especially tasty. The sundry teas and shaved-ice treats are also in demand.
🍴 40 📶 🚭 🍴 All major cards

TAROKO GORGE

🏨 GRAND FORMOSA TAROKO
$$$$/$$$
18 TIAN TIANSIANG (TIAN-XIANG) RD., SIOULIN (XIULIN) TOWNSHIP, HUALIEN COUNTY
TEL (03) 869-1155 OR 2560-3266 (TAIPEI)
FAX (03) 869-1160
A low-rise hotel in the magnificent Taroko National Park. The setting makes it an ideal place to stay if you plan to spend a few days. Rooms open to balconies and splendid views. Lots of aboriginal-motif decor in the lobby. Restaurants cater to nonfussy diners. Shuttle service provided from Hualien airport or railway station.
🛏 225 🅿 🔄 📶 🚭 🏊 🍴 🍷 🍴 All major cards

THE SOUTH

DONGGANG

🏨 CHANG FAMILY RESTAURANT
$$$
65-1 GUANGFU ROAD, SEC. 2, PINGTUNG COUNTY
TEL (08) 833-7251

In a fishing port known for its fresh seafood, this large and bustling place stands out. (President Chen Shui-bian has chosen this place twice to dine.) Be sure to try the town's specialty, the "three treasures of Donggang"—shrimp with sliced cabbage sautéed in chicken broth, ribbon fish eggs marinated in Shaohsing wine, and otoro, from the belly section of the bluefin tuna.
🍴 150-plus 📶 🚭 🍴 No credit cards

HENGCHUN

🏨 YOHO LANDIS BEACH CLUB
$$$
27-8 WANLI RD.
TEL (08) 886-9999
FAX (08) 886-9998
www.yoho.com.tw
Located on the beachfront in Kenting National Park, some of the rooms offer ocean views. Huge swimming pool is the main attraction. Also has a special Kids' Club and Kids' Pool. The hotel's glass-walled Seaview Restaurant affords ocean panoramic views. The club is a bit removed from Kending Town but has scheduled shuttle service to Kaohsiung airport.
🛏 415 🅿 🔄 📶 🚭 🏊 🍴 🍷 🍴 All major cards

🍴 BOSSA NOVA CAFÉ
$$
100 NANWAN RD., PINGTUNG COUNTY
TEL (08) 889-7137
Located in South Bay or Nanwan, this small establishment serves up tasty sandwiches and simple meals (chicken burritos, spicy Thai chicken, spaghetti). The idyllic spot has a big front patio with shaded tables.
🍴 45 📶 🚭 🍴 No credit cards

🍴 CHAO LI
$$
98-1 HEPING DISTRICT, NANWAN WARD,

PINGTUNG COUNTY
TEL (08) 889-6587
Located in a shady grove along the main highway (26), this was the first (and still best) of a clutch of well-known roadside restaurants serving up a Hengchun specialty, puffer fish—locally caught. Most dishes here are Hengchun-based, using local seafood and vegetables. Also try the parrot fish with Hengchun chili peppers.
🔳 50 🔳 Closed Wed. 🔳
🔳 No credit cards

KAOHSIUNG

🏨 GRAND HI-LAI HOTEL
$$$$
266 CHENGGONG 1ST RD.
TEL (07) 216-1766 OR
(02) 2751-7527 (IN TAIPEI)
FAX (07) 216-1966
www.grand-hilai.com.tw
The lobby and public areas are furnished in a neoclassic European style, while the spacious guest rooms are more subdued. The so-called Health Rooms have their own exercise bike, but the harbor and ocean views are the treat. The huge family rooms are furnished with two king-size beds. Fifteen food & beverage outlets spread throughout the hotel provide for your every hunger pain.
🔳 540 🅿 🔳 🔳 🔳 🔳
🔳 🔳 All major cards

🏨 THE SPLENDOR KAOHSIUNG
$$$$
1 ZIHCIANG (ZIQIANG) 3RD RD.
TEL (07) 566-8000
FAX (07) 566-8080
www.gfk.com.tw
Rising 85 stories from the edge of Kaohsiung Harbor, this is one of the world's tallest hotels. Needless to say, the views are spectacular. Guest rooms (including 92 suites) are comfortably appointed, and all bathrooms come with an inviting soaking tub. Ladies-only floors are

available, as are rooms for the physically challenged.
🔳 592 🅿 🔳 🔳 🔳 🔳
🔳 🔳 All major cards

🏨 AMBASSADOR HOTEL
$$$
202 MINSHENG 2ND RD.
TEL (07) 211-5211
FAX (07) 281-1115
www.ambhotel.com.tw
This international class hotel features American maple wood furnishings and neutral European wool carpets. The Spanish marble bathrooms with German fittings, and Japanese duvets, complete the multinational contributions. Most rooms have harbor views; the pool is set in tropical gardens, and the rooftop garden provides grand views.
🔳 453 🅿 🔳 🔳 🔳 🔳
🔳 🔳 All major cards

🏨 THE GRAND HOTEL— CHENG CHING LAKE
$$$
2 YUANSAN RD., NIAOSONG TOWNSHIP
TEL (07) 370-5911
FAX (07) 370-4889
www.grand-hotel.org
The scaled-down sister of Taipei's landmark Grand Hotel is located on Chengcing Lake (see p. 167) parklands north of the city. Guests become temporary members of the Yuan Shan Sports Club, which allows use of a driving range, six tennis courts, squash courts, well-equipped gymnasium, sauna, and Olympic-size swimming pool.
🔳 107 🅿 🔳 🔳 🔳 🔳
🔳 🔳 All major cards

🏨 HOWARD PLAZA HOTEL
$$$
311 CISIAN (QIXIAN) 1ST RD.
TEL (07) 236-2323
FAX (07) 235-8383
www.howard-hotels.com
It's a little difficult finding the check-in counter (on the fifth floor), but once you do, you can settle into large, comfortable guest rooms. It's

worth paying the extra for the Rosewood Club executive floors, offering bigger rooms and more attentive service. There are 12 food and beverage outlets, including a popular breakfast, lunch, and dinner buffet served in the towering atrium lobby.
🔳 328 🅿 🔳 🔳 🔳 🔳
🔳 🔳 All major cards

🍴 ARTIST
$$$
CORNER OF WUFU 3RD RD. & JHONGHUA (ZHONGHUA) RD.
TEL (07) 282-9777
This popular 24-hour eatery turns out pizzas, casseroles, hot pots, salads, soups, and Chinese stir-fry dishes. All can be accompanied by an array of alcoholic and non-alcoholic drinks.
🔳 60 🔳 All major cards

🍴 BRASS RAIL TAVERN
$$$
21 WUFU 4TH RD.
TEL (07) 533-5747
This bar/restaurant is famous for pizza, especially its seafood variety. Other favorite dishes include the U.S. prime filet, and fish and chips. The restaurant also serves noodles, rice, stir-fry meats, and seafood dishes. There is a large variety of international beers and a surprisingly extensive wine list.
🔳 70 🔳 All major cards

🍴 MAYADA
$$$
226 MINGCHENG 2ND RD.
TEL (07) 558-1099
A tasteful Southeast Asian ambience replete with Thai woodcarvings, pottery, and other ornaments sets the tone for some authentic Thai dishes, including lemongrass shrimp with raw shrimp dipped in a piquant homemade sauce.
🔳 50 🔳 All major cards

🍴 ROOF LOUNGE BAR & CAFÉ
$$$
15F, 165 LINSEN 1ST RD.

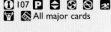

TEL (07) 241-6666
As the name suggests, the restaurant sits high in the sky. The ambience is casual and comfortable and the Southeast Asian menu has dishes from Thailand, Malaysia, Indonesia, and Yunnan Province in China.
🔲 55 🅢 All major cards

🍴 EASTERN VS. WESTERN MUSIC RESTAURANT
$$
490 HEDI RD.
TEL (07) 954-6406
An interesting fusion—or jumble—of Eastern and Western decor. However, the food until recently remained solidly Western with its famous Texas roast ribs—cooked over imported walnut and acacia charcoal. Thai dishes are now being added.
🔲 75 🅢 All major cards

🍴 LIU FAMILY STICKY RICE DUMPLINGS
$$
171-2 ZUOYINGDA RD.
TEL (07) 588-9885
Dumplings resembling tamales and called *rouzong* are stuffed with delicious meat, mushroom, and seafood fillings. Very inexpensive, so you can feast on a variety of these tasty morsels.
🔲 55

🍴 MUSHROOM KITCHEN
$$
197 MINGHUA 1ST RD.
TEL (07) 556-1821
A refreshing and comfortable place with garden dining. Mushrooms, as the name suggests, dominate the menu. Chicken, fish, or various meats are added to hot pots filled with a staggering array of mushrooms for a savory and fulsome taste. A nice touch are the drawers in the dining tables that contain napkins, spoons, chopsticks, and toothpicks. Different dishes, spoons, chopsticks,

and pots are used for vegetarian customers.
🔲 45 🅢 All major cards

🍴 NAKA BASHI
$$
23 CISIAN (QIXIAN) 2ND. RD.
TEL (07) 285-2843
Crowds flock here during the late evening to enjoy generous portions of Japanese-style hot pots and barbecues. Hot pots incorporate chicken, pork, beef, and seafood with a broad range of vegetable and tofu accompaniments. A sweet rice dessert follows each meal. The model train whizzing around the restaurant makes for an interesting diversion.
🔲 60 🅢 All major cards

KENTING

🏨 HOWARD BEACH RESORT
$$$$
2 KENTING RD.
TEL (08) 886-2323
FAX (08) 886-2359
www.howard-hotels.com
Located at the east end of Kending, you will find no end to the facilities at this sprawling resort. A handy tunnel connects the hotel to Small Bay. Rooms are large enough for more than two people, making it a favorite with families. Try for a room with the balcony overlooking the swimming pool and Kending Beach; then settle there to watch the sunset. Airport transfers are available to and from Kaohsiung.
 ① 405 🅟 🔌 🅢 🅢 🌊 📺 🅢 All major cards

🏨 CAESAR PARK HOTEL
$$$
6 KENTING RD.
TEL (08) 886-1888 OR
(02) 2717-5125 (IN TAIPEI)
FAX (08) 886-1818
www.caesarpark.com.tw
Smaller and more intimate than the neighboring Howard Beach Resort, the rooms are furnished for

comfort and relaxation. Glass doors to balconies with views of either the ocean or an expansive swimming pool set amid tropical gardens. The hotel's buffet breakfast (usually complimentary) is excellent. Airport transfers to and from Kaohsiung.
 ① 245 🅟 🔌 🅢 🅢 🌊 📺 🅢 All major cards

🍴 CACTUS CAFÉ
$$
126 DAWAN RD.
TEL (08) 886-2747
A nice and inexpensive place for a hearty North American-style breakfast. Choose from eggs, home fries, crispy bacon, burritos, French toast, buttermilk pancakes, and fruit and yogurt. Lunch, dinner, and bar menus are available throughout the day. Ocean views are included free.
🔲 35 🅢 All major cards

🍴 MAMBO
$$
46 KENTING RD.
TEL (08) 886-2878
This crowded shopfront restaurant serves up a full range of Thai dishes in a densely tabled, casual, and unaffected atmosphere. In keeping with its location at one of Taiwan's most popular beach resorts, the menu has a wide selection of seafood. If you are with a group, share the sea bass with sweet chili; steamed garoupa in lemon; prawn satay; and the perennial favorite: shrimp cakes.
🔲 120 🅢 All major cards

STRAIT ISLANDS

JINCHENG

🏨 HOTEL RIVER KINMEN
$$
100 SIHAI (XIHAI) RD., SEC. 3
TEL (082) 322-211
FAX (082) 323-322
The best of the bunch on these isolated islands, the

Hotel River Kinmen has large, clean rooms and budget hotel facilities. The travel service in the hotel is good for booking trips around the islands.

ⓘ 122 🅿 🔲 🔳 🏧 MC, V

NANGAN ISLAND

🏨 SHENNONG HOTEL
$$
84-2 CINGSHUEI (QINGSHUI) VILLAGE
TEL (0836) 26333
FAX (0836) 26330
www.shennong.com.tw
The Mazu Islands are just finding their feet in terms of tourism resources, and this young hotel is one of the few choices. It sits on a high point near the middle of the island and provides fine ocean views from the upper floors. All rooms are clean and bright, and the staff aims to please but can be unfamiliar with the expectations of international travelers.

ⓘ 63 🅿 🔳 🔲 🔳
🏧 All major cards

🍴 GRANDMA'S EATERY
$$$/$$
143 NIOUJIAO (NIUJIAO) RHINO HORN VILLAGE
TEL (0836) 26125
In this lovely restored inn-style residence made of local stone, the cuisine is north Fujian-style with an emphasis on seafood. The most unusual dish is barnacles, which the staff will teach you how to eat and a good value—at least in terms of adventure. Beyond the Chinese beer, the spirits are all made on the islands.

🍴 50 🔳 🔳 🏧 None

PENGHU

🏨 HOTEL EVER SPRING
$$
6 JHONGJHENG (ZHONG-ZHENG) RD., MAGONG
TEL (06) 927-3336
FAX (06) 927-2112
Options here are limited to budget tourist hotels. At the

Hotel Ever Spring, you will find a clean room, a comfortable bed, satellite television, and a bar fridge: What else do you need? The bar fridge will be empty, by the way, so you will need to stock it with supplies.

ⓘ 88 🅿 🔳 🏊 🔳
🏧 MC, V

ALISHAN

🏨 ALISHAN HOUSE
$$$
16 ALISHAN, SHANGLIN VILLAGE, CHIAYI COUNTY
TEL (05) 267-9811
FAX (05) 267-9596
www.alishanhouse.com.tw
A small, charming hotel perched high in the mountains and set amid lovely gardens. Rooms are elegant; all have views. Choices in Alishan Forest Recreation Area are limited, so best to book early because it is small and can fill quickly. Among the few extras is a running track, but you're here for hiking anyway.

ⓘ 54 🅿 🔳 🔲 🔳 🏧 MC, V

CHIAYI

🏨 CHIAYI CHINATRUST HOTEL
$$
257 WENHUA RD.
TEL (05) 229-2233
FAX (05) 229-1155
www.chinatrust-hotel.com.tw
You will likely need to stay in Chiayi overnight if you want to catch the morning train to Alishan. This hotel is typical of those run by Chinatrust around the island. The rooms may lack the large city decor, but they are clean and comfortable.

ⓘ 170 🅿 🔳 🔲 🔳
🏧 MC, V

🍴 WU LI MUSEO STORICO DEGLI SPAGHETTI
$$$

29-1 CHUEIYANG RD.
TEL (05) 223-8941
Standard Italian fare of pasta, seafood, and fowl dishes. Roast chicken with lemon and butter sauce is a popular choice, along with a tasty variety of pizza. The cappuccino, latte, and au lait are the best you'll find in the city.

🍴 40 🏧 All major cards

SUN MOON LAKE

SOMETHING SPECIAL

🏨 THE LALU
This resort hotel is in the gold standard league for Taiwan. Dark wood floors, glass curtain windows, and minimalist, sharp-lined modern furnishings create a super-stylish simplicity. Suites have balconies with uninterrupted views of the lake, while one- and two-bedroom courtyard villas come with their own swimming pools and an outdoor dining pavilion. The China Tea House serves dim sum and the Japanese Restaurant offers teppanyaki. Room rates in a league of their own make you wonder why guests are charged to use the tennis courts.

$$$$$
142 JHONGSING (ZHONGXING) RD., YUCHIH (YUCHI) TOWNSHIP, NANTOU COUNTY
TEL (049) 285-5311
FAX (049) 285-5312
www.thelalu.com.tw
ⓘ 241 🅿 🔳 🔳 🏊 🔳
🏧 All major cards

TAICHUNG

🏨 EVERGREEN LAUREL HOTEL
$$$$
6 TAICHUNG GANG (HARBOR) RD., SEC. 2
TEL (04) 2313-9988
FAX (04) 2313-8642
www.evergreen-hotels.com
Rosewood furniture and neutral tones add a pleasant feel. All rooms have four-star accouterments, including an

in-room safe-deposit box, satellite television, and marble-clad bathroom. A nice, and for Taiwan unusual, addition are squash courts.

ⓘ 354 🅿 🔲 🔳 🔲 🔲 🔲 🔲 ♿ All major cards

🏨 HOWARD PRINCE HOTEL
$$$$

129 ANHE RD.
TEL (04) 2463-2323
FAX (04) 2463-3333
www.howard-hotels.com
The picture windows allow in plenty of natural light to the well-furnished spacious rooms. The French, continental, Cantonese, and Shanghainese restaurants are well patronized, and the lobby bar is a friendly, chatty place. The Business Center is conveniently open 24 hours.

ⓘ 168 🅿 🔲 🔳 🔲 🔲 🔲 All major cards

🏨 THE LANDIS TAICHUNG HOTEL
$$$$

9 TAICHUNG GANG (HARBOR) RD., SEC. 2
TEL (04) 2326-8008
FAX (04) 2326-8060
www.landis.com.tw
The guest rooms use woods and gold hues to sync with its modernist furniture and fittings in an understated and agreeable style. The cool, crisp bed linens and lightweight goose-down duvets are a delight.

ⓘ 260 🅿 🔲 🔳 🔲 🔲 🔲 ♿ All major cards

🍴 BA BU
$$$$$

61 WUCYUAN (WUQUAN) WEST 1ST ST.
TEL (04) 2372-0777
Located inside a mansion surrounded by courtyard and garden, Ba Bu's atmosphere flows from its polished floors to crisp linen. European style is reflected in its combination of French, German, Swiss, and Italian dishes. Examples include

pan-fried prawn and scallops served with mushroom rice; sablefish filet Meunière; filet steak Café de Paris; and knuckle of veal Aargau style. The shark's fin and abalone are departures from the European influence.

🪑 55 🃏 All major cards

🍴 SERIOUS DAVID SHEN'S STEAK & SEAFOOD HOUSE

David Shen is certainly serious about presentation and taste in this high-end establishment. Wood floors, leather furniture, and attentive tuxedoed-clad service staff lend a cigar-smoking, brandy-sipping ambience to the place. The restaurant uses only USDA Prime Beef. Carnivore delights include a petite eight-ounce New York steak, 12-ounce ribeye steak, an improbable 30-ounce Porterhouse, and short ribs. The restaurant's "surf and turf" meals mix steak with lobster.

277 MINCUAN (MINQUAN) RD.
TEL (04) 2322-6156
$$$$$
🪑 90 🃏 All major cards

🍴 FIVE-CENT DRIFTWOOD HOUSE
$$$$

SHIHJHENG (SHIZHENG) NORTH 3RD RD.
TEL (04) 2254-5678
Antique pottery, carvings, sculptures, stone walls, trees, and even a carp-filled mini-lagoon embellish the restaurant's elegance. Once seated, you can tuck into innovative Chinese cuisine. The "Simple Meal" lets you combine a variety of dishes, including fish, beef, pork, lamb, goose, shrimp, and crab. Popular among the à la carte dishes are goose in a wine sauce and tender crabmeat laid on spicy bean threads.

🪑 110 🃏 All major cards

🍴 CHILI'S GRILL & BAR
$$$

1F, 120 HENAN RD., SEC. 3
TEL (04) 3602-8838
Chili's serves up huge portions of Tex-Mex food in a convivial atmosphere. Diners munch on tangy buffalo wings with bleu cheese dressing, baby back ribs, and chicken, followed by generous salads for starters. Other favorites include the Cajun chicken sandwich and a wicked chipotle bleu cheese bacon burger. Desserts are big men, although you may find trouble fitting them in after the starters and main course.

🪑 110 🃏 All major cards

🍴 SPOOL RESTAURANT
$$$

154 DALONG RD.
TEL (04) 2329-9590
This restaurant is located amid beautiful tropical gardens, while the inside is adorned with palms, ferns, and Asian art (many pieces for sale). A sizable Western menu renowned for its attention to detail is available, along with a large selection of chilled tropical alcoholic and non-alcoholic drinks.

🪑 75 🃏 All major cards

¶ WU GUO JIEH RESTAURANT
$$$
191 DONGSING (DONGXING) RD., SEC. 2
TEL (04) 2472-6200
Nicknamed "No Frontiers" to indicate the range of food choices available. It can create Chinese and European dishes with equal flair. Popular Chinese entrées include rock sugar pig's feet and vinegar fish, while butter bream, roasted lamb chops, and special German-style pork chops are favored European meals. Set-course dinners are available.
🛏 65 🖚 All major cards

¶ GU JIN SHAO
$$
94 JINGMING 1ST ST.
TEL (04) 2328-9228
Gu Jin Shao is a small, unobtrusive eatery with a big reputation. The restaurant imaginatively combines Chinese and Japanese cuisine into its own creations. Its Japanese chicken rolls, crispy oyster rolls, and shrimp rolls make delicious starters. The surprisingly inexpensive juicy tender pork has all the fat removed and is simmered in soy sauce; it comes with all the extras. Tasty and various noodles, rice dishes, fish and beef hot pots, and dumplings are also available.
🛏 30 🖚 All major cards

¶ ZEN CURRY
$$
299 TAIJHONGGANG (TAICHONGGANG) RD., SEC. 1, B1 SOGO STORE
TEL (04) 2329-9222
A stylish, relaxing, and contemporary place serving up a wide variety of Japanese curries that can be ordered in different degrees of spiciness. Reasonably priced set meals are available.
🛏 50 🖚 All major cards

TAINAN

⌂ TAYIH LANDIS
$$$
660 SIMEN (XIMEN) RD., SEC. 1
TEL (06) 213-5555
FAX (06) 213-5599
www.tayihlandis.com.tw
Another classy offering from Taiwan's Landis group. Large, stylish rooms, efficient staff, and complimentary services you usually pay for at other hotels are standard, The lobby bakery sells tasty gourmet sandwiches, savories, and cakes to go, making for a tasty mobile meal while on a walking tour of the nearby temples.
ⓘ 257 🅿 ⊟ 🅢 🚭 🏊
🍴 🕭 🖚 All major cards

¶ TYCOON RESTAURANT
$$$$
258 SHIHMEN (SHIMEN) RD., SEC. 4
TEL (06) 251-2706
Traditional decor sets the scene for quality Cantonese and Hunanese cuisine. House specials are extensive, with the prawn salad, black pepper steak, and garlic steamed *yudai* topping the list. Wallet-depleting specials such as shark's fin and abalone are available for those who wish to impress their guests. Ginseng chicken and Peking-roast duck need to be ordered in advance. Guests are entertained by costumed musicians between 7 p.m. and 9 p.m.
🛏 110 🖚 All major cards

¶ TERRAZZA RISTORANTE
$$$
7F, 52 GONGYUAN RD.
TEL (06) 223-2698
The plush, somewhat pretentious, decor belies the reasonable prices in this top-notch Italian restaurant. Large varieties of pasta and risotto dishes are available. Delicious salads incorporating wild mushrooms, beef and smoked salmon are mandatory

starters. Closed Mon.
🛏 40 🖚 All major cards

¶ HUNDRED HOUSE FRAGRANCE VEGETARIAN RESTAURANT
$$
15 CHANGRONG RD., SEC. 3
TEL (06) 208-6928
An MSG-free vegetarian restaurant with fresh, simple, and healthy meals delivered to your table quickly and without fuss. For delicious dessert variety, try the gel-milk cubes, sweet potato balls, or peanut tofu.
🛏 40 🖚 All major cards

¶ PLEASURED TREASURE VEGETARIAN RESTAURANT
$$
15 FUCIAN (FUQIAN) RD., SEC. 1
TEL (06) 213-3405
One of Tainan's favorite vegetarian restaurants, with homey atmosphere and friendly service. An extensive menu of fried vegetables, tofu, rice, noodles, and stews. Rice cakes accompany the tasty selection of soups, including the restaurant's spicy noodle concoctions.
🛏 35 🖚 All major cards

WULING

⌂ HOYA RESORT
$$$
3-16 WULING ROAD, HEPING TOWNSHIP, TAICHUNG COUNTY
TEL (04) 2590-1399
FAX (04) 2590-1118
www.hoyaresort.com.tw /wuling
Located at Wuling Recreational Farm high in the mountains with magnificent scenery, this high-end facility was opened in 2003. Forty-two of the rooms are designated as family guest rooms, oversized with a separate room for the kids. The farm offers numerous hiking paths.
ⓘ 143 🅿 ⊟ 🅢 🚭 🏊
🖚 All major cards

SHOPPING IN TAIWAN

Taiwan's shopping scene is extensive and vibrant, with upscale boutiques, modern shopping centers, discount stores, and lively and colorful night markets. During the evening in some sections of the city, shopping possibilities expand even further when thousands of small-time vendors lay claim to a patch of sidewalk or roadside to hawk their low-priced, often knockoff goods. Shopping outside Taipei in the small towns can be a source of quality goods.

Fashions and consumer goods are no cheaper here than in other Asian cities, and possibly more expensive than you would find in the West. However, department store sales offer tremendous discounts.

Remember that Asian sizes are smaller than Western. A T-shirt with a tag reading XL will likely be equivalent to a medium (M) back home.

Good buys are on products that are not readily available anywhere else (see Specialized Shopping p. 261). Among the locally made items, you'll find carved jade jewelry, silks, woodcarvings, calligraphy scrolls, tea sets, lacquerware, and foodstuffs.

For inexpensive knickknacks try the **Antique Market,** a collection of small shops at the corner of Bade and Sinsheng (Xinsheng) Roads. For a more extensive range, the government-run **Chinese Handicraft Market** (see Antiques & Artifacts) has good variety.

Rip-offs are refreshingly rare in Taiwan. What you buy is what you get. Staff who speak English, a rare commodity, are usually friendly and helpful.

SHOPPING AREAS

Jhongsiao (Zhongxiao) East Rd., Sec. 4
A popular locale in the Dinghao Area with department stores, high- and mid-end shops, music stores, and restaurants.
Renai Circle/Dunhua South Rd.
Designer-label shops are found in this area just south of Jhongsiao (Zhongxiao) East Rd., Sec. 4.
Simending (Ximending)
This area in western Taipei just north of Wanhua is bounded by

Jhonghua (Zhonghua), Jhongsiao (Zhongxiao) West, Huanhe South, and Chengdu Rds. Here are movie theaters; chic stores; camera shops; and hundreds of tiny shops. Pedestrian streets and open areas draw young hordes.
Sinyi (Xinyi) District
Around the Taipei World Trade Center, this large concentration of department stores and shopping malls, with entertainment facilities, is a favorite of young people and families.

ANTIQUES & ARTIFACTS

Cherry Hill Antiques
288 Minsheng West Rd.,
tel 2555-4555
www.cherryhill.antiques.com.tw
Imported and restored wood furniture, panels, and mirrors from mainland China. Other items include porcelain figurines and silk embroidery.
Chinese Handicraft Mart
1 Syujhou (Xuzhou) Rd.,
tel 2393-3655
www.handicraft.org.tw
This government-run emporium is an ideal place to shop for arts, crafts, and antiques; the store has everything from small gifts to expensive artifacts.
Pacific Cultural Foundation Art Center
38 Chongcing (Chongqing) South Rd., Sec. 3, tel 2337-7155
www.pcf.org.tw
Contemporary art, ink painting, oil, watercolor, photography, sculpture, and mixed media.
Stanny International Culture Center
137 Yuntong Rd., tel 2242-6444
www.stanny.com
Antiques, artifacts, and art exhibitions.

ARCADES & MALLS

The Taiwanese often make shopping a family outing—eating and relaxing. Shopping malls generally have a department store, smaller shops, and restaurants and food courts. Many have cinemas and other entertainment facilities. Most open daily around 10:00–11:00 a.m. and close between 9:00– 9:30 p.m.
Breeze Center
39 Fusing (Fuxing) South Rd.,
tel 6600-8888
Busy mall with mid- and up-scale fashions and accessories.
Core Pacific City Living Mall
138 Bade Rd., Sec. 4, tel 3762-1688 or 3762-1888
The striking, globe-shaped exterior and circular interior atrium provide a stunning layout for these shops. Besides retail outlets, you'll find a cinema complex and restaurants.
Formosa Regent Boutiques
B1, Lane 39, Jhongshan (Zhongshan) North Rd., Sec. 2, tel 2256-9121
A comfortable, ritzy ambience with lots of expensive price tags carrying luxury fashions and accessories; a favorite of Japanese tourists.
Taipei Metro (The Mall)
203 Dunhua South Rd.,
tel 2378-6666
Skylights, greenery, ponds, and fountains set the tone in this mall. Famous brandname stores are featured, along with outlets selling jewelry, watches, trendy home furnishings, and endless fashionable accessories.

BOOKS

Caves Books
103 Jhongshan (Zhongshan) North Rd., Sec. 2, tel 2537-1666
This bookstore has a large range of English-language fiction, non-fiction, travel, textbooks, and foreign magazines.
Eslite Bookstore
245 Dunhua South Rd., Sec. 1, tel 2775-5977
Taiwan's biggest bookstore chain has a large selection of English-

language fiction and non-fiction. The adjoining coffee shop and 24-hour operations make this a favorite haunt for night-owls.

DEPARTMENT STORES

Department stores tend to have shorter hours than shopping centers, opening from about 11 a.m. to 9:30 p.m.
Pacific SOGO
45 Jhongsiao (Zhongxiao) East Rd., Sec. 4, tel 2771-3171
A popular Japanese department store loaded with upscale and brandname fashions and accessories. Eagerly awaited big-discount sales.
Shin Kong Mitsukoshi
66 Jhongsiao (Zhongxiao) West Rd., Sec.. 1, tel 2388-5552
This branch of the Japanese department store is located nearby Taipei Main Train Station. Name fashions share floors with mid-price clothing and accessories, electronics, housewares, watches, etc.

FOOD & DRINK

Chez Jimmy–Fine Foods and Wines
1F, 15 Alley 178, Jhongjheng (Zhongzheng) Rd., Sec. 2, Tianmu, tel 2876-5388
Imported gourmet foods and quality wines, along with pastries and cheeses.
G&G Delicatessen
435 Jhongshan (Zhongshan) North Rd., Sec. 6, Tianmu, tel 2873-9769
Fresh breads and imported cheeses and meats, along with frozen foods and wines. The deli also has a café.
Sansone Salumeria
756 Jhongshan (Zhongshan) North Rd., Sec. 6, Tianmu, tel 2873-2444
A bakery specializing in imported and hard-to-find gourmet foods and groceries.
Tien Mu Grocery
39 Jhongshan (Zhongshan) North Rd., Sec. 7, Tianmu, tel 2871-4828
Stocks a multinational array of

foods, groceries, and wines. The owners speak English.

MARKETS

Dihua Street Traditional Dried Goods Market
Mid-morning–evening
Taiwan's oldest dry-goods, herbs, and traditional crafts market. Some of the sealed foodstuffs make good gifts.
Huasi (Huaxi) Street Tourist Night Market
6 p.m.–1 a.m.
The once famous Snake Alley has cleaned up its act, but the snake-handling shows still attract large crowds. You can try snake, and drink snake's blood, in the snake blood-and-bile soup. There are also a number of seafood restaurants, foot massage places, and footwear shops.
Raohe Tourist Night Market
6 p.m.–1 a.m.
Crowded market with vendors selling herbal medicines, handicrafts, and Taiwanese snack foods (corn on the cob, squid on a stick, steamed peanuts, chicken feet). It's very colorful.
Shihlin (Shilin) Night Market
Off Wenlin Rd. northwest of Jiantan MRT station, 4 p.m.–1 a.m.
Taipei's largest market. It's a great place to try Taiwanese foods. Hundreds of shops and market vendors compete for business in and around the packed market. Retailers sell cheap clothing, shoes, souvenirs, toys, appliances, CDs, gifts, tools, kitchenware, and much more.
Taipei Holiday Flower Market
Under the Jianguo elevated expressway, south of where it passes over Renai Rd.
10 a.m.–6 p.m. Sat. & Sun.
Located adjacent to the Holiday Jade Market. Fragrant and colorful vendors sell a wide variety of flowers and plants.
Taipei Holiday Jade Market
Under Jianguo elevated expressway, north of Renai Rd. overpass
10 a.m.–6 p.m. Sat. & Sun.
Plenty of good-quality jade. Lots of cheap trinkets starting at

NT$100. Vendors also sell Chinese macramé that can be used to make a necklace or bracelet, Buddhist prayer bead bracelets, flashy costume jewelry, and jewelry supplies.

SPECIALIZED SHOPPING

Taiwan has a number of towns and regions that specialize in certain products. In some cases, the whole town is built around the manufacture and sale of a particular product.
Jioufen (Jiufen) This lovely quaint town north of Taipei (avoid on weekends) has become an artist enclave, and much of their work is displayed and sold in boutique galleries. You find most in the narrow streets off Jishan Road.
Kaohsiung—Tailian St. For sheer numbers and variety, the city's famous "Shoe Street" is in a league of its own. If it fits on a foot, the retailers have it. The range is staggering and the prices the lowest in Taiwan.
Lugang—Jhongshan Rd.
This historic town has numerous factory shops—some more than 100 years old—turning out traditional, quality handicrafts, including woodcarving, tin-ware, fans, lanterns, and pottery.
Sanyi The center of Taiwan's woodcarving industry, with hundreds of outlets selling a staggering variety of wood products from delicate sculptures to solid-timber furniture. Famous for its woodcarvers sculpturing away in their workshops.
Yingge This is the pottery center of Taiwan—south of Taipei. Here, streets are lined with factories shops turning out and selling everything from miniature clay tea sets to porcelain toilet bowls. You'll find a variety of pottery objects, including simple earthenware products, musical instruments, Ming and Qing dynasty reproduction pieces, and exquisite glazed porcelains.

ENTERTAINMENT & ACTIVITIES

Taipei has a wealth of entertainment choices. Its Chinese heritage is celebrated in drama and art, while elsewhere there are big-name international performers on stage. Taiwan's museums hold priceless collections of artifacts and antiquities, while smaller galleries display and sell works by contemporary artists. First-run Hollywood movies compete with the island's active film industry. The major cities have no shortage of nightlife options—themed pubs, a wide choice of nightclubs, and discos, from the down-at-the-heel karaoke bars to trendy be-seen-at clubs. Outdoor activities abound from the active—kayaking, white-water rafting, hiking, mountaineering, windsurfing, rock climbing, hang gliding, and parasailing—to spectator sports where fans can join raucous locals at a baseball game between teams in Taiwan's national league.

ENTERTAINMENT CENTERS

National Concert Hall
21-1 Jhongshan (Zhongshan) South Rd., tel 3393-9888, www.ntch.edu.tw
Home of the Taipei Symphony Orchestra, the hall also hosts international orchestras and other large-scale music concerts. Also housed here is the Recital Hall for chamber music, workshops, and lectures.
National Dr. Sun Yat-sen Memorial Hall
505 Renai Rd., Sec. 4, tel 2758-8008, www.yatsen.gov.tw
The complex hosts musical performances and drama, both local and international. Also available are a number of galleries, a café, and a museum dedicated to Sun Yat-sen.
National Theater
21-1 Jhongshan (Zhongshan) South Rd., tel 3393-9888
Along with the National Concert Hall, this imposing building forms the National Chiang Kai-shek Cultural Center. Regular productions of Chinese opera, traditional Chinese folk arts, Western opera, drama, ballet, and other dance forms are held here.
Novel Hall for Performing Arts
3 Songshou Rd., tel 2722-4302 www.novelhall.org.tw
Holds regular performances of various forms of Chinese drama, including the Beijing, Taiwanese, and Liyuan Operas.

Red Theater
10 Chengdu Rd., tel 2311-9380, www.redplayhouse.com.tw
Opened in 1908 as a market, the Red Theater now has a second-floor performance area under a beautiful timber-domed ceiling that welcomes small productions, including puppetry and children's theater.

CINEMA

The Taiwanese love movies, especially first-run Hollywood films. Most cinemas have a number of theaters, and are in or near shopping centers. Local English-language papers have daily listings.
Ambassador Theater
88 Chengdu Rd., tel 2361-1222 Powerful surround-sound system makes the 1,500-seat cinema popular.
Lux Theater
85 Wuchang St., Sec. 2, tel 2311-8628
Four cinemas and a digital audio system.
President
4F, 59 Jhonghua (Zhonghua) Rd., Sec. 1, tel 2388-5576
Ergonomic seats and an impressive sound system.
Spring Cinema Galaxy
10F, 52 Hanjhong (Hanzhong) St., tel 2381-1339 or 2381-1399
The cinema's two theaters show art-house movies.
Warner Village
18 Songshou Rd., tel 8780-1166 or 2757-2345 (reservations)
An 18-theater Cineplex located in a shopping mall.

NIGHTLIFE

There is no shortage of pubs, bars, and nightclubs in Taipei, from British-style pubs to trendy dance clubs. Opening hours vary from 11:30 a.m. for lunch to 5 p.m. Most close between 1 and 3 a.m. —some not until dawn. A small bottle of imported beer or glass of wine costs between NT$100–200, with mixed drinks around NT$200 or higher.
@live
2F, 15 Heping West Rd., Sec. 1, tel 2393-2222
Huge pulsating dance club DJs playing techno and trance music. There is a lounge bar on the second floor.
Blue Note
4F, 171 Roosevelt Rd., Sec. 3, intersection of Shihda (Shida) Rd., tel 2362-2333
A popular jazz club with local and international performers. It is small so get there before 9 p.m. if you want a table. Pleasant atmosphere with good service. Minimum charge.
Carnegie's
100 Anhe Rd., Sec. 2, tel 2325-4433
Among the most popular bars in Taipei, it carries a staggering list of 300 shooters. Raunchy action inside accounts for the long lines of people outside on weekends.
Brown Sugar
101 Songren Rd., tel 8780-1110 International and local bands perform on a stage in an intimate, lively atmosphere. Music is jazz and blues.
Jurassic
196 Bade Rd., Sec. 2, tel 2741-0550
Dinosaur Beer House would be an appropriate name given the Jurassic decor and the roof's dinosaur skeleton. Long tables, flowing beer, scurrying waiters, and noisy, cheerful patrons make for a lively atmosphere. Feed on the Taiwanese and Chinese snack foods while drinking.
Juliana
29 Lane 31, Daan Rd., Sec. 1 tel 8773-7337
A popular, plush lounge bar and

ENTERTAINMENT & ACTIVITIES

sports bar combo with décor and music from the 60s through 80s. Excellent food. Wireless Internet access.

My Other Place
303 Fusing (Fuxing) North Rd., tel 2718-7826
This friendly and welcoming pub serving British beer is located downtown. It draws expatriates and business people mainly for its generous lunch and early evening happy hour.

The Ploughman Inn
8 Lane 232, Dunhua South Rd., Sec. 1, tel 2773-3268
One of Taipei's oldest pubs, it draws expatriates and locals equally. The friendly staff makes you feel welcome. Happy hour is from 6 p.m. to 9 p.m. Many take advantage of the Mongolian BBQ in the basement. Cover.

The Post Home
31 Lane 35, Jhongshan (Zhongshan) North Rd., Sec. 6, tel 2835-6491
Easygoing, American-style bar atmosphere. Happy hour lasts until 7:30 p.m.

Q-Bar
16 Alley 19, Lane 216, Jhongsiao (Zhongxiao) East Rd., Sec. 4, tel 2771-7778
Chic after-work hangout with inexpensive imported beers that belie its up-market ambience. The staff is friendly and the patrons chatty.

The Tavern
415 Sinyi (Xinyi) Rd., Sec. 4, tel 8780-0892
Nautical theme attracts foreign and local businessmen here to enjoy the extensive range of beers. A giant television screen shows international sporting events, while pool tables keeps patrons occupied.

The Zone
Often also called the Combat Zone. A section of cheek-by-jowl bars that were once favored by U.S. troops on R&R during the Vietnam War—a lot quieter these days. Some bars have been refurbished, while others have changed little since the 1970s. Mainly expatriate male clientele. To enter the Zone, head to the neon-lit lanes

and alleys along Shuangcheng St., behind the Imperial Hotel.

ACTIVE SPORTS

Taiwan presents numerous opportunities to get involved with sports. The sporting associations and clubs are well organized, helpful, and generally welcoming to visitors—although language problems may be encountered. The most popular and accessible outdoor pursuit is hiking. There are numerous quality golf courses and some good beaches for swimming. Adventure sports like diving, paragliding, white-water rafting, and rock climbing can be organized with relative ease.

CYCLING & MOUNTAIN BIKING

Taiwan's compact size and beautiful scenery make it ideal for mountain biking and cycling —although be careful on heavily traveled roads. The hilly terrain makes for some long and exhilarating downhill rides, along with challenging climbs. Numerous off-road possibilities exist. Any cycle shop will put you in touch with a biking/cycling club.
Yangmingshan Cycling Club
www.taipeiycc.blogspot.com

GOLF
Golf courses are open to guest membership for foreign visitors; this can usually be arranged at the hotel concierge desk or through travel agencies. Excellent courses can be found on the outskirts of major cities. Clubs, shoes, and caddies are available at most clubs.
ROC Golf Association
12F-1, 125 Nanjing East Rd., Sec. 2, Taipei, tel 2516-5611
www.twgolf.com.tw

HIKING & MOUNTAINEERING
Hiking in the mountains is one of the favorite active activities of the Taiwanese. There are many hiking clubs that take busloads of hikers to the mountains for day or overnight trips. If you prefer

more solitude, registered guides can be hired. In some cases, mountain permits are needed—generally for ascents above 9,800 feet (3,000 m) and for protected areas. Permits can be obtained by contacting the associations listed below or the National Park authorities.
Alpine Association
10F, 185 Jhongshan (Zhongshan) North Rd., Sec. 2, Taipei, tel 2594-2108
Mountaineering Hiking and Association
50-A Longjiang Rd., Taipei, tel (02) 2751-0938

HOT AIR BALLOONING
Colorful hot air balloons float in the southern sky over Pingtung and Kaohsiung Counties.
Shyang An Enterprises Co., Ltd.
68-6 Jhongshan (Zhongshan) Rd., Yangpu Township, Pingtung County, tel (08) 793-8827

KAYAKING
Taiwan's mountains and heavy rainfall contribute to some good runs, mainly during the wet season and especially after a typhoon. The most popular areas are the East Coast's Syiuguluan (Xiuguluan) River in Hualien County and Laonong River in Kaohsiung County.
Chinese Taipei Aruba Kayaking Association
1F-1, 3 Lane 238, Yangping Rd., Yonghe, Taipei County, tel 2552-8000
Chinese Taipei Canoe Association
260 Guangming St., Sindian (Xindian), Taipei County, tel. 2918-5151

MARTIAL ARTS
After a few lessons you can join the tens of thousands of people at dawn who practice tai chi in temple courtyards and parks around the island. The most popular places for tai chi in Taipei are 2-28 Peace Park, Chiang Kai-shek Memorial Plaza, and Sun Yat-sen Memorial Plaza.

National Tai Chi Chuan Association
6F, 20 Jhulyuen (Zhulun) St., Taipei, tel 2778-3887

PARAGLIDING
The three most popular paragliding launch sites are on the north coast at Green Bay and in the mountains at Luye Plateau fronting tea plantations, in the Taitung County's East Rift Valley, and at Saijia Aero Sports Park in Sandimen Township, Pingtung County.

Chinese Taipei Aero Sports Association
9F, 20 Jhulyuen (Zhulun) St., Taipei, tel 2775-8755

Taipei Aero Sports Association
10 Alley 5, Lane 305, Yuandong Rd., Jhonghe (Zhonghe), Taipei County, tel 2247-5905

ROCK CLIMBING
The sea cliffs of Longdong on the northeast coast are regarded as the best for rock-climbing because of the surface variations and climbs. The area suits beginning and experienced climbers.

Taipei Rock Climbing Association
1F-1, 3 Lane 238, Yangping Rd., Yonghe, Taipei County tel 8923-5476

Shao Hu Tz Rock Climbing Enterprise (XHS Adventure Life)
1 Lane 16, Alley 60, Shuangcheng St., Sindian (Xindian) City, Taipei County, tel 2215-9019

Rock Wall Climbing
Taipei Youth Activity Center 17 Renai Rd., Sec. 1, Taipei tel 2343-2388

SNORKELING & DIVING
The corals fringing Kenting, Green Island, and the Penghus offer excellent and varied dives. Kenting has a number of dive shops that offer PADI courses for a reasonable fee.

PADI Dive Centers and Resorts
www.padi.com

Inner Space Dive Center
1F, 55 Bade Rd., Sec. 5, Taipei, tel 2767-1124

SURFING
An enthusiastic and welcoming surfing community makes the best of the swells off the island's east coast. The popular spots are the northeast coast's Honeymoon Bay and Fulong Beach, and the Kenting National Park's east coast. The best conditions are after a typhoon.

Chinese Taipei Surfing Association
5F, 11 Lane 20, Alley 155, Bade Rd., Sec. 3, Taipei, tel 2577-1666

Sun Brothers Surf Shop
39 Waidasi (Waidaxi) Rd., Toucheng, Ilan County, tel (03) 978-1781

SWIMMING
The best beaches by far are in Kenting National Park in the south. The better hotels have swimming pools. Public pools tend to be shallow, noisy, and crowded.

TENNIS
Tennis is a popular sport in Taiwan, and there are numerous courts around the country. Some hotels and resorts have tennis courts that are open to non-guests for a fee.

Chinese Taipei Tennis Association
7F, 20 Jhulyuen (Zhulun) St. Taipei, tel 2772-0298

WHITE-WATER RAFTING
The most popular area is the Syiuguluan (Xiuguluan) River in Hualien County, the only river on the island that carries enough water year-round for white-water rafting. The wet season is the best time. After a typhoon, the rivers swells and delivers plenty of thrills. Full-day trips including transportation and equipment can be booked through travel agents.

Nansen Amusement Co., Ltd.
Taipei, tel 8809-4688
Hualien, tel (03) 833-4369
www.nansen.com.tw

Wanjiang Amusement Co., Ltd
138-6 Guolian 1st Rd., Hualian City, tel (03) 835-6285

Bao May Rafting Water Inc.
1 Jhongjheng (Zhongzheng) Rd., Boalai Village, Liouguei (Liugui) Township, Kaohsiung County, tel (07) 688-2580

WINDSURFING
Windsurfing gear can be rented from popular beaches around the island. The best conditions for the sport are found on the windswept Penghu archipelago in Taiwan Strait between October and April.

Liquid Sports
36 Huimin 1st Rd., Magong, Penghu, tel (06) 926-0361
www.liquidsport.com.tw

SPECTATOR SPORTS
Spectator sports in Taiwan do not draw big crowds to stadiums or arenas, although some have a large television following. Outdoor stadiums are generally small, with the largest only holding 10,000 spectators. Baseball attracts the largest, most vocal, and fanatical crowds, although attendance per game is not high. There is also a basketball league. Big-event regional and international martial arts and table-tennis competitions draw larger crowds.

Taipei Municipal Stadium
10 Nanjing East Rd., Sec. 4, tel 2570-2330, #147
The Taipei Municipal Stadium holds 16,000 in its Taipei Track and Field Stadium, but only a fraction of the seats are filled for the meets and soccer games held there. Its indoor stadium, Taipei Gymnasium, hosts basketball and seats 2,000.

Tianmu Baseball Stadium
77 Jhongcheng (Zhongcheng) Rd., Sec. 2, tel (02) 2873-6548
Two or three games are played weekly during the 9-month season. The stadium holds 10,400. Crowds are generally only a few thousand except for the season's opening game and at playoff time, so you can always get a ticket by just turning up.

ILLUSTRATIONS CREDITS

TTB = Taiwan Tourism Bureau

Front cover (left), Getty; (center), Ron Watts/CORBIS; (right), David Hartung. Spine, Getty. Back cover Maltings Partnership, Derby, England.

1, AFP/CORBIS; 2-3, Taxi/Getty Images; 4, Chen Chia Hsing/TTB; 9, Eugene Yeh,TTB; 11, Chia-Hung Yuan/TTB; 12-13 & 14-15, National Geographic Photographer Jodi Cobb; 16-17, Chia-Yung Tung/TTB; 18-19, David Hartung; 20, Sun-In AV Corp./TTB; 21, David Hartung; 22-23, Ying-Ting Huang/TTB; 24-25, Macduff Everton/CORBIS; 25, David Hartung; 26, Sun-In AV Corp/TTB; 27, Eugene Yeh/TTB; 28-29, David Hartung; 31, Library of Congress; 32, Asian Art & Archaeology, Inc./CORBIS; 34-36 (all), Bettmann/CORBIS; 38-39, AFP/CORBIS; 41, David Henley/CPA Media; 42-43, Sheng-Hung Huang/TTB; 44-45, Jing-Ho Chi/TTB; 46-47, David Hartung; 48, Karen/CORBIS Sygma; 50-51, National Palace Museum, Taipei, Taiwan, Republic of China; 51, Hsien-Ming Lu/TTB; 53, Reuters NewMedia, Inc./CORBIS; 54, David Hartung; 55, Jim Zuckerman/CORBIS; 57, CORBIS; 58, Chen Chia Hsing/TTB; 61, Hsiao-Shih Huang/TTB; 62 & 63, Hsu-Shih Jung/TTB; 64 & 65, Gary Conner/Index Stock Imagery; 66-67, Jui-Tsung Yeh/TTB; 68, David Henley/CPA Media; 69, Bohemian Nomad Picturemakers/CORBIS; 70-71, Maltings Partnership, Derby, England; 72-73, Macduff Everton/CORBIS; 74, Eugene Yeh/TTB; 75, Big River Company Ltd./TTB; 76, National Palace Museum, Taipei, Taiwan, Republic of China; 77, Chen Chia Hsing/TTB; 78-79, Rich Communication Services/TTB; 80, TTB; 82, Maltings Partnership, Derby, England; 84, David Hartung; 85, National Palace Museum, Taipei, Taiwan, Republic of China; 86, David Henley/CPA Media; 87, Chen Chia Hsing/TTB; 89, Hsu-Shih Jung/TTB; 90, David Hartung; 91, Yan Liu/CORBIS; 92, David Henley/CPA Media; 94-95, Hsu-Shih Jung/TTB; 96, David Hartung; 97 (upper), Xu Kun-Lun/TTB; 97 (center), Chen-Hui Kuo/TTB; 97 (lower), Eugene Yeh/TTB; 98, David Henley/CPA Media; 99 Shu-Yu Chang/TTB; 100, TTB; 101, Chen Chia Hsing/TTB; 103, Maltings Partnership, Derby, England; 104, Chen Chia Hsing/TTB; 105, David Henley/CPA Media; 106-107, Shen Yen Wen/TTB; 108-109, Robert Hsiao/TTB; 110, TTB; 111 (upper), Shen Yen Wen/TTB; 111 (lower), Hsu-Shih Jung/TTB; 113, Kun-Sung Yen/TTB; 114, David Hartung; 116 Hsu-Shih Jung/TTB; 117 David Reid; 118, Hsin-Chiang Lin/TTB; 119, Eugene Yeh/TTB; 120, Chen Chia Hsing/TTB; 121, Eugene Yeh/TTB; 122-123, Chen Chia Hsing/TTB; 124 & 125 (all), David Hartung; 126, TTB; 127, Rich Communication Services/TTB; 128, Chen Chia Hsing/TTB; 129, Kuei-Mei Liao/TTB; 130, Su-Fei Pan/TTB; 132, David Henley/CPA Media; 133, David Hartung/OnAsia; 134, Ching-Lin Wu/TTB; 135, Chen Chia Hsing/TTB; 136, Christian Kober/Robert Harding World Imagery/Getty; 138, Liu-Ya Yang/TTB; 140, Chia-Nien Chang/TTB; 143, David Henley/CPA Media; 144, Chen Chia Hsing/TTB; 145 Eugene Yeh/TTB; 146, TTB; 147, Han-Yun Liang/TTB; 148-149, National Geographic Photographer Jodi Cobb; 149, Reuters NewMedia, Inc./CORBIS; 150, David Henley/CPA Media; 151, TTB; 152, David Hartung; 153, Che-Hui Hsu/TTB; 154, Yeh Chui-Jing/TTB; 155, Tsai Deng-Huei/TTB; 157, Eugene Yeh/TTB; 158, David Henley/CPA Media; 160, Mu-Sheng Hung/TTB; 162, David Hartung; 163, Chen Chia Hsing/TTB; 164, David Henley/CPA Media; 165 (upper), Sun-In AV Corp./TTB; 165 (center), Chen Chia Hsing/TTB; 165 (lower), Eugene Yeh/TTB; 165 (right), David Henley/CPA Media; 167, Chung-Kuang Lo/TTB; 168, David Henley/CPA Media; 170, TTB, 171, O-Shan Tseng/TTB; 172, Kun Lun Hsu/TTB; 173, David Hartung; 174-175, Guan Chun Company/TTB; 176, Tung-Chin Tsai/TTB; 177 (upper left, center & lower), Wen-Hua Lee/TTB; 177 (upper right), Wen-Chi Wu/TTB; 178, Henry Westheim Photography/ Alamy; 180-181, Eugene Yeh/TTB; 182, Guan Chun Company/TTB; 183, Kun Lun Hsu/TTB; 184, AFP/CORBIS; 185, Sun-In AV Corp./TTB; 187, Maltings Partnership, Derby, England; 188, Eugene Yeh/TTB; 189, Chen-Yang Shih/TTB; 190, Sun-In AV Corp./TTB; 191, TTB; 192, You Fu-Lian/TTB; 194, Jui-Chun Tsai/TTB; 195, Chen-Yuan Lee/TTB; 196-197, Alberto Buzzola/OnAsia; 198, Yeh Ping Hsun/TTB; 199, Lin Ming-Ren/TTB; 200, Chien-Tso Lai/TTB; 201, Hui-Wen Liu/TTB; 202, Hsu Shih Jung/TTB; 203, TTB; 204 & 205, AFP/CORBIS; 206, TTB; 207, Sun-In AV Corp./TTB; 208, Robert Hsaio/TTB; 210-211 & 212, CORBIS; 213 & 214, Rich Communication Services/TTB; 215, Sun-In AV Corp./TTB; 216-217, Hsu Shih Jung/TTB; 218, Sun-In AV Corp./TTB; 219, TTB; 220-221, Shu-Der Ko/TTB; 222, Ching-Shiuan Tzou/TTB; 223, Eugene Yeh/TTB; 224 (upper); Chia-Sheng Liu/TTB; 224 (lower) Paul Almasy/CORBIS; 225, Yi-Fu Hsu/TTB; 226, Eugene Yeh/TTB; 227, Kun Lun Hsu/TTB; 228-229, David Hartung; 230-231, Feng-Yi Chen/TTB; 232, Eugene Yeh/TTB 233, David Henley/CPA Media; 234, Ke-Jia Lu/TTB; 235, David Henley/ CPA Media.

Founded in 1888, the National Geographic Society is one of the largest nonprofit scientific and educational organizations in the world. It reaches more than 285 million people worldwide each month through its official journal, NATIONAL GEOGRAPHIC, and its four other magazines; the National Geographic Channel; television documentaries; radio programs; films; books; videos and DVDs; maps; and interactive media. National Geographic has funded more than 8,000 scientific research projects and supports an education program combating geographic illiteracy.

For more information, please call 1-800-NGS LINE (647-5463) or write to the following address: National Geographic Society,1145 17th Street N.W.,Washington, D.C. 20036-4688 U.S.A.

For information about special discounts for bulk purchases, please contact National Geographic Books Special Sales: ngspecsales@ngs.org

Printed in Spain

Published by the National Geographic Society

John M. Fahey, Jr., *President and Chief Executive Officer*
Gilbert M. Grosvenor, *Chairman of the Board*
Nina D. Hoffman, *Executive Vice President; President, Book Publishing Group*
Kevin Mulroy, *Senior Vice President and Publisher*
Leah Bendavid-Val, *Director of Photography Publishing and Illustrations*
Marianne Koszorus, *Director of Design*
Elizabeth L. Newhouse, *Director of Travel Publishing*
Carl Mehler, *Director of Maps*
Barbara A. Noe, *Series Editor*
Cinda Rose, *Art Director*
Jennifer A. Thornton, *Managing Editor*
Gary Colbert, *Production Director*

Staff for this book:

Kay Kobor Hankins, *Illustrations Editor and Designer*
Patricia Daniels, Judith Klein, *Text Editors*
Caroline Hickey, *Senior Researcher*
XNR Productions, *Map Edit, Research, and Production*
Richard S. Wain, *Production Project Manager*
Sharon Berry, *Illustrations Assistant*
Connie D. Binder, *Indexer*
Jane Sunderland, Catharina L. Gill, *Contributors*

Staff for 2007 edition:

Lawrence M. Porges, *Project Manager*
Rick Charette, *Editorial Adviser*
Michael McNey, Carol Stroud, Ruth Thompson, Maura Walsh, John Wagley, Rob Waymouth, Meredith C. Wilcox, *Contributors*

Map art drawn by Chris Orr & Associates, Southampton, England
Artwork by Maltings Partnership, Derby, England

ISSN: 1547-559X

National Geographic Traveler: Taiwan, Second Edition (2007)
ISBN: 978-1-4262-0145-5

Printed and bound by Mondadori Printing, Toledo, Spain.

Visit the society's Web site at http://www.nationalgeographic.com

The information in this book has been carefully checked and to the best of our knowledge is accurate. However, details are subject to change, and the National Geographic Society cannot be responsible for such changes, or for errors or omissions. Assessments of sites, hotels, and restaurants are based on the author's subjective opinions, which do not necessarily reflect the publisher's opinion. The publisher cannot be responsible for any consequences arising from the use of this book.

NATIONAL GEOGRAPHIC
TRAVELER
A Century of Travel Expertise in Every Guide

- **Alaska** ISBN: 978-0-7922-5371-6
- **Amsterdam** ISBN: 978-0-7922-7900-6
- **Arizona** (2nd Edition) ISBN: 978-0-7922-3888-1
- **Australia** (2nd Edition) ISBN: 978-0-7922-3893-5
- **Barcelona** (2nd Edition) ISBN: 978-0-7922-5365-5
- **Berlin** ISBN: 978-0-7922-6212-1
- **Boston & environs** ISBN: 978-0-7922-7926-6
- **California** (2nd Edition) ISBN: 978-0-7922-3885-0
- **Canada** (2nd Edition) ISBN: 978-0-7922-6201-5
- **The Caribbean**
  (2nd Edition) ISBN: 978-1-4262-0141-7
- **China** (2nd Edition) ISBN: 978-1-4262-0035-9
- **Costa Rica** (2nd Edition) ISBN: 978-0-7922-5368-6
- **Cuba** (2nd Edition) ISBN: 978-1-4262-0142-4
- **Egypt** (2nd Edition) ISBN: 978-1-4262-0143-1
- **Florence & Tuscany**
  (2nd Edition) ISBN: 978-0-7922-5318-1
- **Florida** ISBN: 978-0-7922-7432-2
- **France** (2nd Edition) ISBN: 978-1-4262-0027-4
- **Germany** (2nd Edition) ISBN: 978-1-4262-0028-1
- **Great Britain**
  (2nd Edition) ISBN: 978-1-4262-0029-8
- **Greece** (2nd Edition) ISBN: 978-1-4262-0030-4
- **Hawaii** (2nd Edition) ISBN: 978-0-7922-5568-0
- **Hong Kong**
  (2nd Edition) ISBN: 978-0-7922-5369-3
- **India** (2nd Edition) ISBN: 978-1-4262-0144-8
- **Ireland** (2nd Edition) ISBN: 978-1-4262-0022-9
- **Italy** (2nd Edition) ISBN: 978-0-7922-3889-8
- **Japan** (2nd Edition) ISBN: 978-0-7922-3894-2
- **London** (2nd Edition) ISBN: 978-1-4262-0023-6
- **Los Angeles** ISBN: 978-0-7922-7947-1

- **Madrid** ISBN: 978-0-7922-5372-3
- **Mexico** (2nd Edition) ISBN: 978-0-7922-5319-8
- **Miami & the Keys**
  (2nd Edition) ISBN: 978-0-7922-3886-7
- **New York** (2nd Edition) ISBN: 978-0-7922-5370-9
- **Naples & southern Italy**
  ISBN 978-1-4262-0040-3
- **Panama** ISBN: 978-1-4262-0146-2
- **Paris** (2nd Edition) ISBN: 978-1-4262-0024-3
- **Piedmont & Northwest Italy**
  ISBN: 978-0-7922-4198-0
- **Portugal** ISBN: 978-0-7922-4199-7
- **Prague & the Czech Republic**
  ISBN: 978-0-7922-4147-8
- **Provence & the Côte d'Azur**
  ISBN: 978-0-7922-9542-6
- **Romania** ISBN: 978-1-4262-0147-9
- **Rome** (2nd Edition) ISBN: 978-0-7922-5572-7
- **St. Petersburg** ISBN 978-1-4262-0050-2
- **San Diego** (2nd Edition) ISBN: 978-0-7922-6202-2
- **San Francisco**
  (2nd Edition) ISBN: 978-0-7922-3883-6
- **Shanghai** ISBN: 978-1-4262-0148-6
- **Sicily** ISBN: 978-0-7922-9541-9
- **Spain** ISBN: 978-0-7922-3884-3
- **Sydney** ISBN: 978-0-7922-7435-3
- **Taiwan** (2nd Edition) ISBN: 978-1-4262-0145-5
- **Thailand** (2nd Edition) ISBN: 978-0-7922-5321-1
- **Venice** ISBN: 978-0-7922-7917-4
- **Vietnam** ISBN: 978-0-7922-6203-9
- **Washington, D.C.**
  (2nd Edition) ISBN: 978-0-7922-3887-4

AVAILABLE WHEREVER BOOKS ARE SOLD